ZERO

BOOKS BY ROBERT PAYNE

Published by The John Day Company

SUN YAT-SEN: *A Portrait* (With Stephen Chen)

THE WHITE PONY

THE REVOLT OF ASIA

REPORT ON AMERICA

ZERO: *The Story of Terrorism*

Published by Dodd, Mead and Company

FOREVER CHINA

TORRENTS OF SPRING

DAVID AND ANNA

THE ROSE TREE

THE BEAR COUGHS AT THE NORTH POLE

CHINA AWAKE

THE YELLOW ROBE

ZERO

THE STORY OF TERRORISM

ROBERT PAYNE

WITH AN INTRODUCTION BY

PEARL S. BUCK

Originally published in 1950

ISBN: 978-0-9835784-5-1
Digitally Reproduced in 2011 by:
CONVERPAGE
23 Acorn Street
Scituate, MA 02066
www.converpage.com

for
CHARLES AND CONSTANCE OLSON

Introduction

THINKING minds in many parts of the world today are trying to understand our age and specifically why, when civilization has in some aspects reached its highest point in human history, there should exist at the same time the greatest savagery and cruelty.

In this important and timely book Robert Payne has explained, I believe, the essential reasons for the dualism. Our Western World, which through science and modern industry has bestowed upon us such amazing benefit, has also by the same means afforded unparalleled opportunity for the development of man's blackest nature, the impulse toward destruction and death, expressed most dangerously in that love of terror known as nihilism.

It is well, indeed, that Mr. Payne calls our attention so powerfully to the nihilism at present everywhere, as evident in the murders perpetrated by one American killing thirteen innocent people in a street in Camden as in the mass murders of millions in Russia and Germany. The nihilist at large today is making his perverted enjoyment of despair and death into a philosophy for other perverted minds. It is nihilism which has provided the specious doctrine that means and ends are not all of a piece, ignoring the fact proved often in history, that good ends are invariably destroyed by evil means.

We need to be reminded again and again of the fantastic

INTRODUCTION

folly and danger of nihilism and of its horrible potency over certain types of persons. We must be reminded lest being unaware we fall victims once more. Yet I confess that after my first reading of Mr. Payne's book, then in manuscript, I asked myself whether it was worthwhile to present to the public, even in so brilliant a form, this picture of renewed horror. Mankind is sick and disgusted with the knowledge of its own evil. The impetus toward nihilism today is simply one aspect of that sickness and that disgust. There is no healing in the mere knowledge of evil, little use even in its continued warning, unless there is at the same time the presentation of that other and hopeful side of human nature, that alternate to death, which is the love of life.

Mr. Payne and I then entered into a correspondence upon this matter, and he added some very fine pages to the book. I still felt, however, that for balance and proportion these last pages should be expanded further, not to expound doctrines of love and sympathy, which however valuable they may be as an individual's attributes, are the flowering rather than the fundamental techniques for expressing the natural and instinctive goodness inherent in the dualism of human nature. Love and sympathy tend to become personalized in their effects. We feed those peoples who agree with us, for example. This is not enough to change the evil of our dangerous times. What we need today, what our young people, reared in the knowledge of terror and evil, supremely need, is to know how we can all conquer nihilism and replace terror with safety, cruelty with mercy, evil with good.

Searching back into the history of the last hundred and fifty years for an answer to this question, it seemed to me evident that Darwin was responsible to a great degree for the strengthening of nihilism in our modern times. His discovery and statement of that natural law commonly called the sur-

INTRODUCTION

vival of the fittest gave excuse to all those who preferred and profited by contest and competition, without mercy toward the weak. I venture to suggest that people, in whatever country or age, are the product of their teaching, and emphasis upon one or the other aspect of our human dualism may result in entirely different types of humanity. Thus emphasis upon the survival of the fittest and consequently upon competition and contest, during a time when machines which greatly extended the power of the individual were also developing so rapidly, certainly resulted in new ruthlessness in the human creature.

Yet Darwin himself suggested another law which he said might be even more important. Survival, or life, is the supreme test of strength in any group, animal or human, and in terms of survival those groups which have not competed within their own species have always been the strongest. That is, they have lived on while the others destroyed one another. Other scientists followed Darwin in this research and there was developed the law of mutual aid. Kessler, the great European zoologist, lecturing upon the subject in 1880, said, "I obviously do not deny the struggle for existence, but I maintain that the progressive development of the animal kingdom, and especially of mankind, is favoured much more by mutual support than by mutual struggle."

Kropotkin, the Russian anthropologist, later wrote a book entitled *Mutual Aid*, wherein he developed still further the thesis that the law of mutual aid is far more important than the survival of the fittest in the struggle for life and the progressive evolution of the species. He supported his thesis by many data drawn from animal and human history and existence, proving beyond doubt that those groups remaining upon the earth without extinction have been those which early discovered and practiced the law of mutual aid. This

INTRODUCTION

explains, I believe, more than any other cause, the thousands of years of continuing history of the peoples of China and India. In their family and tribal customs they have consistently practiced the law of mutual aid. It will be interesting to see whether modern statism can provide an equally strong means for survival through mutual aid. Certainly it was a catastrophe for the world that Kropotkin was too old at the time of the modern Russian revolution to exercise influence upon it, although he was sadly aware of the destructive turn it took and would, had he been younger, have endeavored to stem it, as he tells us in the autobiographical preface to his *Ethics*. Ways of expressing and practicing goodness have to be taught the young human creature as definitely as anything else has to be taught. The rational basis for such teaching is, I believe, to be found in a revival of the teaching and application of the law of mutual aid. I was pleased recently to discover an excellent essay by M. F. Ashley-Montagu, entitled "Man and the Social Appetite," in the *Saturday Review of Literature* (November 19, 1949), and so to know that others, too, are thinking along the same lines.

It is unfair, perhaps, to write this foreword when the author of the book may not wholly agree with it. That Mr. Payne is quite willing for me to do so is a proof of the largeness of his mind and the integrity of his spirit. That I do so is proof of my intense interest in his book and my conviction that it is an exceedingly important work, especially at this most perilous moment in our perilous times.

PEARL S. BUCK

CONTENTS

Introduction by Pearl S. Buck	vii
I. The Nechayev Monster	1
II. The Nature of the Nihilist Mind	39
III. Hitler and Nechayev	62
IV. The Fault in the Culture	79
V. Man = Zero	108
VI. The Nihilists in the Camps	146
VII. The Destruction of the World	175
VIII. The Continuing Terror	204
IX. The Task Before Us	233
Index	263

ZERO

I.
The Nechayev Monster

HE had a long dark face, a flat nose, thick hair which fell over his forehead, and piercing blue eyes; he was small and physically frail, and lived on his nervous energy. He was charming to women, whom he seduced at leisure, and he could keep awake for days on end, and all his friends observed his extraordinary untidiness, his bootlaces always undone, and his shirt falling to ribbons. Living with an intensity which frightened other men, who recognized that he possessed superior powers, superbly confident of his own insolence, plotting destruction, he dominated the Russian scene for a few brief years; and then disappeared into the underground cells of the Peter and Paul fortress in Petersburg; but even then, like a dark ghost, he terrorized from behind the prison bars, and even today we have reason to fear him. His name was Sergei Gennadiyevich Nechayev.

Only one photograph of Nechayev has survived; it occurs in a revolutionary handbook, and the small medallion in which it is framed has dimmed with age. It shows him bearded and brooding, with enormous eyes, the look of a man in a cage about to snap at the bars, the lips pursed and the cheeks sunken. But such a photograph might have been taken of any one of hundreds of young nihilist students who worked through the night, plotted and murdered and found themselves at last in exile or prison, or else—as often happened—they abjured their nihilist convictions and became small bureaucrats. Only the intensity of the gaze alarms. Though the medallion is fading, the eyes are full of life. It is what one might have expected. He was the founder of modern terrorism, the author of the wildest plan of destruction ever known, and the first nihilist to carry nihilism to its logical conclusions. He was a murderer, a thief and a blackmailer, but those were his lesser crimes.

Sergei Nechayev, the son of a village priest who was once a serf on Count Cheremetiev's estate, was born at Ivanovo, near Vladimir, a hundred miles northeast of Moscow, in 1847. Ivanovo was then a comparatively small town, which blossomed later into the great textile city of Ivanovo-Voznessensk. From his father Nechayev learned to recite long passages from the Bible, and received his first training in divinity; to the end of his life Nechayev wrote Russian with biblical rhythms. Of his mother, we know only that she had once been a servant in the houses of the nobility, and for some time she was a dress-maker. His father intended him for the priesthood, and when we have our first glimpse of him, he is twenty-one, wearing his peasant clothes and teaching divinity in a school in Petersburg: for some time previously he seems to have been a sign-painter in his native village. During the late autumn of 1868 he attended evening lectures at Petersburg University. From the beginning he was noticed. He had a sharp tongue, and a caustic contempt for his professors. He began to read voluminously. He read Babeuf, Blanqui, and Fournier, gave lectures on Louis Blanc, and struggled with the French dictionary, but never knew French well enough to understand exactly what was being said. He began to teach less and less divinity, spent his days in bed and plotted all night, living on borrowed money.

THE NECHAYEV MONSTER

The strange slovenly revolutionary with the extraordinary pallor began to be noticed in the higher revolutionary circles. He met Tkachev, whose manifestoes were being eagerly copied by the students. Tkachev had announced the possibility of a technique of revolt, and suggested that the revolution should begin from within the universities, with small bodies of determined students defying the police and the soldiers. "The social revolution can be accomplished by the use of a small force of determined young men ready to assume the task of destroying the government." Though Tkachev later became an anarchist and went into exile in Switzerland, for a brief while his influence was supreme, and his pamphlet called *To the Public* became the bible of the Petersburg students. A simultaneous revolt of all the students in the colleges of Petersburg and Moscow was planned for the Spring of 1869. Delegates were sent from the University of Petersburg to the University and colleges of Moscow. Nechayev remained in Petersburg, exhorting the students in secret conferences to arm themselves, produce clandestine literature, and go among the peasants. Then it was learned that the delegates sent to Moscow had been arrested. Shortly afterwards Nechayev disappeared from the scene, leaving the student revolutionaries to lead the revolt as best they could. The expected revolt in Petersburg spluttered out, but in Moscow the medical school revolted on March 19th 1869, and shortly afterwards the technological school and the University followed. These revolts were crushed, and it began to be suspected that Nechayev had been an *agent provocateur* who deliberately lit the fuse and then disappeared.

It is, however, unlikely that Nechayev was in any way in league with the police or with the famous Third Division which threw a net of *agents provocateurs* over the whole length and breadth of Russia. Perhaps his nerve failed him, or perhaps he fled because the police were already on his track. From his hiding-place he heard rumors that his disappearance was having a disquietening effect on the student revolutionaries, and since he was determined to maintain his leadership, and even to re-inforce it, he employed a ruse which became known later as "the Nechayev trick." He simply wrote to the young revolutionary Vera Zasulich, at that time a handsome girl of seventeen, two unsigned letters which he sent by ordinary post. The first read:

> While I was walking in the Vasilievski Park this morning, I passed the police prison van. As it came by me, a hand appeared at the window and threw out a slip of paper. I heard a voice saying: "If you are a student take this to the enclosed address." I am a student, and I felt it my duty to obey this summons. Destroy my letter.

The second letter, in Nechayev's well-known handwriting, read:

> They are taking me to prison. I do not know which prison. Tell the comrades that I hope one day to see them again. May our work go on.

Vera Zasulich was not a credulous person, and she seems to have been doubtful of the authenticity of Nechayev's prison van from the beginning, but she could not make up her mind —it was at least possible that Nechayev had been arrested— and she was prepared to assist Nechayev in every way. He was already a legend, brusque-mannered, consumately in command of himself, the student revolutionary who inspired most awe and most loyalty. She summoned a meeting of the students, showed the letter to Nechayev's sister, and it was agreed to call a mass meeting to demand the prisoner's release. Meanwhile the prisoner had gone into hiding in Moscow. He stayed there a fortnight, and then borrowing the passport of his friend Nikolaev he slipped over the border and made his way to Switzerland, where he stayed with Mikhail Bakhunin in Geneva, announcing to the world that he had escaped from the Peter and Paul fortress.

Mikhail Alexandrovich Bakhunin was now no longer at the height of his fame. He was fifty-four, enormously stout and toothless, and he suffered from a kind of palsy of the hands. He was a former artillery officer and a descendant of a long and famous line of landed gentry, and even though his life had been one long succession of revolutionary failures, he still commanded respect as the exponent of revolutionary anarchism. His pale blue eyes in a ruddy face, his great mane of iron-gray hair, his flamboyance and great height inspired trust; he was still the symbol of revolt. To this man, aging, complaining of gout, poverty-stricken, forever in search of sources of money and of excitement, the youth Nechayev came as a gift from heaven.

The relations between the two were soon intimate. Bakhunin marvelled at Nechayev's stories about the ceaseless revolts of the University students and implicitly believed Nechayev when he spoke of his own major role in the Russian revolution and his escape from the Peter and Paul fortress. He called Nechayev "Boy," and Nechayev called Bakhunin "Matrena," a diminutive for "Maria." There is some evidence that Nechayev seduced the old revolutionary. What is certain is that Bakhunin's flagging spirits were revived, and for six months—from March to August 1869—they worked and lived together. Bakhunin was so overwhelmed by the young student who possessed all the instincts of revolutionary intrigue that in May he had already given Nechayev a certificate embossed with the double axe and bearing the seal of the Central Committee of the European Revolutionary Alliance. The signed certificate read:

ZERO

> The bearer of this certificate is one of the accredited representatives of the Russian section of the World Revolutionary Alliance, No. 2771.
>
> MIKHAIL BAKHUNIN

The certificate was hardly more than a mark of affection and confidence, not unlike the letter he wrote to Nechayev during this period promising obedience "even to the forging of bank-notes." He was in love with Nechayev, or with the idea of Nechayev, and he was prepared to guide and obey and serve him; and confronted with the anarchic audacity of the youth who had escaped from the fortress and lit the revolutionary flames within Russia, he was prepared to take a subordinate position. He was famous; Nechayev was not; and he was perfectly prepared, during those first months of their friendship, to let their roles be reversed.

In five months, seven pamphlets of quite extraordinary violence were produced between them. On the whole, the style is Nechayev's, though here and there can be found the well-known sign manuals of Bakhunin's style. We can recognize passages which have been inserted by Bakhunin, who liked to use the phrase "without phrase" to suggest completeness; some twists and turns of sentences, an occasional haziness. What is direct and uncompromising remains Nechayev's; and the most impudent and terrifying product of their six months leisure, a short pamphlet called *The Revolutionary Catechism*, which was for a long time kept in cipher, shows the authentic accents of the twenty-one-year-old revolutionary.

The Revolutionary Catechism consists of twenty-six articles, divided into four sections. The catechism states bluntly that the purpose of the revolutionary is destruction, nothing less. All existing institutions are to be destroyed and the people must revert to brigandage. It is not the purpose of the revolutionary to put anything in the place of the existing state. Total destruction—Nechayev uses the doubly emphatic Russian word *vserasrouchitelnoi*—continues through the catechism like a refrain. He does not care if anything survives the flames, and even if nothing survives, this must be a matter of entire indifference to the revolutionary. He draws in the introductory articles a careful portrait of the agent of destruction, a mysterious impassive figure who is devoid of human emotions, an artist of revolution, comparable with Baudelaire's Dandy, who also believed in the injunction: *Perinde ac cadaver.* The people who take part in the revolution, and the people who will oppose it are placed in their necessary categories, and even the position of women in the revolution is resolutely analyzed. There are ominous underscorings, hints of undisclosed powers, moments when the pen seems about to falter, but Nechayev goes on to the very end, introducing with the utmost calm the prophetic portrait of the modern terrorist and sketching out the blue-print for the revolution of destruction. It is as though Hitler and Lenin, in their different ways, had read *The Revolutionary Catechism* and then set about following step by step the commands of the half-forgotten nihilist.

THE REVOLUTIONARY CATECHISM

The Duties of the Revolutionary towards himself

1. Every revolutionary must be a dedicated man. He should have no personal affairs, no business, no emotions, no attachments, no property and no name. All these must be wholly absorbed in the single thought and the single passion for revolution.

2. The revolutionary knows that in the very depths of his being he has broken all ties with society, both in word and

in deed. He breaks all ties with the civilized world, its laws, its customs, its morality, all those conventions generally accepted by the world. He is their implacable enemy, and if he has intercourse with the world, it is only for the purpose of destroying it.

3. The revolutionary despises all dogmas and all sciences, leaving them for future generations. He knows only one science: the science of destruction. For this reason, but only for this reason, he will study physics, mechanics, chemistry and perhaps medicine. With the same end in view he will dedicate himself day and night to the science of life: he will study men, their characteristics, the roles they play, all the phenomena of modern society in all its forms. The object is perpetually the same: the quickest and surest way of destroying the whole filthy order.

4. The revolutionary despises public opinion, he despises the present social morality and hates all its manifestations. The revolutionary defines as moral only that which assists the revolution, and defines as immoral and criminal that which stands in his way.

5. The revolutionary is wholly dedicated. He must show no mercy to the State or towards the civilized classes of society; nor does he ask for mercy for himself. Between him and society there is waged a mortal war, declared or concealed, a relentless and irreconcilable fight to the death. He must accustom himself to torture.

6. Tyrannical towards himself, the revolutionary must be tyrannical towards others. All the emotions that move human beings, all the soft and enervating feelings of kinship, love, friendship, gratitude and honor, must give way to a cold and single-minded passion for revolution. For him there exists only one pleasure, one consolation, one reward, one satisfaction—the success of the revolution. Night and day he must

have but one thought, but one aim—merciless destruction. Coldly, relentlessly, he pursues his aim, and he must be prepared to perish himself, as he must be prepared to destroy with his own hands those who stand in his way.

7. The nature of the true revolutionary is to exclude all sensitivity and all romantic enthusiasm; he must exclude equally all thoughts of hatred and vengeance. The revolutionary passion, practiced at every moment of the day until it has become a habit, is to be employed coldly, with calculation. At all times the revolutionary must obey, not his personal impulses, but only those which serve the cause of the revolution.

The Duties of the Revolutionary towards his Revolutionary Comrades

8. The revolutionary can have no friendship or affection except for those who have proved by their actions that they, like him, are agents of the revolution. His degree of friendship, devotion and obligation towards a revolutionary comrade must be determined only by the comrade's degree of usefulness to the cause of total revolutionary destruction.

9. It is superfluous to speak of solidarity among revolutionaries; it is here that the main strength of revolutionary activity lies. Comrades who possess the same revolutionary passion and understanding should, wherever possible, deliberate among themselves on all important matters; their decisions must be unanimous. When the decision is made, and the attack is carried through, then the revolutionaries wherever possible must rely solely on themselves, never running for advice or assistance unless the situation dictates such a course.

10. All real revolutionaries should have second and third string revolutionaries under their command: that is, they must be able to control those who are not yet completely initiated.

ZERO

These lower members of the revolutionary order should be regarded as revolutionary capital placed at their disposal. This capital should, of course, be spent as economically as possible in order to derive from it the greatest possible profit. The real revolutionary regards himself as capital placed at the disposal of the successful revolution, but this capital—himself—must not be expended by any decisions of his own. He is expendable only when there is unanimous agreement to this effect among the fully initiated comrades.

11. When a comrade is in danger, it may be necessary to determine whether he is expendable. The decision must not be arrived at on the basis of sentiment; only the eventual success of the revolution has any importance at this juncture. The revolutionaries must therefore make an equation between the revolutionary usefulness of the comrade who is in danger and the number of comrades who may become expendable in the effort to save him. The actual equation must be examined, and action must be taken solely in accordance with the solution of the equation.

The Duties of the Revolutionary towards Society

12. The new member, having given proof of his loyalty not by words, but by deeds, can be received into the society only by the unanimous agreement of all the members.

13. The revolutionary enters the world of the state, of the classes and of so-called civilization, and he lives in this world only because he has faith in its quick and complete destruction. He no longer remains a revolutionary if he keeps faith with anything in this world. *He should not hesitate to destroy any position, any place, or any man in this world.*[1] He must hate everyone and everything with an equal hatred. All the worse for him if he has in the world relationships with parents,

[1] The italics are in the original.

friends, or lovers; *he is no longer a revolutionary if he is swayed by these relationships.*

14. Since the final aim is implacable destruction, the revolutionary can and sometimes must live within society, while pretending to be completely other than he is. A revolutionary must penetrate everywhere; he must enter high society as well as the middle classes; he must penetrate the shops, the churches, the palaces of the aristocracy, the official, military and literary worlds; he must be found among the members of the Third Division and even in the Imperial Palace.

15. In the foul society we live in, it is necessary to divide people into several categories; the first category comprises those who must be condemned to death without delay. Comrades must make the registers of the condemned according to the relative gravity of their crimes, always remembering what is useful for the success of the revolution; and when the registers have been compiled, the executions should be so arranged that those who are first on the register should actually be executed before the others.

16. When a list of those who are condemned to death is made, he who makes it must in no way allow himself to be influenced by considerations of hatred; nor can the hatred evoked among others but be of advantage to the revolution, if it causes a ferment among the people. Whenever a man is murdered, our duty is to concern ourselves only with the question—in what way has his death profited the revolution? So we must first destroy these people whose existence is most inimical to the revolutionary organization; their violent and sudden death will put fear into the heart of the government, break its will, and deprive it of its most energetic and intelligent agents.

17. The second group composes those to whom we concede life provisionally in order that, by a series of monstrous acts, they may drive the people into inevitable revolt.

18. The third group consists of animals in high positions remarkable neither for their intelligence nor their energy, but who have wealth, connections, influence and power as a result of their position. These we must exploit in every conceivable manner; we must blackmail them, ferret out their dirty secrets, and make them our slaves. In this way their power, their position, their influence, and their wealth become an inexhaustible treasure, and a precious asset in our adventure.

19. The fourth group is composed of various ambitious people in the service of the state; and liberals of varying shades of opinion. The revolutionaries will pretend to be blindly conspiring with them, obediently following their aims. But we shall do this only the more successfully in order to bring them under our power, *so as to reveal their secrets and completely compromise them.* Thereupon, no path of retreat will be open to them, and they can be used to create disorder within the state.

20. The fifth group comprises doctrinaires, conspirators, and revolutionaries; those who orate away at meetings, or on paper. They must be constantly driven into ambiguous positions; they must be compelled to come out into the open and assume real and dangerous tasks. The majority of these will disappear, but of the rest we shall make genuine revolutionaries.

21. The sixth group is extremely important. These are women; and we shall divide them into three classes. First, completely frivolous women, unintelligent and without the least signs of sensitivity—these are to be used in exactly the same way as the third and fourth groups among men. Second, women who are ardent, capable, and devoted to the revolution, but who do not belong to us because they have not reached the stage of complete understanding of revolutionary action; these are without phrase, and we shall use them as we use the

fifth group among men. Finally, there are the women who are completely with us: those who are wholly with us and have accepted our program in its entirety. These we are to regard as the most precious of our treasures, and without them nothing can be done.

The Duties of the Revolutionary Association towards the People

22. The purpose of our society is the entire emancipation and happiness of the people, namely the laborers. We are convinced that this happiness and emancipation can only come about as a result of an all-destroying popular revolt. The society will use all its resources to increase and intensify the evils and miseries of the people, believing that at last their patience will be exhausted and they can be incited to a revolutionary *levée-en-masse*.

23. By a popular revolution, the society does not mean a revolution which follows the classic patterns of the West, a pattern which finds itself completely restrained by the existence of property and the traditional social orders of so-called civilization and morality; and so the western concept of revolution has hitherto meant only the exchanging of one form of political organization for another, thus creating the so-called revolutionary state. The only revolution which can do any good to the people is that which destroys, from top to bottom, every idea of the state, overthrowing all traditions, social orders, and classes in Russia.

24. With this end in view, the society has no intention of imposing on the people from above any other organization. The future organization will no doubt spring up from the movement and life of the people, but this is a matter for future generations to decide. Our task is terrible, total, inexorable, and universal destruction!

25. It follows that in drawing closer towards the people, we must unite, above all, with those elements of the people who have never ceased to protest since the foundations of the State of Muscovy, not only in words, but in deeds, against everything directly or indirectly connected with the state; against the nobility, against the bureaucracy, against priests, and every kind of tradesman; against all the exploiters of the people. We must unite with the adventurous bands of robbers, who are the only true revolutionaries of Russia.

26. To concentrate the people into a single force wholly destructive and wholly invincible—this is our aim, our conspiracy, and our task! [2]

The sources of the extraordinary pamphlet of Nechayev are to be found in the times he lived in; he did not invent the philosophy of destruction; there were hints of it all through the nineteenth century. The French Revolution had failed; there was no clear-cut social revolution following in the wake of the industrial revolution, and men were becoming more disposed to violence as they saw themselves harnessed to machines, those instruments possessing violent powers. The Wreckers had destroyed the machines; other wreckers were to come, and they would not sing to a gentle dance tune the song of *The Tazzling Mill*, with its plaintive invocation of a desire to burn down all the mills of Lancashire. There was sterner stuff in Michelet who, after contemplating the history of the French Revolution, wrote:

> Let this society perish, then, through the fury of its factions and the fierceness of its civil wars. Let the cities return to their original state of forests, let the forests become the dens of men, and then, after many centuries have elapsed, when their wickedness and perversity have disappeared beneath the rust

[2] *Mikhail Bakhunin's Sozial-politischer Briefwechsel,* edited by Mikhail Dragomirow, Stuttgart, 1895, pp. 374-380.

THE NECHAYEV MONSTER

of barbarism, and they have sunk back again into primitiveness, then they will be ready once more to be civilized.

The same delight in absolute destruction occurs in many of the anonymous pamphlets which heralded the Revolution of 1848. Here the romantic violence of the revolutionaries reaches verbal heights (or depths) rarely surpassed. Writing anonymously in the Dresden *Volksblatter*, Richard Wagner, while still retaining his position as Royal *Kapellmeister*, said:

> The old world is in ruins from which a new world will arise; for the sublime goddess REVOLUTION comes rushing and roaring on the wings of storm; destroying and blessing she sweeps across the earth; before her pipes the storm; it shakes so violently all man's handiwork that vast clouds of dust darken the air, and where her mighty foot treads, all that has been built for ages past in idle whim crashes in ruins, and the hem of her robe sweeps the last remains of it away.

The theory that it was becoming necessary to destroy the State and revert to a primitive barbarism was perhaps peculiarly French; Blanqui, Louis Blanc, Proudhon, and later Sorel spoke approvingly of the utmost use of violence, without ever defining exactly what other aims beside destruction could be accomplished. Violence was in the air men breathed, a legacy of the revolutionary Terror and the Napoleonic wars, and even Flaubert occasionally lashed himself into a furious rage against the *bourgeoisie*, consigning them to imaginary extinction, though it was the *bourgeoisie* who bought his books, defended him in the courts, and continually admired him. "We have faith in poison," wrote the French poet Arthur Rimbaud. "We know how to surrender our whole selves every day. Now comes the time of the assassins."

From French sources, ill-read and sometimes misunderstood, Nechayev derived the intellectual delight in violence;

but other elements were at work. There was his own desire to take vengeance on the world, the memory of his father's serfdom, the knowledge that it was only by acts of dramatic violence that he could ensure his leadership among the students. Violence had become a code. The students who took part in the attempted assassinations of the Russian ministers saw themselves as the heroic leaders of their country; they knew how "to surrender their whole selves every day." Their nihilism had roots deep in Russian history. Bazarov in Turgenev's *Fathers and Sons* says: "The nihilist is the man who bows before no authority. We must act according to what appears most useful, or rather the most useful thing of all is to deny. There is not a single institution of our society which should not be destroyed," and when Bazarov is reminded that only a handful of nihilists in Russia were fighting against the huge inertia of the court and the peasantry, he answered: "You should remember that a farthing candle was enough to put all Moscow to the flames." Nechayev was disposed to be the farthing candle, and he too denied, denying like Goethe's romantic Mephistopheles all the potentialities of the human spirit, consigning the human race to a state of perpetual brigandage for the sake of a final act of destruction. It is significant that he paid no attention at all to the kind of social state which followed the holocaust. All that remained was a pious hope that something better would emerge, and even if it did not emerge this was a matter of entire indifference. "Fire the cities," he wrote, "then plow them under: afterwards every peasant will be his own master." The strange theorem of *The Revolutionary Catechism* outlined, not so much a technique of revolution, but a technique for punishing the human race, or at least all those who were not peasants.

The emergence of the nihilist was not something new in Russia. To be a nihilist meant to set no value to human life, human thought, or human creativeness. The Russian peasant in the immense loneliness of the Russian plains sometimes gave way to desolate rages; at such moments he struck out at the world around him, suffered intolerably and thought fiercely about suicide. At some period in the middle of the seventeenth century there had emerged the strange sect of the *raskolniki* [3] or schismatics, who pronounced against Father Nikhon's desire to revise the translations of the scriptures. These schismatics were persecuted by their enemies, and resorted in despair to self-holocausts, *noyades,* self-burials, hunger-deaths and the "red" or beautiful death which took the form of strangulation by request. They were the apostles of violence; it hardly mattered whether the violence was directed inward or outward. Dostoyevsky was fascinated by them, immersed himself in their history and contemplated writing a long novel about them; the most nihilistic of his characters he called Raskolnikov. He recounts Raskolnikov's dream as he lies ill on a hospital bed at Easter. Raskolnikov, who murders an old woman in order that he might obtain power equal to Napoleon's, dreams of a plague which sweeps over Europe from the heart of Asia, and the vision of death and destruction is hardly different from Nechayev's:

> In this plague, as I saw it in a dream, everyone was to be destroyed with the exception of a few, a few of the elect. There appeared new trichinae, microscopic beings penetrating the bodies of people. Yet these beings were spirits, endowed with a mind and a will. People who absorbed them instantly became mad and raved. But never, never did people consider themselves so understanding and unshakable in truth as the infected ones considered themselves: their verdicts, their scientific deductions, their moral convictions and beliefs—all

[3] The term is derived from two Russian words *ras,* asunder, and *kolot,* to split. The *raskolniki* are discussed at greater length in Chapter IV.

were unshakable. Whole villages and people became infected and went mad. All were troubled and did not understand one another; everyone thought that he alone possessed the truth, and was tormented when he looked at others . . . People killed one another in senseless malice. One people rose up against another people, armies against armies; but the armies on the march suddenly began to torment themselves, their columns became disordered, and their soldiers thereupon threw themselves on one another, bit and clawed and murdered one another; and in the cities all day long the alarm sounded. Fires began to break out, famines came, everyone and everything was coming to an end. The plague grew and swept on further and further. In the whole world only a few men could save themselves—these were the pure and the elect, destined to start a new race and a new life, to renew and purify the earth.[4]

Nechayev, however, was not concerned with the elect, and had no intention of renewing and purifying the earth; it was enough that everyone and everything was coming to an end. He would provide the initial stimulus in the shape of the revolutionary committees dedicated to pure revolutionary destruction, and the curiously impassive figure of the *anonymous assassin*, with no will of his own, no friendships, no attachment except his attachment to destruction, possessed of a delusive calm which concealed a deep hatred against the world, hatred inspired by years of poverty, neglect, disappointed hopes, and humiliation. "Now, friends, let us start the drama," wrote Nechayev in another pamphlet; and the drama consisted of the destruction of the entire world.

Nechayev and Bakhunin, plotting quietly and contentedly in Geneva, were faced with one obstacle to their hopes; destruction is always expensive. They looked around for money. In 1858 an eccentric Russian landowner with communist lean-

[4] *Crime and Punishment,* Epilogue, II.

ings had handed over to the revolutionary Alexander Herzen the sum of eight hundred pounds sterling deposited in a bank in London; then he went out to found a colony of communists in an island of the Pacific. Nothing more was ever heard of him. Eleven years later the capital of the Bakhmetiev fund was still intact. Nechayev heard of the money, sought out Alexander Herzen and induced him to sign over half of the fund to Bakhunin. Nechayev spoke of the revolutionary cells he had founded in Russia, and described his escape from the Peter and Paul fortress. Herzen argued bitterly against surrendering the fund, but he was too old to resist Nechayev's eloquence; and by the end of July the money was already in Nechayev's hands. Bakhunin was still living in a dream world, bathing in the reflected glow from the young revolutionary and willingly surrendering the ten thousand Swiss francs which represented one half of the residue from the Bakhmetiev fund and their total resources for the revolution of destruction. They went for long walks in the mountains together. Bakhunin represented his small successes as being veritable revolutions which had compelled the states of Europe to fear him; Nechayev pretended to be in continuous correspondence with the highest Russian officials and the most dedicated students. Bakhunin, suffering from gout, dropsy, and boils, becoming shaggier as the summer passed, began to believe that Russia was ripe for the new kind of revolution. When Nechayev prepared to return, armed with the certificate of the Revolutionary Alliance and a poem called *Enlightened Personality*—which had been written for him by the poet Nikolai Ogarev, who was himself the least successful of revolutionaries—Bakhunin blessed his departure and invoked the assistance of some Bulgarian revolutionaries who accompanied Nechayev to Bucharest and helped him across the frontier.

Nechayev was now in his element. He proclaimed that the

world revolution would break out on February 9, 1861, the tenth anniversary of the freeing of the serfs. There would be war lasting through the summer, and perhaps—he was not quite certain—there might be a Universal Congress in October. His mind moved now with delighted incomprehension among the simplicities of revolution. Asked why he had chosen the spring of 1870 for the time of revolt, he explained that if the revolt failed, this would at least allow the revolutionaries to fight along the Volga and the Dnieper, and the people would be able to find shelter in the forests. As he drew nearer to the center of the revolt, he no longer talked of destruction, but of vast upheavals, great revolutionary surges, whole masses of the population joining the brigands in the forests. There was nothing immature in this picture of the Russian Revolution. The peasant leaders, Stenka Razin and Pugachev, had led the peasants into the forests in the time of Catherine the Great. Destroy the cities, let the peasants loose—this had been the clear call of Russian revolutionaries in the middle ages. So it remained, until the Communists entirely reversed the procedure of revolution and gave power to the industrial proletariat over the peasants. Nechayev's admiration for the brigands had been expressed in several pamphlets:

> Brigandage [he wrote] has always been one of the most honoured forms of Russian national life. The brigand is the hero, the defender, the popular avenger, the irreconcilable enemy of the state, and of all social and civil order established by the state. He is the wrestler in life and in death against all this civilization of officials, of nobles, of priests and kings. . . He who does not understand brigands cannot understand the history of the Russian masses. He who is not sympathetic with them cannot sympathize with the lives of the people, and lacks the strength to avenge the ancient, interminable wrongs suffered by the people: he belongs in the camp of the enemy, the

THE NECHAYEV MONSTER

partisans of the state. . . . It is only through brigandage that the vitality, ardour and strength of the people can be established indisputably. . . . The brigand in Russia is the true and unique revolutionary. . . . He who desires to make a serious revolution in Russia must enter their world. The season is at hand. The anniversaries of Stenka Razin and Pugachev are approaching, and it is time to celebrate these warriors of the people. Let us all prepare for the feast.[5]

But if the appeal to brigandage formed a part of the necessary propaganda for the revolution, the means of destroying the state remained obscure. In his larger ideas, Nechayev could be subtly convincing; he was less happy when he came down to details. In a closely argued pamphlet called *Principles of Revolution* he wrote, "We recognize no other activity except the work of utter destruction, but we admit that the form our activity will take may be extremely varied—poison, the knife, rope, etc. In this struggle the revolutionary sacrifices everything." The instruments of violence are somehow not convincing, and it was perhaps characteristic of Nechayev, but not of his philosophy, that his total success in violence consisted in the strangling of a defenseless student.

Meanwhile, Nechayev was determined upon his revolution. His chief credentials were Bakhunin's certificate and Ogarev's poem, which praised Nechayev as the forerunner of a new race. Working in secrecy and under many names—at various times he called himself Ivan Petrov, Ivan Pavlov, Dmitri Feodorov, Captain Panin and Special Agent Number 2664—he first formed the Moscow Group of the Russian Section of the World Revolutionary Alliance, with 150 members from the University and colleges. Later, there appeared nine sections of the World Revolutionary Alliance in Petersburg, with Tkachev as the head. Later still, more mysterious societies

[5] James Guillaume, *L'Internationale; documents et souvenirs*, I, 63.

emerged, with names like Confederation of the Ax, Committee of the Five. Detailed lists of those to be condemned to death were drawn up, in accordance with paragraphs fifteen and sixteen of *The Revolutionary Catechism*. At the head of Nechayev's list was Trepov, the Chief of Police, followed by General Mezentsev, who was in charge of the Third Division. The life of the Tsar was to be temporarily spared, so that "the free peasantry, having broken the chains of slavery, on the day of vengeance break his head, and at the same time pull down the tattered cloaks of the obsolete imperial system." Nechayev made his headquarters in Moscow, and on the advice of his friend Ouspensky, he lived quietly in the Petrovsko-Razoumovskaya Akademia, a small agricultural school on the outskirts of the city. From this hiding place he received dues, authorized the admission of revolutionary students into the World Alliance, collected firearms, printed pamphlets, and introduced a system of so blackmailing the members of the Alliance that they were forever at his mercy. He would, for example, order one of the members to steal money. He would receive the money, and hold over the thief the threat of revelation. It was during this period that there occurred the incident that brought Nechayev's downfall. So far, he had employed all the minor arts of terrorism; he had used blackmail, and threats; now he was to use murder.

Among the students at the agricultural college there was a youth bearing the curious name of Ivan Ivanovich Ivanov. He seems, from every account, to have been one of those dedicated youths who lived only for the workers and peasants. He went out to the villages to teach the peasants how to read; he assisted poor students and starved himself in order to establish cheap lodging houses. Nechayev had selected these cheap lodging houses for the meetings of his revolutionary groups. He ordered Ivanov to post a pamphlet called "From those who are united to those who are scattered" in the messhalls, and the police, on their tours of inspection, were not long in discovering the pamphlet and ordering that the lodging houses be closed down. Ivanov was heart-broken. The fault was Nechayev's. He said so openly. Nechayev explained that he had merely handed on the instructions of the Secret Committee. "Which Secret Committee?" asked Ivanov. "Why, everyone knows the Secret Committee, or rather no one knows," Nechayev answered. Ivanov said: "I don't know anything about the Secret Committee. Every time you disappear and consult the Committee, you come back and tell us that it has endorsed your views. I don't believe the Secret Committee exists." Saying this, Ivanov signed his own death warrant. Nechayev, who had never encountered such determined opposition, conscious of the truth of Ivanov's statement, and worried by the growing uneasiness and growing disloyalty of the students, determined upon a dramatic act. He would kill Ivanov. As many members of the Alliance as possible would be made to participate in the murder, and thereby he would be able to hold over them the threat of exposure. He called meetings of the students. Ivanov was summarily condemned to death, Nechayev explaining that the youth was secretly connected with the Third Division and was about to betray the Alliance. On November 21, 1869, Ivanov was enticed into the cellar of the agricultural college on the promise that he would then be shown the secret printing presses of the organization. There, with two assistants, Nechayev at first tried to strangle him, then shot him in the head, then strangled him with a silk scarf tied round his neck. Ivanov had fought hard, and when the murder was over Nechayev was covered from head to foot in blood. Afterwards there were discussions on how to dispose of the body; and it was Nechayev who answered that there was nothing simpler: all you had to do was to throw the weighted body into a pond. That same night a hole was cut in the ice of a pond in the Petrovsk Park, bricks were heaped into the pockets of Ivanov's coat and the revolutionaries observed with satisfaction that the ice was already reforming over the body as they slipped stealthily away. Four days later the body rose to the surface, breaking through the thin layer of ice, the police were summoned, the whole plot was uncovered, and immediately a hue and cry was raised for Nechayev. Once again Nechayev slipped across the frontier, nursing the swollen thumb which had been bitten by Ivanov in the death agony.

The conspirators were rounded up, and the court trial, held in Petersburg, occupied the attention of journalists for two months, from 1st July to September 11th 1871. There had been more than a year's delay, but now all the details of the secret societies were known; the extent of Nechayev's tyrannical power over hundreds and perhaps thousands of students was revealed. The defendants included the youth Ouspensky who had taken part in the murder of Ivanov, the revolutionary Peter Tkachev, an obscure Frenchman with the extraordinary name of Pajou de Moncey, and a number of amateur revolutionaries including Prince Tcherkassov. Most of the defendants were young and connected with the agricultural college: the secretary of the college, Pryjov, was also implicated. Other inexplicable murders were attributed to the group, probably without cause. *The Revolutionary Catechism*, and a further essay on *The Principles of Revolution* were found and decoded. The *bourgeois* were fascinated and terrified by the emergence of "the Nechayev Monster," knowing only too well that the blue-print for total destruction, which Nechayev had gathered hazily out of the intellectual air of his time, was more than a theoretician's dream;

they recognized that in the Russia of their time "total destruction" had become only too possible. The members of the Alliance, who were arrested and placed on trial, were given light sentences; it was recognized that the mind behind the murder was Nechayev's.

Nechayev's glory was already departing. He made his way back to Geneva with the money he had found in Ivanov's pocket and with the funds of the Alliance. Bakhunin was away in Locarno. Nechayev stayed with Ogarev, who gave him a lukewarm reception and seems not to have believed his story that he had once again broken out of the Peter and Paul fortress. But Bakhunin greeted him as a long-lost friend, and is supposed to have jumped with so much joy that he cracked his head against the ceiling.

The long idyll with Bakhunin continued as before. Nechayev recounted his exploits and received absolution for his murder, while Bakhunin, wearying of his long struggle to foment anarchist revolutions, in bad health, immersed in a translation into Russian of Karl Marx's *Das Kapital*—which a Russian publisher had commissioned against a payment of twelve hundred rubles ($500)—and perhaps annoyed by the presence of the illegitimate child which his unfaithful wife had just presented him, saw in Nechayev the heaven-sent instrument who would bring the reign of anarchy to birth. There were problems to be solved. They must find money. Nechayev objected to the older revolutionary wasting his time on a translation of Karl Marx, and suggested that the matter could be easily resolved. All that was necessary was that they should send, under the seal of the secret committee of the *Narodnaya Rasprava* (the People's Vengeance)—one of the organizations created by Nechayev in Moscow—a letter addressed to the publisher Polyakov, threatening him with unpleasant consequences if he continued to demand that Bakhunin should waste his time on the translation. The publisher, remembering the fate of Ivanov, could thereupon infer that the advance payment of three hundred rubles had been forfeited. Bakhunin was delighted with the trick, but he reminded Nechayev that the three hundred rubles had already been spent. Were there other sources of money? Nechayev remembered the Bakhmetiev fund. Herzen was dead. Ogarev and Herzen's son were the surviving trustees of the fund. The trustees were called upon to surrender the remaining portion of the fund, and in Geneva the remaining ten thousand Swiss francs were handed over in a solemn ceremony by the young Herzen to Ogarev, by Ogarev to Bakhunin, and by Bakhunin to Nechayev.

Meanwhile, the affairs of Nechayev were no longer doing well. He was growing increasingly contemptuous of Bakhunin, and Bakhunin in turn was wondering whether it would ever be possible to tame this strange monster of revolution. Nechayev revived the old revolutionary journal, *The Bell*. In it, there were veiled attacks against Bakhunin, and the crude vigor of these attacks alarmed other revolutionaries who might otherwise have been sympathetic to Nechayev's cause. The Polyakov *affaire* was already becoming known; Marx seized upon the extraordinary threat to the Russian publisher as an excuse for an open attack on Bakhunin; and since Nechayev's complicity was well-known, Nechayev was also in danger of Marx's wrath. Worse still, the Russian government was demanding the extradition of Nechayev as a common criminal. There was only one course, and Nechayev took it. Stealing as many incriminatory papers belonging to Bakhunin as possible, he fled to London.

Bakhunin was in a quandary. He suspected with good reason that Nechayev would publish the papers or sell them to the highest bidder. Marx or the British Government might

THE NECHAYEV MONSTER

see their way to buy them—these diaries and manifestoes and secret lists of the adherents of the World Revolutionary Alliance. From Neuchâtel, where he had gone into hiding, Bakhunin wrote an urgent letter to his friend Talandier in London:

My dear friend,

I have just heard that N. has been received by you, and that you have given him the address of our mutual friends. I am forced to the conclusion that the two letters which O [Ogarev] and I sent to you, warning you to hold him at arm's distance, have arrived too late. Without the least exaggeration I can say that this delay may have terrible consequences.

It may seem strange to you that we warn you against a man to whom we have given letters of introduction—letters which were written in the warmest terms. But these letters were written in May, and since then we have been compelled to face some extremely grave incidents—incidents which have made us break off all relations with N. At the risk of appearing casual and inconsequential, we find ourselves possessed of the sacred duty of warning you against him. I will try to explain the reasons for the change.

It is perfectly true that N. is the man who has been most persecuted by the Russian government, which has covered the whole continent of Europe with a cloud of spies in order to find him; and they have demanded his extradition both from Germany and Switzerland. It is also true that N. is one of the most active and energetic persons I have ever known. When he serves what he calls *the cause*, he never hesitates, stops at nothing, and is wholly merciless towards himself and towards others. This was the chief quality which attracted me to him, and made me seek his help and advice over a long period. There are some who say he is a fraud; this is untrue. He is a devoted, but at the same time, a dangerous fanatic; and with him an alliance can never but be disastrous. And this is why;

he belonged first to a secret society which actually existed in Russia. This society exists no more; all its members have been arrested. N. alone remains, and alone he represents the "committee." The Russian societies having been destroyed, he is compelled to form new ones on Russian territory. All this is perfectly natural, legitimate, and useful, but the means with which he undertakes these measures is detestable. . .

Let me warn you! He will spy on you, and attempt to get possession of all your secrets; if he is left alone in your room in your absence, he will open all your drawers, read all your correspondence, and if he finds a letter which in some way compromises you or your friends, he will steal it and guard it carefully for his own purposes of intimidation. Then, too, if you introduce him to your friend, his first aim will be to sow dissension, scandal, and intrigue between you, and make you quarrel. If your friend has a wife or a daughter, he will try to seduce her and get her with child, forcing her beyond the limits of conventional morality, and so place her, that she is compelled to make a revolutionary protest against society. Do not, I beg of you, cry out that this is an exaggeration! All this has happened and can be proved. When he is unmasked, this poor N. is so childlike, so simple, in spite of his systematic perversity, that he believed he could even convert me. . . He has betrayed the confidence of us all, stolen our letters, horribly compromised us—in a word, he has behaved like a villain. His only excuse lies in his fanaticism. Without knowing it, he is terribly ambitious, because he has at last identified the revolutionary cause with his own person. He is not an egotist in the worst sense of the word, because he terribly risks himself and leads the life of a martyr, submitting himself to great privations and incredible labour. . . He is a fanatic, a loyal fanatic—and at the same time a very dangerous one—association with whom may be fatal to all concerned. His methods are abhorrent. He has come to the conclusion that in order to create a workable and strong organization, one must use as a basis the philosophy of Machiavelli and adopt the motto of the Jesuits "Violence for the Body; lies for the Soul."

With the exception of a small group who are to be the chosen leaders, all the members of this organization will serve as blind tools in the hands of the leaders, obedient and loyal. It is permissible to deceive these members, compromise them in every way, rob them—even murder them if necessary. They are cannon-fodder for his conspiracies. For the good of the cause he must be allowed to gain full mastery over your person, even against your will. When we came together and opposed him, what did he say? He said, "This is how we do things. Anyone who disapproves of us, anyone who refuses to use terror against our enemies, we shall deceive. They must come with us the whole way, or face the consequences. . ."

So you understand he remains very dangerous, because he daily commits acts of terror, abuses men's confidence and is treacherous; and it is all the more difficult to guard against these things because one hardly suspects the possibility.[6]

One hardly suspects the possibility . . . Bakhunin was bemused, as he had never been bemused before; it was beyond all comprehension, he said, and yet there was nothing performed by Nechayev which he had not himself encouraged, and done himself a hundred times. Even the name of his friend terrified him; he dared not write it down in full; and he went bitterly complaining against the injustice of "Boy" to anyone who cared to listen to him.

Meanwhile Bakhunin had performed a useful service to humanity; the letter to Talandier from Neuchâtel, dated July 24, 1870, provides the perfect summary of the nihilist character, and belongs to the great series of "Characters" written during the seventeenth and eighteenth centuries; and this was the last, the most reprehensible, the most dangerous

---

[6] Michel Bakhunine, *Correspondence*, edited by Michel Dragomirow, Paris, 1889, p. 310-311.

of all. Bakhunin saw the danger and recoiled in horror. The huge terrifying insolence of Nechayev frightened him, as later it pleased Lenin; and what is apparent throughout this long letter is a kind of envy of Nechayev, a deep love, and even an understanding; it is as though Bakhunin was saying, "He is terrible beyond words; he has compromised me; but he is singularly great in his terrible way." Bakhunin had only been playing with destruction; this was the real thing. He had written once, "The desire for destruction is at the same time a desire for creation." He had only half believed it. Now for the first time he saw this belief parading in the flesh.

Stung into fury by his loss, Bakhunin writes with quite extraordinary penetration of the nihilist character. Himself a nihilist or nearly a nihilist, he is able to relate the construction of the nihilist mind. Mostly, it is only the nihilists who write convincingly about the nihilist character. So Dostoyevsky describes Kirillov with immense understanding, and Hitler (though he was pretending to be doing something else) describes his own nihilism in the speech he delivered after the blood bath of 1934. Bakhunin was so frightened of Nechayev that he remained in hiding for six weeks; he wrote innumerable letters of warning to his friends, and it was only when he received news that Nechayev was poverty-stricken in London that he dared escape from his hiding place and come to Geneva.

Little is known of Nechayev's brief visit to London. He edited a revolutionary journal, *The Commune*, which survived for two numbers; here Bakhunin is once more bitterly and trenchantly attacked, and there is a vitriolic account of the way in which the trustees of the Bakhmetiev fund were compelled to hand over the money. Nechayev asks what has happened to the interest, amounting to fourteen hundred Swiss francs, which had accumulated through the years; and the theme of total destruction is repeated in the obscure revolutionary journal printed by an obscure revolutionary in the placid backwaters of London.

Nechayev left London, where there was no welcome for him—Bakhunin had been only too successful in warning everyone against him. In January 1871 he was in Paris. In March he was once again in Zurich, working as a house-painter with a Serbian passport. It was said that he even visited Lyons during the few days when Bakhunin placed himself at the head of the Committee of Public Safety, during the Commune. All that is known for certain is that Nechayev wandered over France and Switzerland penniless, and what survived of the famous suitcase stuffed with incriminating papers was surrendered for the price of a night's lodging. He still spoke of "the essential tasks of the revolution," he was still surrounded by a loyal but improvident band of followers, but the original impetus was wearing out; and when the Russian government renewed its demand for his extradition, Nechayev allowed himself—perhaps deliberately—to be betrayed by the Pole, Adolf Stempkowski, who had taken part in the insurrection of 1863, only to become a Russian secret agent. He met Stempkowski in the early summer. In September the trap was laid, and Nechayev was captured in a café where Stempkowski had arranged to meet him. In October he was already in the Peter and Paul fortress. Bakhunin says he made a special journey to Zurich to warn Nechayev of his impending fate. It seems unlikely, for Bakhunin himself was under police observation. However, he wrote in a letter to Ogarev:

> Something within me tells me that this time Nechayev, who is utterly lost and certainly knows it, will retrieve all his old energy and steadfastness from the depths of his character, which may be confused and vitiated, but is not low. He will

ZERO

go under as a hero, but this time he will betray no one and nothing.

From the moment when Nechayev was handed over to the Russian police, he behaved as Bakhunin had prophesied.

The trial, which took place in Petersburg in January 1873, was brief and explosive. Nechayev saw himself as the heroic defender of terrorism, refused to answer questions, hurled abuse at the prosecutor, defended the killing of Ivanov as "a purely political matter," and denied the competence of the Court to prosecute him. He refused to employ a lawyer. Asked by the judge whether he was guilty of murdering Ivanov, he replied: "I am an exile! I am no longer a citizen of the Russian Empire! I utterly despise all your formalities of justice, and I am ashamed to allow you to judge my conduct. I refuse to be the slave of your despotic government. Long live the Zemski Sobor!" This reference to the States-General instituted in the time of Peter the Great and then abandoned is the only reference to any kind of representative government he ever made. He was not interested in government, but he was, very curiously, interested in conceptions of personal honor, and when the judge finally asked him whether he had anything further to say in his defense, he repeated the claim he had made to all those who had examined him previously. He said: "It is humiliating to defend myself against these obvious calumnies. All Russia knows that I am a political criminal. I repeat what I have already said to Count Levachov—the government can take my life away, but not my honor!" At last he was sentenced to twenty-five years in Siberia, and was dragged from the Court shouting "Down with despotism!" He was not sent to Siberia; instead he was imprisoned in the Ravelin Alexis of the Peter and Paul fortress. But before being imprisoned there occurred, as always in Russia, the ceremony of public degradation. The government was so afraid he might be rescued that the ceremony took place at night, with the prisoner placed in a hollow square of soldiers and policemen. There, in the dark, while the drums were beating, he cried out: "The guillotine will soon be standing in the place where I am, and it will lop off the heads of those who brought me here. Down with the Tsar! Long live freedom!" The Tsar himself sent a message to the military governor of the city. It was very simple, and read: "Put Nechayev discreetly and forever in the fortress." This was done, and after they achieved power the Bolsheviks found in the Peter and Paul fortress an order written by Bogorodetsky, the governor of the fortress, dated January 29, 1873: "I order that Sergei Nechayev, deprived of all his rights and imprisoned yesterday under the order of His Majesty in the Ravelin Alexis shall be put in cell number 5 in the greatest secret and guarded with the greatest vigilance; his name is never to be pronounced, and he is to be known only by the number of his cell."

Since the beginning of the eighteenth century the Ravelin Alexis, where Alexis, the son of Peter the Great, had been imprisoned throughout the greater part of his life, was known as the darkest, most solitary, and most honorable prison in the whole of Russia. Bakhunin, Dostoyevsky, Kropotkin, Chernichevsky and many other famous revolutionaries had been imprisoned there. Nechayev was given a small, dark, low-roofed cell, two paces broad and seven feet high, in a small moated tower in the center of the fortress, where the walls were two metres thick. In one corner there was a straw bed with a woolen counterpane which had worn as thin as paper; in another corner there was a high wooden pail with a cover called a *parashka;* there was a Bible—nothing else. For days on end, Nechayev was chained to the stone walls; occasionally he was allowed out of his cell for ten minutes every forty-eight hours.

The achievements of Nechayev had only just begun. Shackled, and in solitary confinement, he was still a power in the world. "That man is a force, he has immense energy," wrote Bakhunin once. The old leaven was still working. Count Levachov had invited him to serve the Third Division immediately after his arrest in Switzerland. Now the offer was repeated, and indignantly refused. In 1876 General Potapov, chief of the Corps of the Gendarmerie, repeated the offer, and Nechayev struck him so hard that blood covered his face. This, at any rate, was the story told by the guards later. They half-approved of him and called him "our eagle," and they even presented him with a plan of the fortress. He was always plotting, and one of his most daring plots concerned the annual visit of the imperial family to the chapel of the Peter and Paul fortress. Nechayev hoped to arrest the whole family there, murder the Tsar and proclaim the Tsarevich emperor. It is almost certain that he was visited secretly by the revolutionary Andrei Zhelyabov. All this was unknown outside the prison, where he was treated with inhuman severity and occasionally received from the guards unexpected privileges, though these were uncommon and derived from the sheer dominance of his character, his endless speeches and his threats of reprisals, and the sudden gentleness which he could show whenever he wanted to. For seven years no one outside knew what had happened to him. His name was still dreaded, and there were rumors that he had appeared mysteriously and briefly in the great cities. He was converting his jailers, who gave him newspapers and allowed him writing materials, though the thousands of pages he wrote in the early years in prison were destroyed; but by 1881, when the revolutionary Stepan Shiraev was imprisoned with him, Nechayev was already beginning to have his messages sent out. Shiraev brought him news of the *Narodnaya Volya* (The People's Will), a revolutionary society which had swept through the educated classes of Russia. One evening in January 1881, when the ice was frozen, the terrorist Vera Figner was staring out of her window on the Voznessensky Prospekt. She had been making bombs, preparing for an attack on the Tsar. Then her friend Grigory Isayev entered the room quietly, removed his coat and made his way to the table. He held in his hands a little roll of paper, and said, as though it was a matter of no importance at all, "A letter from Nechayev."

It was the beginning of a period during which Nechayev wielded vast and secret power over the destinies of the foremost revolutionary society in Russia. The long letter, written sometimes in his own blood, recounted all that had passed during his nine years' confinement, all his hopes for the future. He had, he said, converted some of the guards to the revolutionary cause; he had been offered his liberty if he would turn police informer; he had been often flogged to unconsciousness, and he was beginning to wonder whether he would survive. If the name Nechayev meant anything to the younger generation, he hoped they would rescue him from the Ravelin Alexis.

The message was handed to the executive committee of the *Narodnaya Volya*, presided over by the revolutionary Andrei Zhelyabov, who was later to assassinate the Emperor Alexander II. The legend of Nechayev had assumed such proportions that for a while the committee deliberated between rescuing Nechayev and killing the Tsar. "The Tsar's death must come first," Nechayev wrote from his prison, adding that it was his desire that Zhelyabov should assume the function of the "Revolutionary Dictator" as soon as the Tsarist regime had been overthrown. It was a cunning move. He must have known that he would himself be offered the greatest powers if the revolution succeeded. His letters became more numerous. He told his jailers that he belonged to the "Successors' Party" and would be released immediately after the death of Alexander II. The jailers went in fear of him. The old impudent messages to the world were refashioned. He sent hundreds of messages to different revolutionary leaders, and sometimes, under the promptings of Nechayev, they found themselves at each others' throats. He was a master of the false proclamation. He suggested to the *Narodnaya Volya* that it should distribute millions of copies of a "proclamation" from the Tsar:

> We, Alexander II, Emperor and Autocrat of all the Russias, Tsar of Poland, Duke of Finland, etc. etc. etc. have on the counsel of Our Most Beloved Consort, Her Imperial Majesty the Tsarina, and at the entreaty of the Princes and the Grand Dukes, and in consequence of the request of the entire nobility, thought it fitting to return the peasants into slavery at the hands of the landed proprietors, to prolong the period of military service, and to overthrow the houses of prayer of the Old Believers ...

Having failed to bring about rebellion by a proclamation reintroducing serfdom, he suggested after the assassination of Alexander II, a forged proclamation from the Holy Synod that the new Emperor was insane:

> Almighty God, having seen fit to put Russia to this supreme trial, we have the misfortune, O brethren, to inform you that the new Tsar, Alexander III, suffers from a confusion of the mind, and no longer understands affairs of State. Therefore the loyal clergy are in duty bound to offer secret prayers at the altar for his miraculous return to health; and let none of you confide this secret to anyone.

It was almost the last act of the outrageous drama he had performed. When the assassins of Alexander II were at length

THE NECHAYEV MONSTER

rounded up and placed on trial, and the *Narodnaya Volya* was temporarily extinguished, Nechayev still hoped to create a new party, but his power was failing. He still sent messages through his jailers; he still prepared forged proclamations and hoped to obtain supreme power, but his strength was waning. The final blow came late in 1881 when Leon Mirsky, the youth who had shot at the Chief of Gendarmerie Drenteln, was imprisoned in the Ravelin Alexis with him. No two revolutionaries could have been more different. Mirsky was small, handsome and dapper, the pure amateur of revolution where Nechayev was the professional. On March 13, 1879, Drenteln was driving through the streets of Petersburg in his carriage. Riding a beautiful white racehorse, Mirsky followed him, fired several shots through the carriage window, and then made off only to be pursued by the general who ordered his driver to give chase. When the white horse stumbled and fell, Mirsky, with superb presence of mind, simply beckoned to a policeman and said: "My good man, this horse is hurt; just look after it while I go and get the groom." Then he took a droshky and went into hiding. Meanwhile, it had been discovered that the horse had been hired from a riding school by a medical student named Mirsky. The hue and cry was on, but it was several months later before Mirsky was traced to Taganrog. The house where he was staying was surrounded; he tried to fight his way out; he was wounded, arrested, and placed on trial. In the courtroom the audience applauded him for his immaculate appearance, his black morning coat, and white tie; the newspapers said "he presented a very gentlemanly appearance." In all this he was so different from the normal revolutionary—who used the courtroom for a forum and loudly protested against the Tsarist regime—that some doubt arises on the nature of his crime. He seems to have shot at the Chief of Gendarmerie in a mood of careless bravado.

ZERO

He behaved like an aristocrat, contemptuous of legal assistance, smiling impassively, courteous to everyone, never once raising his voice, and when he was condemned to death there was a gasp of horror in the Court.

Mirsky was not hanged, as the murderers of Alexander II were hanged; he was sent to the Ravelin Alexis of the Peter and Paul fortress, sharing the same cell with Nechayev. Occasionally he would disappear from the cell, summoned on a mysterious errand by the secret police. At such moments, he divulged whatever secrets he had been able to extort from Nechayev, and the Third Division were also given incriminating evidence that the prison guards were not fulfilling their functions. The director of the fortress, Bogorodetsky, was arrested, together with twenty of the guards: they were all sentenced to long terms of imprisonment. By the end of 1881 there was sufficient information to condemn Nechayev to a slow death. Mirsky was reprieved; his death sentence reduced to exile in Siberia, and there long afterwards Otto Deutsch met him. "He used to sit around the cooking fires," Otto Deutsch said. "He was unusually well-mannered, and never spoke about the past."

For Nechayev, it was the end. The jailers who had helped him were arrested. Nothing more was ever heard of him. Rumor said that he was taken to an even more secluded cell, his only companion a raving lunatic, that his hair had turned white, and that he had the look of an old man. A few more efforts were made to pardon him, but they came to nothing. The prison records say that he died in the night of May 8, 1883, at the age of thirty-five, having spent eleven years in the Peter and Paul fortress. The prison records also say that he died of tuberculosis. It was widely believed that he was hanged by order of the governor of the prison in a corner of his cell.

II.
The Nature of the Nihilist Mind

WITH Nechayev, for the first time, the pure revolutionary of destruction steps out into the open. Careless of human suffering, asking for no mercy and giving none, possessed of no aim except destruction, he left on the world indelible traces, the two most destructive revolutionary movements of our time were influenced by him, and without him they might never have come into being.

Nechayev was not the first nihilist, but he was the first to draw up a code of revolutionary laws which represented—pushed to their "logical" extremes—the romantic protest against the age of reason. He did not employ the word "nihilism," but he was its most embittered defender and most dangerous exponent. The word was invented by Chernichevsky who described in his novel, *What Should Be Done?* an anarchist paradise where "no one works unless he desires to, and the cheerful peasant may sit beside his table spread with huge cups of wine, while the wind fans him; he lives, contented with himself, in a delightful dream."

Nechayev, however, was not in the least interested in delightful dreams, and it is possible that he never read Chernichevsky's book. He was interested in the technique of revolution—in the technique of the revolution of destruction. His aim was nothing less than universal destruction, not only without mercy, but without passion. Karl Marx, who shared with Nechayev a complete contempt for mankind and could lose himself in similar dreams of "the destruction of the existing *bourgeoisie*," was appalled when he read the secret statutes of the brotherhood which Nechayev was attempting to form. The documents compiled by Nechayev and Bakhunin fell into Marx's hands in London; both were summarily ejected from the *International*. The statement that displeased Marx most came from the section called *General Programme and Objective of the Organization of the International Brotherhood*:

> The association of the International Brotherhood desires the universal, social, philosophical, and political revolution; and all these at the same time, so that the present order of things —founded on property, exploitation, ruthless domination of authority, whether religious or metaphysical or deriving from doctrinaire *bourgeois* sanctions, or from Jacobin revolutionary enthusiasm—shall be destroyed. The revolution we have in mind will destroy all these, first in Europe, and then in the whole world, leaving not one stone upon another; and all this will come about because the workers cry for peace and freedom from their lords, the exploiters and masters of all kinds. We desire that all these gentlemen shall die. We desire to destroy all the states and all the churches, with all their institutions and their laws, whether religious, judicial, political, or financial; whether they stem from the universities, or from economic principles, or from society. To the end that all these millions of poor human beings, who are deceived, enslaved, exploited, and condemned, shall be delivered from their rulers and official well-doers; and thereafter all associations and all individuals shall live in complete liberty.

THE NATURE OF THE NIHILIST MIND

This strange document, which showed the wooliness of Bakhunin's mind and the absolute ruthlessness of Nechayev's, had, according to Marx, nothing to recommend it except its sympathy for the oppressed. This was not revolution; this was playing with revolution; it was worse—it was exceedingly silly. Having condemned these documents he seems to have forgotten all about the existence of Nechayev and Bakhunin, for he does not refer to them again in his letters; and he did not know that the principles Nechayev had outlined were to be followed, often to the very letter, by revolutionaries who called themselves Marxian Communists.

The survival of nihilism as a phenomenon of our own times is not altogether difficult to explain. It appealed to neurotic, complex minds weighed down by the strains of modern existence; it offered astonishingly simple solutions. That the solution was invalid in human terms only whetted the nihilist's appetite for inhumanity. He could go along the road to the very end, stepping lightly over all obstacles; for all that is necessary is to destroy. With no patience for the practical details of unwinding the knot, he cuts it smoothly, and in the act of cutting the knot he has exerted his will, demonstrated his power, shown to everyone that he is in command of his destiny; and everything would be well enough if it was not that there were hidden flaws in the argument. The nihilist aims too high. Not content with destroying some small thing, he must destroy the whole; not content with a practical revolution, he demands "the universal, social, philosophical and political revolution, and all these at the same time." But what happens if a nihilist comes to power, and the revolution which Nechayev spoke about becomes a reality? Marx laughed at the simple solutions, perhaps because he preferred complexities. Lenin, who worshipped Nechayev, did not laugh at them, and one by one he carried out the precepts of *The Revolutionary*

ZERO

Catechism and demanded everything which Nechayev and Bakhunin together had hazily formulated in the *General Programme of the Organization of the International Brotherhood*. He was completely open and unsecretive in this demand, and he said that it was Nechayev who had given him both the weapon and the armor for bringing about a successful revolution. What delighted him above all was the simplicity of Nechayev's revolutionary technique. He said:

> People completely forget that Nechayev possessed unique organizational talent, an ability to establish the special technique of conspiratorial work everywhere, an ability to give thoughts such startling formulations that they were forever in one's memory. It is sufficient to recall his words in one of his leaflets, where he replies to the question, "Which member of the reigning house must be destroyed?" He gives the succinct answer, "The whole responsory."[1] This formula is so simple and so clear that it could be understood by everyone living in Russia at a time when the Orthodox Church held full sway; when the vast majority of the people, in one way or another, for one reason or another, attended Church, and everyone knew that every member of the Romanov house was mentioned at the great responsory. The most unsophisticated reader, asking himself, "But which of them are to be destroyed?" would see the obvious, inevitable answer at a glance. "Why, the entire Romanov house." But this is simple to the point of genius![2]

When Lenin came to power, the same ruthlessness was employed to the same chaotic ends, and he very quietly ordered the destruction of "the whole responsory," invented slogans which he had no intention of fulfilling, and set all opposing parties at each others' throats, while waging a war of complete

---
[1] The prayer for the royal house recited in the Orthodox Church.
[2] David Shub, *Lenin: A Biography*, New York, 1948, p. 371.

THE NATURE OF THE NIHILIST MIND

extermination against them. He had no plans for the social reconstruction of Russia, but developed out of the force of circumstances an arbitrary dictatorship which still survives. He climbed to power on the slogan "All power to the Soviets," and then disbanded the Soviets. He signed a declaration returning the land to the peasants, then in a single stroke ordered the peasants to surrender their land to the State. He followed Nechayev in all particulars except one. Nechayev's program had included the defiant statement, "We deny free will and the assumed right of society to punish." Lenin denied free will, but he exercised the right to punish to the uttermost. To the State was given the power which formerly belonged to the Tsar, and there was no difference except in name to the violent autocracy which seemed fated indefinitely to rule over the Russian people. But this time there was a Tsar who had learned at the school of nihilism.

The mind of the nihilist possesses subtleties which are not immediately apparent. He is the end-product of a long historical development. He does not destroy only because destruction provides an easy method of escaping from his obsessional neuroses; the obsessional neuroses themselves provide the strength with which he destroys. Confused, perplexed, under intolerable strains, his mind as complex as the brightly colored wires in a telephone central, despairing of ever transforming the messages he receives into a satisfying formal pattern, he decides to exert all his powers in one final vindictive act of destruction. He is therefore a creature of the will, but his will is sharpened by despair, and he dare not fail, for if he fails he must once again accept the established order. "We dare not fail," said Lenin. "This is why we must be merciless to our opponents. Those who even think of opposing us must be extirpated from the roots." The same desperate summons was uttered by Hitler on his road to power. The marked similarities between Lenin and Hitler were inevitable, and so too was the war between Soviet Russia and National Socialist Germany, for nihilism fights most desperately against nihilism, because nihilism represents the pure destructive will intolerant of all opposition.

Nihilism, as an historical phenomenon, occurs for the first time in Russia, but it is not essentially Russian in origin. It arises whenever the will is divorced from common humanity, and it is often the product of industrial society, arising from the mass misery of the industrial proletariat. It is significant that it came to birth simultaneously with the first wave of strikes which swept over Tsarist Russia. But Russia was the last of the European countries to undergo the industrial revolution; there were Nechayevs before Nechayev; the fantastic portrait of the pure revolutionary of destruction stems directly from the romantic hero, from the thousands of romantic novels which described the torments of the romantic, faced with the development of the industrial society where imagination has no place and everything is calculated with mathematical laws. In Germany, in particular, in the novels of Tieck, Hölderlin, and Jean-Paul Richter, the tortured portrait is drawn with immense power. Tieck makes his romantic hero, William Lovell, say:

> My outer self thus rules my inner self, the spiritual world. Everything is subject to my will. I can summon every phenomenon, every action I please. The animate and inanimate worlds are on the leading-strings of my mind, and my whole life is only a dream, and I can form the dream according to my will. I, myself, am the only law in nature, and everything obeys my law.

It was nonsense, but the dangerous nonsense had come to stay. The romantic imagination, seeing the material forces of the

THE NATURE OF THE NIHILIST MIND

world encroaching upon its preserves, struck out and claimed imaginary victories. The philosophers were caught up in the same fierce dream. When Fichte said: "I am, absolutely because I am," or Hegel more dangerously defined the new German state as "the pure spirit of the new world, whose object is the realization of absolute truth as endless self-determination of freedom," they were saying no more than Nechayev was to say later. Byron's Giaour, Lermontov's Demon, Baudelaire's Dandy all sprang from the same source; the determination to celebrate the will, whatever the consequences. Nechayev merely showed how, in an industrial society, all these lawless forces could succeed in establishing the reign of destruction.

There appeared in St. Petersburg in 1873, the year of Nechayev's trial, in three small badly printed volumes with yellow covers, a book by Dostoyevsky which describes, better than anything which has ever been written, the nature of the nihilist mind. The book was called *The Possessed*. The title was carefully chosen. It was about nihilists, and Dostoyevsky repeatedly compares them with the man of Gadarene who was possessed by devils. He had worked on the book for many years. In his notes, we can watch him fumbling towards solutions. At one time he intended to make Nechayev one of the characters of the novel, under his real name. He dismissed the idea, re-wrote large parts of the novel, but the book never took complete shape in his mind. Part of the novel is devoted to an academic nihilist, the remaining part to revolutionary nihilists. There are really two novels; and it is in the second part—particularly in a terrible chapter called *A Busy Night*, where all the conspirators meet, and the murder of the student Shatov takes place—that Dostoyevsky offers his wisest comments on the nihilist mentality which he knew so well, because he shared it. In *The Diary of a Writer* he wrote, "I myself am an old Nechayev, or else—perhaps—I might have been a follower of Nechayev, I am not sure. In the days of my youth it might certainly have happened." But all the evidence of his novels shows that he understood the nihilist mind better than he understood any other.

Originally *The Possessed* was to be called *The Life of a Great Sinner*. The book gradually became focused, not on a great sinner, but on the greatest sinner of all—the pure nihilist, who cares nothing for life, passes through all the stages of nihilism and at last sees himself as someone dedicated to remove the burden of the pain of death from men's minds. This he does by suicide. The desire to relieve men of their pain is not a real desire; he does not care sufficiently; it is almost as though he was offering a meaningless sacrifice. He lives in grotesque dreams, and at the same time he sees through the falsities of ordinary life. He is caught in a trap, and the trap is not of his own making. In all this Dostoyevsky is stating a universal theme; translated into modern terms, Dostoyevsky is describing the life and death of the mentality which brings about the concentration camp.

In the notes to the book Dostoyevsky observes that "all nihilists love terribly to profit." The story, as it unravels, describes accurately the profit-and-loss accounts of the revolutionary nihilists. But at the same time it concerns the *mystique* of destruction, chiefly as it appears in the minds of Shigalov, Kirillov and Pyotr Verkhovensky. They are all facets of the nihilist character. They merge into one another, and are never completely differentiated. When Kirillov kills the student Shatov in exactly the same circumstances that Nechayev killed Ivanov, he explains that he was compelled to exert himself, and there is left to him only one further act of will—to kill himself:

THE NATURE OF THE NIHILIST MIND

Terror is the curse of man, but I will exert my will. I am bound to believe what I don't believe. I will begin, and make an end of it, and open the door, and save. I will kill myself; that's the only thing that will save mankind, and recreate the next generation physically; and with his present physical nature, man can't get on with God, I believe. For three years I have been seeking the attribute of my Godhead, and I've found it; the attribute of my Godhead is self-will.[3]

He explains that he must annihilate God—that is the last, the most important of the tasks to be performed. He rages violently, and sometimes we can only guess at the meaning. When he says, for example, that henceforth history must be divided into two parts "from the Gorilla to the annihilation of God and from the annihilation of God to the transformation of earth and man physically," we must remember the beliefs of the old *raskolniki*. Kirillov is the *raskolnik* emerging into the nineteenth century with renewed vigor, the schismatic who refuses under any circumstance all orthodoxy, all custom, all law. On him, Dostoyevsky sheds the greatest light, but the other characters are made to speak in the same tones, and all derive their revolutionary nihilism from him. Some of the most terrifying speeches are put into the mouth of Pyotr Verkhovensky:

> Everyone belongs to all, and all to everyone. All are slaves, and equal in their slavery. In extreme cases there are slander and murder, but the chief thing is equality. To begin with, the level of education, science, and talents is lowered. A high level of science and talents is suitable only for great intellects, and great intellects are not wanted. . . Slaves are bound to be equal. Without despotism there has never been freedom or equality; but within the herd, there is bound to be despotism.

[3] *The Possessed*, III, vi, *A Busy Night*.

ZERO

Listen, Stavrogin, to level the hills is a good idea. Down with culture! We've had enough science! Without science we have enough material to go on with for a thousand years, but one must have discipline. The one thing wanting in the world is discipline. The thirst for culture is an aristocratic thirst. The moment you have family ties or love, you get the desire for property. We will destroy that desire; we will make use of drunkenness, slander, spying; we'll make use of incredible corruptions; we'll stifle every genius in its infancy... Slaves must have directors. Absolute submission, absolute loss of individuality; but once in thirty years Shigalov would let them have a shock, and they would all suddenly begin eating each other up, to a certain point, simply as a precaution against boredom. Boredom is an aristocratic sensation.[4]

At one point Kirillov speaks of his divine vision of destruction. None are appalled by this vision; they fasten on corruption with delight. The most fantastic fancies occur to them. They talk of giving up the world to the Pope. "Let him come forth on foot, and barefoot, and show himself to the rabble, saying: 'See what they have brought me to!' and they will all rush after him, even the troops. The Pope at the head, and with us all round—that's Shigalovism." But Shigalov is only another name for Nechayev: it is the world seen with the flames of destruction all around.

In the same chapter the vindictive poet Pyotr Verkhovensky suggests the methods by which the revolution of destruction will be brought about. They are the same as Nechayev's, with significant differences—they go further than even Nechayev went, and they are more embracing.

> We shall penetrate into the peasantry. Do you know that we are tremendously powerful already? Our party does not consist only of those who commit murder and arson, fire off

[4] *The Possessed*, II, viii, *Ivan the Tsarevich*.

THE NATURE OF THE NIHILIST MIND

pistols in the traditional fashion, or bite colonels.[5] They are only a hindrance. I don't accept anything without discipline. I am a scoundrel, of course, and not a socialist. Ha, ha! Listen. I've reckoned them all up; a teacher who laughs with children at their God and at their cradle is on our side. The lawyer who defends an educated murderer because he is more cultured than his victims and could not help murdering them to get money is one of us. The schoolboys who murder a peasant for the sake of the sensation is one of us. The juries who acquit every criminal are ours. The prosecutor who trembles at a trial for fear he should not seem advanced enough is ours, ours. Among officials and literary men we have lots, lots, and they don't know it themselves. . . .

It is a terrible and revealing catalogue, and one which should be regarded as having grave relevance to our own times, for the nihilist mentality survives, and Dostoyevsky has only roughed out a sketch of the kind of people involved. Verkhovensky's feverish brain continues to pursue visions:

> One or two generations of debauchery are essential now; unparalleled debauchery, when man turns into a filthy, cowardly, cruel, vicious reptile. That's what we need! And what's more, a little "fresh blood" that we may get accustomed to it. . . We will proclaim destruction. . . Why, why has this idea such a fascination? But we must have a little excuse; we must. We'll set fires. . . We'll set legends going. . . Every "mangy" group will be of use. From these groups I'll search out for you such fellows who will not shrink from shooting, and will remain grateful for the honor. Well, the upheaval will begin! There's going to be such an overthrow as the world has never seen before. . . Russia will be plunged into darkness. The earth will weep for its old gods!

---

[5] Kirillov, at one stage in his life, had dared himself to be offensive to a governor and had bitten his ear.

ZERO

Again and again, as though impelled by some fatal instinct to reveal every successive facet of the nihilist character, Dostoyevsky comes to grips with the problem of the Nechayev monster. He quotes at length Ogarev's poem *Enlightened Personality*—it turns out to be an excessively dull poem. He examines the manifestoes issued by Bakhunin and Nechayev from Geneva, and the examination is closely connected with another problem—whether, in fact, Europe will be destroyed. The revolutionary Karmazinov asks Pyotr Verkhovensky whether he really thinks Europe will survive, and he is answered with a blunt, "How can I tell?" Then Karmazinov launches upon a quite extraordinarily revealing discussion on survival:

> If the Babylon out there [he means Europe] does fall, and great will be the fall thereof (about which I quite agree with you, yet I think it will last my time), there's nothing to fall here in Russia, comparatively speaking. There won't be stones to fall, everything will crumble into dirt. Holy Russia has less power of resistance than anything in the world. The Russian peasantry is still held together somehow by the Russian God; but according to the latest accounts the Russian God is not to be relied upon, and scarcely survived the emancipation; it certainly gave Him a severe shock. And now, what with railways, what with you. . . I've no faith in the Russian God.
> And how about the European one?
> I don't believe in any. I was shown the manifestoes here. Everyone looks at them with perplexity because they are frightened of the things put in them, but everyone is convinced of their power, even if they don't permit it to themselves. Everybody has been rolling downhill, and everyone has known for ages that they have nothing to clutch at. I am persuaded of the success of this mysterious propaganda, if only because Russia is now pre-eminently the place in all the

THE NATURE OF THE NIHILIST MIND

world where anything you like may happen without any opposition. . . Holy Russia is a country of wood, of poverty . . . and of danger, the country of ambitious beggars in its upper classes, while the immense majority live in poky little huts. She will be glad of any way to escape, you have only to present it to her. It's only the government which still means to resist, but it brandishes its cudgel in the dark and hits its own men. Everything here is doomed and awaiting its own end. Russia as she is has no future. I have become a German and am proud of it.

But you began about the manifestoes. Tell me everything. Do you look at them?

Everyone is afraid of them, so they must be influential. They openly unmask what is false, and prove that there is nothing to lay hold of among us, and nothing to lean upon. They speak aloud while all is silent. What is most effective about them (in spite of their style) is the incredible boldness with which they look the truth straight in the face. To look facts straight in the face is only possible of Russians in this generation. No, in Europe they are not yet so bold; it is a realm of stone; there, there is still something to lean upon. So far as I see and am able to judge, the whole essence of the Russian revolutionary idea lies in the negation of honor. I like its being so boldly and fearlessly expressed. No, in Europe they wouldn't understand it yet, but that's just what we shall clutch at. For a Russian a sense of honor is only a superfluous burden, and it always has been a burden through all its history. The open "right to dishonor" will attract him more than anything. I belong to the older generation and, I must confess, still cling to honor, but only from habit.[6]

It is in passages such as these that Dostoyevsky reveals precisely what is at stake. The lies, the corruptions, the subterfuges practiced by the Russian Communists are explained fifty years before they came to power with remarkable pre-

[6] *The Possessed*, VI, v.

cision; and the danger is seen to lie, not only in the absolutely self-willed men, but in those who "still cling to honor, but only from habit." In such passages Dostoyevsky maps out the extent of the physical and mental decay, the breath of corruption, the ultimate and eternally threatening Zero, the evil of our time.

In Dostoyevsky's notebook Nechayev is described as the last of the nihilists. In fact, Nechayev was the first, and everything Dostoyevsky wrote concerning Nechayev was more prophetical than historical, for what he was describing is something which at last has become only too familiar to us, and we refuse his warnings at our peril. Their ravings sound like idiocy, but it is the idiocy we were accustomed to see in Hitler and Lenin, and both might have said, like Shigalov: "I am perplexed by my own data; my conclusion is a direct contradiction of the original idea with which I start. Starting from unlimited freedom, I end with unlimited despotism." Both came to the same conclusion: "One-tenth receives freedom of individuality and unlimited power over the remaining nine-tenths. They must surrender all individuality and become, so to speak, a herd, and through boundless submission, and by a series of regenerations, they will attain a primitive innocence, something like a primeval paradise, although they will have to work."[7] For such people Dostoyevsky reserved, in *The Brothers Karamazov*, the most terrible curses. Father Zossima cries out on his deathbed, "There are those who remain proud and fierce even in Hell—they cry out that the God of life should be annihilated, that God should destroy himself and his own creation, and they will burn in the fire of their own wrath forever, and yearn for death and annihilation, and they shall not be annihilated."

Shigalov's phrase stated the dilemma of nihilism in its most

[7] *The Possessed*, II, vii.

THE NATURE OF THE NIHILIST MIND

naked terms. "Starting from unlimited freedom, I end with unlimited despotism." At another time Dostoyevsky said perhaps the same thing when he wrote, "The will is closest to nothing; the most assertive are closest to the most nihilistic." [8] All of *The Possessed* and all of Nechayev can be summed up in this phrase, which provides in our own time the necessary commentary to the Communist and National Socialist experiments.

In *The Diary of a Writer*, Dostoyevsky denied repeatedly —six or seven times—that he was influenced by the Nechayev case in his portrayal of *The Possessed*. He wrote from Dresden to his friend Katkov that he knew nothing of Nechayev except through the newspapers, and had even come to the conclusion that Nechayev was a half-comical figure, but the notes reveal his indebtedness. When he returned to Petersburg, he threw himself into the Nechayev case. His brother-in-law had been a close friend of Ivanov, Nechayev himself may have been a family connection—the name Nechayev appears in his family tree—and he was continually seen poring over reports of the trial. He had written preliminary studies of the nihilists before. They were the "thoughtless" or "resolute" men he had known in Siberia, men defeated by the world and determined to defeat the world on their own terms. Nechayev was the end product, the last, the most terrible of all, and Dostoyevsky never foresaw that the monster would one day sweep over two continents.

The figure of the nihilist occurs again in modern literature in Thomas Mann's Naphta who broods within *The Magic Mountain*, developing the same thesis that terror is necessary to save the world:

[8] Dostoyevsky's idea was not entirely new. Hobbes was saying the same when he wrote: "The passion, whose violence, or continuance, maketh madness, is either great vainglory, which is commonly called pride or self-conceit; or great dejection of mind." (*Leviathan*, I, viii.)

53

ZERO

> No, liberation and development of the individual are not the key to our age, they are not what our age demands. What it needs, what it wrestles after, what it will create is—Terror.

Naphta explains that he is seeking after the single principle which unifies asceticism and domination; he finds this principle within the proletariat:

> The proletariat has taken up the task of Gregory the Great; his religious zeal burns within it, and as little as may be it withholds its hand from the shedding of blood. Its task is to strike terror into the world for the healing of the world, that man may finally achieve salvation and deliverance, and win back at length to freedom from law and from distinction of classes, to its original status as a child of God.[9]

But for Naphta the case is loaded, and Thomas Mann explains how he came to these conclusions. Naphta was a poor Jewish boy, brought up in Poland, accustomed to seeing the throats of animals slit by his father, a kosher butcher, and then later he became a novice in a Jesuit school, where he learned the classical nihilistic phrase, *Perinde ac cadaver*. The figure of Naphta lacks the strength of the figures of Dostoyevsky. He enters the sanatorium like a dark shadow, but there are so many shadows, so many lesions in the hearts and lungs of the patients that he is no longer exceptional; all Mann's characters suffer from the disease of nihilism, but the real terror comes from the sanatorium itself, as it came later from the eagle's nest in the Bavarian hills, where Hitler plotted the destruction of the world. The Dadaists were hardly more convincing than Naphta. Like him they resurrect the old abracadabras; the witch's brew is stirred; but when they deny, their heart is not in it. The manifestoes and paintings of the Dadaists and Sur-

---

[9] Thomas Mann, *The Magic Mountain*, V, *Of the City of God and Deliverance from Evil*.

THE NATURE OF THE NIHILIST MIND

realists prophesied the coming era of destruction with extraordinary accuracy, but they were rarely powerful or convincing; it is as though they were too frightened of the coming storm to speak of it with genuine emotion. The famous *Manifeste Dada* stated that "all that is divine in us springs from the awakening of our anti-humanity. Let every man exclaim; there is a great destructive and negative task before us; let everything be swept away." A later manifesto by Tristan Tsara was more explicit:

> No more painters, no more writers, no more musicians, no more sculptors, no more religions, no more republicans, no more royalists, no more imperialists, no more anarchists, no more socialists, no more bolsheviks, no more proletariat, no more democrats, no more bourgeois, no more aristocrats, no more weapons, no more police, no more countries, enough of all these imbecilities, no more of anything, *nothing, nothing, nothing*.[10]

The horror is there, but it is not convincing. The nihilist is babbling the required formulas without believing in them, and perhaps it was inevitable that Tristan Tsara, the founder of Dadaism, should have become in the end a practicing Communist.

It is when we come to Leonid Andreev that we hear once more the authentic notes of nihilism. Writing at the same time as Thomas Mann, toward the end of the first world war, he makes his nihilist cry out in the play *Shadows*:

> O you who can see, tear out your eyes, for it is shameless to look upon those who have been blind from birth. And if with our little lanterns we cannot light up the shadows, then turn out the fires and let us wander in darkness. If para-

[10] "Manifeste du Mouvement Dada," *Littérature*, XIII, 1.

dise is not for all, I wish to have none of it. Let us drink to the day when all the fires go out.

Here, however greatly perverted, there is religious feeling. In somewhat the same way the young Buddhist will often, as he enters the Buddhist church, swear an oath that he refuses the salvation of *nirvana* until all that has ever lived has been received into *nirvana*. For the Buddhist, as for the nihilist, there is no easy way to the promised land, and both, but in different ways, applaud the destruction of the world.

Nihilism was not an easy faith. The most intense and the most intelligent young Russian students accepted it with uncomprising loyalty. They possessed a logic of their own, one which, assuming their basic assumptions, is incontrovertible. They discarded tradition. They saw men as the instruments of their own will. Nothing was noble or base in the world. There were no values. A relentless dynamism ruled, and since men were at the mercy of forces beyond their control, it was incumbent upon men to exert their wills to the uttermost. They half recognized that this exaltation of the human will would lead to chaos or the most highly organized totalitarian state, but they saw no way out. They forgot that the will, as Dostoyevsky said, is closest to nothing.

Or perhaps they accepted it. There was not one nihilistic tradition, but every nihilist was attempting to work out his own nihilist salvation, flouting the acceptable human laws and trying desperately to discover new laws—or rather attempting to discover what happened when all the man-made laws were held in abeyance, for perfect liberty demanded nothing less. If the will was nothing, what then? If there was perfect liberty the Tsar must go, the State must go, all the established institutions must follow them; man must be left to his own resources, he must become a brigand.

THE NATURE OF THE NIHILIST MIND

Karl Marx had characterized *The Revolutionary Catechism* as a hodge-podge of Schiller's *The Robbers* and Dumas' *The Count of Monte Cristo*. But it was more than that, and he was himself consciously or unconsciously involved in a nihilistic philosophy of life, seeing everything in terms of dubious Hegelian categories and statistics, and romanticizing revolutionary destruction. Like the nihilists he possessed a curious belief in the truth of the romantic equation, $\frac{1}{0} = \frac{2}{0}$, and to his dying day believed he had invented new principles of the differential calculus based upon an identical equation.[11] In this fallacious equation lies the intellectual excuse for nihilism; for the nihilist says that all values become equal when compared with the infinity of the desert, or of eternity, or of God's infinite power to destroy and create. Man was too small to be of importance, and only the human will—the undifferentiated desire for perfect freedom—retained any meaning at all for the nihilist.

Nihilism was not an ignoble philosophy; it was a philosophy abstracted from all human values, but it possessed a kind of validity, and involved a pure form of asceticism without grace and without tradition. It posited man's ultimate insignificance, and deduced the consequences. That they were terrible consequences only spurred the nihilist to greater effort; and that they were vile never concerned him.

They were not the first to discover the consequences of the assumption that there are no human values. Mme de Rémusat records in her memoirs that Napoleon once said, "Listen, there is nothing noble or base in the world; in my character there is everything that goes to the strengthening of power, and everything that will deceive those who pretend to under-

[11] See Edmund Wilson, *To the Finland Station*, Appendix B.

stand me." Human psychology is such that only "the strengthening of power" remains as an incentive when human values are jettisoned; ordinary human morality and "the strengthening of power" are incompatible. Lenin therefore was following the nihilist code when he wrote in *The Infantile Sickness of Leftism in Communism* that it was necessary "to use any ruse, cunning, unlawful method, evasion, concealment of the truth." The infantile sickness of leftism was simply that it obeyed common morality, and common morality cannot assent to a reign of terror and deceit. Lenin's debt to Nechayev was expressed in one of his most famous slogans, "The proletariat can achieve its aim not by restarting the old machinery of state power, but *by smashing it to atoms and not leaving a stone of it standing.*" From there it was only a small step to abolishing all popular representation and inaugurating Caesarism: "The Soviet Socialist Democracy is in no way inconsistent with the rule and dictatorship of one person; that the will of a class is at times best realized by a dictator who sometimes will accomplish more by himself and is frequently more needed." Above the destruction stands the lone figure of Lenin-Nechayev, contemptuous of human life, but proud of having given men their freedom, for in their efforts to discover the widest bounds of freedom, the nihilists are always prepared to destroy men, and they will not flinch from destroying, if necessary, the whole human race. Lenin might have repeated Napoleon's boast. Certainly both of them were responsible for destroying whole provinces and whole peoples.

It is possible that we shall never know how much havoc and destruction has been wrought by nihilists. Some massacres have left no trace; we are perhaps ignorant of the greatest of them. Hulagu, destroying the seven hundred thousand inhabitants of Baghdad, Tamerlane, killing half the population of

THE NATURE OF THE NIHILIST MIND

northern India are remembered; but we know almost nothing about the still more formidable agent of destruction, Chang Hsien-chung, who came at the end of the Ming Dynasty from north China, and destroyed the rich province of Szechuan, killing thirty million people in the space of a few months. He was twenty-nine when he ordered the deaths of all the scholars of Chengtu because they disputed his title of King of the Great Western Kingdom. Having destroyed the scholars, he set about destroying the merchants, then the women, then the officials; finally he gave orders that his own soldiers should destroy each other. He ordered the feet of his officers' wives to be cut off, and made a mound of them; on top of the mound he placed the feet of his favorite concubine. He carefully counted the ears and feet which his bodyguard hacked from the bodies of villagers from the remote districts, and he stated his own nihilism in terms that could be understood by a Russian nihilist in a tablet which he caused to be erected in Chengtu:

> Heaven brought forth innumerable things to support man; Man has not one thing with which to recompense Heaven. Kill. Kill. Kill. Kill. Kill. Kill. Kill.

The tablet, which was still to be seen in Chengtu forty years ago, stated in twenty-one Chinese characters the nihilist dilemma; since men were unworthy, they might just as well be killed.

The accents of Nechayev and Chang Hsien-chung were heard again during the last stages of the war against Nazi Germany. By Hitler's orders Germany was to become a "traffic-desert." Bands of armed irregulars called Werewolves were to destroy everything: all factories must be dynamited; all wells must be poisoned; all the ancient monuments must be reduced to rubble; the Germans themselves must be destroyed

ZERO

to prevent them from being placed at the service of the enemy. By radio and newspaper, a frenzied paean in honor of the total destruction of Germany came to the ears of the startled German people. In *The Principles of Revolution* Nechayev had stated the basis of nihilist revolutionary action: "There must not rest one stone upon a stone. It is necessary to destroy everything in order to produce perfect amorphism, for if a single one of the old forms is preserved, it would become the embryo from which would spring all the other social forms." Goebbels was saying the same thing when he broadcast over Berlin radio:

> Together with the monuments of culture, there crumble also the last obstacles to the fulfilment of the revolution. Now that everything is in ruins, we are forced to rebuild Europe. In the past, private possessions tied us to bourgeois restraint. Now the bombs, instead of killing all Europeans, have only smashed the prison walls that kept them captive. In trying to destroy Europe's future, the enemy has only succeeded in smashing its past; and with that everything old and outworn has gone.[12]

He had thought he was saying something new, discovering the final justification for National Socialism, but in fact it was only Nechayev's philosophy at second hand. Goebbels had had a vision of the pure zero, the world starting afresh—everything new; but it was not so, and the world went on as before among the rubble. It was the final drama; nothing more final could be imagined; and in the end he discovered that the only finality lay in himself—he was zero, because like Kirillov he could commit suicide. It was, after all, what we might have expected. From the moment when Hitler said, "I am freeing men from the wearisome restrictions of the mind, from the

[12] H. R. Trevor-Roper, *The Last Days of Hitler*, pp. 55-56.

THE NATURE OF THE NIHILIST MIND

duty and degrading self-mortifications of a chimera called conscience and morality, and from the demands of a freedom and a personal independence which only a few will enjoy," [13] the end was already in sight; the utmost freedom leads, by devious roads, to the utmost destruction. Between National Socialism and revolutionary nihilism there was no essential difference—nor should we have expected any—for Hitler, like Lenin, was directly influenced by Nechayev.

[13] Hermann Rauschning, *The Voice of Destruction*, p. 225.

III.
Hitler and Nechayev

THE story of the National Socialist debt to Nechayev goes back to the time when the Tsarist police were still recoiling from the shock of *The Revolutionary Catechism*. At the time of the Great Schism there had been statements as wild as any made by Nechayev, but no one else in recent times had uttered the categorical imperative, "Destroy everything," and shown how it could be done. The publication of the document terrified the *bourgeois;* it also terrified the police. They realized better than others its vast implications, for it meant that the weapons of the secret police might be used against the state, by men as intelligent, uncompromising, and brutal as the men in the secret police. It was not a dream; it was something that could happen. Nihilism had not died with Nechayev's imprisonment; it had gone underground, and all over Russia there were small groups of students who admired Nechayev and discussed the possibilities of a revolt on a scale as widespread as the one Nechayev planned. At any moment, from some unexpected place, there might arise another Nechayev—someone with more intelligence, more personal integrity, who would not throw away his opportunities by murdering a defenseless student. There were abundant signs that *The Revolutionary Catechism* had come to stay.

HITLER AND NECHAYEV

The Third Division of the *Okhrana* found itself in an intolerable position. Nothing was more difficult than fighting nihilism, just as nothing was more difficult than fighting Nechayev, who was still powerful, though imprisoned. Though he was in prison and in chains, he was directly involved in the assassination of Alexander II. Code letters written by him were found on Sophie Perovskaya and Andrei Zhelyabov when they were arrested after the assassination. The letter written to Zhelyabov suggested that Nechayev was either the chairman of the revolutionary committee, or at least so high in their counsels that he possessed an equivalent rank. The letter, which acknowledged the receipt of a new code, a copy of the *Narodnaya Volya*, and 25 rubles, went on to make recommendations concerning recruits to the party, suggested the tasks they should be made to perform, and offered instructions on their payments. It was a long letter, and the instructions were couched in such a form that they might have been taken *verbatim* from *The Revolutionary Catechism*. It was evident that *The Revolutionary Catechism* was not dead, and the Third Division of the Secret Police began to see that the only way of destroying the "Nechayev monster" was to raise an even greater "Nechayev monster" in its stead; they would use the weapons of *The Revolutionary Catechism* against the revolutionaries.

There was nothing, of course, new in using the methods of terror against terrorists. The *Okhrana* descended from the *Opritchina*, the imperial guard of Ivan the Terrible, which consisted of young gentry elected to their positions at the Tsar's whim, and paid out of the dispossessed estates of the nobility; they wore dog's-head masks, black cassocks, and cloth of gold; they carried out with instant obedience all the unsavory crimes demanded of them by the Tsar, torturing so vilely that no one has ever dared to translate into English some of their methods—though these accounts are freely available in Russian. The Russian secret police was accustomed to terror, intrigue, vast networks of espionage. It knew more about such things than any other European power. Faced with the Nechayev terror, it would produce a document as authentic as *The Revolutionary Catechism,* and use it for its own purposes. If necessary the document would be forged, as Ivan the Terrible continually forged documents in order to have an excuse to destroy the Russian nobility.

The task of forgery was made easier by the discovery by the police secret agent in Brussels of an obscure propaganda pamphlet called *Dialogue aux enfers entre Machiavel et Montesquieu, ou la politique de Machiavel au XIXe siécle, par un Contemporain.* The author, who published the pamphlet anonymously in 1864, was discovered to be Maurice Joly—a French lawyer who detested Napoleon III, and hoped to destroy his Machiavellian policy by ridicule, by reducing it to its logical extremes. The pamphlet begins humbly enough with some phrases—which Napoleon III had actually used—placed in the mouth of Machiavelli. But gradually the Caesarism, of which Napoleon III was so nebulous an example, is dramatically and feverishly announced, and a plan of world domination, but not of world destruction, emerges. In this plan all methods are given free reign. All lies, prevarications, treacheries, deceits are allowed. "We shall arm all parties," says Napoleon-Machiavelli. "We shall set up state authority as a target for every ambition, and turn the state into arenas for revolt. A little more patience, and these revolts will be universal; and out of the general misuse of power we shall shake the pillars of society." There was much more in the same vein in the small twenty-four-page pamphlet written by the obscure vindictive lawyer—of whom almost nothing is known except that he was at last discovered, arrested, and sent to prison for fifteen months.

This *Dialogue in Hell*, which went into two small editions and never obtained a circulation of more than two thousand copies, was only one chain in the production of the new, revolutionary document which the Russian secret police hoped to impose on the Russians. The French book had been published in 1864. Four years later a German called Hermann Gödsche, who wrote under the name of St. John Retcliffe the Younger, published a novel called *Biarritz*, which derived from the Gothic romances of Mrs. Anne Radcliffe—whose *The Mysteries of Udolpho*, published ninety years previously, supplied the plot, many of the events, and most of the characterization. In *Biarritz* twelve rabbis meet in the Jewish cemetery in Prague. They speak in Chaldean and plot the overthrow of all established religions except Judaism, and of all governments except their own. They, too, are prepared to use all deceits in accomplishing their aim. Though Hermann Gödsche later published the chapter concerning the meeting in the cemetery in a pamphlet, the Russian secret police had no intention of using his whole work. They took the central incident, married it to some of the speeches of Machiavelli in the *Dialogue*, omitting nearly everything said by Montesquieu, and they were on their way to having the document they desired. Only one thing more was necessary—the destructive message of *The Revolutionary Catechism*. From this they took whole phrases, and the general form of a series of short enunciatory paragraphs describing the aims and the character of the revolutionaries, but instead of using the word "revolutionary" they substituted the words "the Jews." With diabolical cunning they had produced a pamphlet which could rival *The Revolutionary Catechism*. They were powerless to arrest all the students, but at least they could give the students a new aim, and this aim could be clearly stated: "Destroy the Jews, for they have taken over the whole content of *The Revolutionary Catechism* and are out to destroy the world."

All this took time. General Oryevsky, in command of the Third Division, was feeling his way. The first pamphlet, prepared by General Ratchkovsky, the chief of the French division within the secret police, the man who had found Maurice Joly's *Dialogue*, was not yet convincing. It was a hodge-podge of all three sources and leaned heavily on Hermann Gödsche, or rather on an entirely re-written version of the famous meeting in the Prague cemetery. There were scraps of the *Dialogue*, and larger scraps of *The Revolutionary Catechism*, but the pamphlet failed to have the inflammatory quality demanded of it, even though two journalists Golovinsky and Manuilov worked at it at intervals for a number of years. Various editions of the pamphlet were prepared and bought eagerly; the publications increased as the violence of the attacks against the Jews increased. The police stepped up the persecution of the Jews deliberately, whenever there were outbreaks by the students, so that in the eighties and nineties of the last century we can watch two parallel curves: there is the curve of student violence rising and dipping at the same time, and often in the same places, as the curve of violence against the Jews; and the Jews were made to pay for the crimes of the revolutionaries. In 1886 there was a further attempt upon the new Tsar's life. In the same year a brutal government order flung all the Jews out of the judicial service and the administration, and from nearly all the professions, while only five per cent of Jews were allowed in the Universities of Petersburg and Moscow. It had been the same before. The murder of Alexander II was followed by pogroms, though not one of the assassins had been a Jew. Like Hitler later, they attempted in cold blood

HITLER AND NECHAYEV

to head off the revolution by placing the guilt for civil disturbance on the Jews; and their chief propaganda sheet came more and more to resemble *The Revolutionary Catechism*, though now re-written and stated to have been issued by the Jews. In 1897 their chance came. The Jewish Nationalist Movement of the Zionists was born in Basel; Herzl made his plea for a legally assured homestead of the Jews in Palestine. The meeting was open, and full reports of the agenda were available. But the Russian secret police was not interested in these full reports. They pretended that secret sessions had been held, and that the Jews had spoken in Basel with the authentic accents of Nechayev: "We shall everywhere arouse ferment, struggle and enmity—we shall unleash a world war—we shall bring the people to a state of terror, and they will voluntarily surrender their power to us." The fable was piously and patiently invented in all its details. From Basel there had come a courier to the German city of Frankfurt-am-Main—the ancestral home of the Rothschilds—and the secret protocols were to be preserved in the archives of the Rising Sun Lodge of Freemasons. They did not explain why the Freemasons should be so anxious to possess these documents. The fable did not end there. They told how the courier spent the night at Baden, met some officials of the Russian secret police, and voluntarily surrendered the documents, dictating them to a staff of secretaries in the original Hebrew. The secretaries then translated the protocols into Russian, and for some secret and unexplained reason, the originals were destroyed. This, at any rate, was the story told by Sergei Nilus, a Russian clerk in the *Okhrana*, in a work called *Small Signs Prophesy Great Events; the Antichrist Is Near at Hand*. In the appendix to this book, remodelled and now in its final form, there were *The Protocols of the Wise Men of Zion*. Most of Gödsche and Maurice Joly had disappeared, and now there was almost—but not quite, for an amalgam remained—the quintessence of Nechayev's *Revolutionary Catechism*.

Who was Sergei Nilus? The question assumes considerable importance because he is the link between Nechayev and Hitler, and he was directly responsible for the pogroms which spread all over Russia after the publication of the book. The name was clearly a pseudonym. About the name hung a faint aroma of schismatic incense; it suggested some wandering priest who had gone beyond the Urals and founded a monastery after having lived in hiding for years. He was assumed to be a priest, and he wrote the introductions with a rough priestly style, quoting texts at length, with relish, especially II Peter, iii, 7 with its vision of the heavens and earth "reserved unto fire against the day of judgment and the perdition of ungodly men." Whoever wrote it was steeped in the schismatic tradition.

No one has yet discovered beyond any doubt who Sergei Nilus was, but there is reasonable presumption that the greater part of the work, the author of the successive editions and recensions was the journalist Manuilov, who has already been mentioned as the secretary of General Ratchkovsky. His full name was Ivan Manasevich-Manuilov, a Jewish name, and he was in fact a Jew, the son of a merchant in Gurevich who had come to Moscow and received a junior appointment in the Ministry of the Interior. He was small, elegant, and famous for his expensive clothes. He had attracted the attention of Prince Meshchersky, who encouraged him and made him write articles under a pseudonym in his reactionary review *Grazhdanin* (*The Citizen*), which was edited shortly after the trial of Nechayev by Dostoyevsky. He attended Prince Meshchersky's famous Wednesday afternoon salons, and became friendly with Dostoyevsky, for both were violently

Pan-Slav. Manuilov had become an honorary Slav. He was handsome—and the old prince delighted in surrounding himself with handsome young men—and he was also extremely capable. How capable he was did not appear until Prince Meshchersky asked him what position he desired to occupy. He answered, "The chief of the *Okhrana*."

Manuilov was never chief of the *Okhrana*, but he spent his life in the service of the *Okhrana*, performed for it his most dangerous missions, and he exercised over it vast and terrible powers. As a student he had been a member of the *Narodnaya Volya;* he is said to have met Nechayev and admired him, while reporting all Nechayev's actions to the police. He became the confident of Komisarev and Ratchkovsky, and he was put in charge of the Jewish section of the secret police. He was therefore directly concerned with the pogroms. His astonishing career had only just begun. Possessed of a brilliant, heretical, and completely unscrupulous mind, he set about changing the world to conform with his own Pan-Slavic desires. No one else performed such legendary feats for Pan-Slavism. Manuilov sent himself to Vienna, Stockholm, and Antwerp to organize counter-espionage services; he sent himself to Madrid, where he bribed the first Secretary of the German Embassy, and then threatened him with blackmail, and so succeeded in breaking the German code and acquiring telegrams from Berlin *before* they reached the Ambassador. He broke the Japanese naval code. He was the secret agent who rifled Count Witte's safe and produced the documents, subtly altered by himself, which led to the Minister's downfall. But the feat which should have given him a place in history was his intervention with Father Gapon, for it was Manuilov who succeeded in convincing Father Gapon to lead a procession of workers to the Winter Palace on Sunday, January 22, 1905, and so precipitated the first revolution. He was a close friend of Rasputin, and he even has some responsibility for bringing about the Russian Revolution of 1917, in the sense that he created a core of decay at the head of the government, for he became the chief political adviser of the reactionary Prime Minister Stürmer. He was a Jew who hated Jewry, and of those rare people who influence the course of history from behind the scenes, he seems to have been one of the most successful in concealing his motives.

The Protocols of the Wise Men of Zion now became an instrument of the *Okhrana*. It was the bible of Pan-Slavism, as later it would become the bible of Hitler, the one book which he read assiduously and placed under his pillow. The first pogroms were ordered by Plehve, who implicitly believed in the authenticity of the documents. Kishinev, a city in Bessarabia largely inhabited by Jews, was plundered and half the population was massacred in 1903. The Tsar believed in the authenticity of the protocols and countenanced for a while all measures to destroy the Jews. In 1905, a second edition was published with a few minor alterations. They concerned the Japanese War and "proved" that Count Witte had signed the Treaty of Portsmouth because the Jews had blackmailed him into it. They said Count Witte was Jewish, which he was not, and that whatever he had accomplished only assisted the world-empire of the Jews. There were more pogroms. From General Komisarev's headquarters the *Protocols* were sent out to the Pan-Slavs; this was done openly and even against the rulings of Ministers. Though Stolypin at last convinced the Tsar of the book's forgery, and the Tsar refused to allow the book to be read because "a pure cause is not fought with impurity," yet the book—for now it was always published with vast introductory matter attempting to prove or disprove whatever theorem Nilus had in mind, and the text of the protocols, in large italics, was relegated to an appendix—continued to be published, and the last edition in Russia appeared in 1917.

In their final form the *Protocols* still shows signs of its complex origin. Nilus never completely understood the kind of terror he was writing about. From Maurice Joly he takes mainly the figure of the "world-emperor," while from Nechayev he takes the means of destroying existing civilization; and these two hardly compatible ideas—for if the civilization is destroyed, there is nothing left for the "world-emperor" to rule—are never properly fused together. *The Protocols of the Wise Men of Zion* says, quoting, or half-quoting from Maurice Joly:

> An autocrat will assume the rule of the nations. Without unlimited power, no civilization can survive, and this power will come from the leader, whoever he may be, not from the masses, for the masses are only barbarians. In a state where power is insufficiently organized, we shall create a new reactionary party, by seizing the government in accordance with the will of the stronger. Imperceptibly the last traces of constitutional power will vanish, and the time will come when we shall seize all power in the name of the autocrat.

From Nechayev come the more practical passages dealing with the manner in which power is achieved:

> By effective executions, we shall uphold the reign of terror, and blind force, and unconditional obedience. The knowledge that we are merciless will suffice to eliminate our opponents. Our leaders will move to their goal with unparalleled boldness. The highest principles of political art lie in the concealment of our practices. By envy and hatred, by hunger and warfare, even by spreading hunger, destitution, and plague, we shall bring the people to such a pass that their only escape will lie in total submission to our domination.

ZERO

The Russian influence on Hitler was strong. Asked once whether he had read Trotsky's *History of the Russian Revolution*, he answered that he had learned a great deal from it and had found in the writings of the Russian revolutionaries encouragement for his own theories. He adopted Trotsky's slogan of the permanent revolution, though this in turn derived from the Marquis de Sade, and phrases from Trotsky are studded through his speeches. There seems to have been a Slav streak in him: his foster-grandfather, who was perhaps his real grandfather, had the half-Czech name of Johann von Nepomuk Hutler. Some of Hitler's more classic phrases are entirely Slav in origin, and "the night of the long knives" comes from a famous speech of Ivan the Terrible to the *Opritchina*, the blood-curdling lunatic youths in cassocks who guarded him and murdered with curved knives two feet long. He may have even read *The Revolutionary Catechism* in German, for it had been made available by the Swiss anarchists in Geneva. If he did not, he at least knew what survived of it in *The Protocols of the Wise Men of Zion*, which Rosenberg—fleeing from the Russian Revolution in 1917— brought, in a Russian edition, to Munich. Through Rudolf Hess, Hitler came to possess a copy of a German translation. It is unlikely that he knew it when he was living in Vienna, for he speaks about it in *Mein Kampf* only when he comes to discuss the German defeat. There he states that he is not impressed by the way in which the *Frankfurter Zeitung* is continually saying it is a forgery, for "anyone with any intelligence knows that it represents the unconscious desires of the Jewish people." By 1924 he knew the *Protocols* by heart, and it is inconceivable that he was unable to distinguish between the dross of Maurice Joly and the fiery gold of Nechayev.

Hitler was, in fact, horribly fascinated by the picture of the nihilist. Himself the most irresponsible of terrorists, he knew, as no one else, the workings of the nihilist mind, and after the 1934 blood bath he quietly broadcast to the German people an explanation of why he had found it necessary to murder so many of his own lieutenants, and he found the reason, not in the fact that they had threatened his own existence, but in their extraordinary nihilism, in their threat to the whole of existence.

This broadcast speech is one of the most interesting and revealing that Hitler ever delivered. He was on the defensive. The whole world was aghast. No one knew what had been happening in Germany, except that at least seven hundred people had been killed in cold blood. In one of his earlier speeches Hitler had spoken of the reign of unreason, when the people have "the thought of a wild beast, tearing, raging in their unreason, driving everyone to the same ruin." [1]

After the June massacres the reign of unreason itself appeared in Germany, though no one suspected the power or extent of the new dispensation. Curiously enough, Hitler did not embark at first on a defense or explanation of his actions. He speaks of the foundations of the National Socialist state, and seems to be searching for them among the débris. He denies that the National Socialist party came to power as usurpers. No, they received power constitutionally. They were not uprooted anarchists, but men who executed the people's will; and then very strangely and very suddenly he began to speak of his sense of torturing anxiety, an anxiety which had gripped him from the beginning of his rise to power and would only continue to grip him more strongly. It was not, he said, an anxiety over his own personal fate, but over the fate of the Germans. Then, for no reason in particular, he launched into a dissertation on nihilism; and though it seems clear at this

---

[1] *My New Order* (A Collection of Hitler's Speeches), edited by Raoul de Roussy de Sales, New York, 1941, p. 37.

distance that the torturing anxiety and the lecture on nihilism spring from the same sources, it was odd that he should begin one of his momentous speeches with a tortured inquiry into the nature of the nihilist mind. It is clearly a self-portrait. He sees nihilism in four disguises, and every one of these disguises is only one more portrait of himself. What is strange is that he groups them together like Nechayev, and almost in the same form:

> The first group consists of a small body of international disintegrators, apostles of the world-view of communism, who systematically incite the peoples, break up established order, and endeavor to produce chaos. We see evidence of the work of these international conspirators everywhere around us, in street fights, war at the barricades, mass terrorism, the individualistic propaganda of disintegration which disturbs nearly every country of the world...
> The second group consists of discontented political leaders... The more time veils with the gracious mantle of forgetfulness their own incapacity, the more do they think themselves entitled gradually to bring themselves back into the people's memory. But since their incapacity was not formerly limited to any special period, but was born in them by nature, they are today unable to prove their value in any positive and useful work, but they see the fulfilment of their life's task to lie in a criticism as treacherous as it is mendacious.
> The third group of destructive elements is formed of those revolutionaries whose former relation to the State was shattered by the events of 1918; they became uprooted and thereby lost altogether all sympathy with any ordered human society. They became revolutionaries who favored revolution for its own sake and desired to see revolution established as a permanent condition... Amongst the numberless documents which during the last week it was my duty to read, I

have discovered a diary with the notes of a man who, in 1918, was thrown into the path of resistance to the laws and who now lives in the world in which law in itself seems to be a provocation to resistance. It is an unnerving document—an unbroken tale of conspiracy and continual plotting: it gives one an insight into the mentality of men who, without realizing it, have found in nihilism their final confession of faith. Incapable of any true cooperation, with a desire to oppose all order, filled with hatred against every authority, their unrest and disquietude can find satisfaction only in some conspirational activity of the mind perpetually plotting the disintegration of whatever at any moment exists. . . This third group of pathological enemies of the State is dangerous because they represent a reservoir of those ready to co-operate in every attempt at a revolt, at least just for so long as a new order does not begin to crystallize out of the state of chaotic confusion.

The fourth group sometimes carries on its destructive activity even against its own will. This group is composed of those persons who belong to a comparatively small section of society and who, having nothing to do, find time and opportunity to report orally everything that has happened in order thus to bring some interesting and important variety into their otherwise completely purposeless lives. . . Since these men as a result of doing nothing do not possess any living relation to the millions which form the mass of the nation, their life is confined in its range to the circle within which they move. . . Because their whole ego is full of nothingness, and since they find a similar nothingness among their like, they look upon the whole world as equally empty. . . Their anxieties, they imagine, form the cares of the whole nation. . . These people are dangerous because they are veritable bacillus carriers of unrest and uncertainty, of rumors, assertions, lies and suspicions, slanders and fears, and thus they contribute to produce gradually a state of nervousness which spreads

ZERO

amongst the people so that in the end it is hard to find or recognize where its influence stops.[2]

The extraordinary psychological profundity of this portrait of the nihilist makes it all the more horrible. He had seen himself wholly, in the round, and there were only the four faces of nothingness. It is all loaded. The note-book, "the unnerving document," with its "unbroken tale of conspiracy and continual plotting," was clearly his own—and perhaps he was even conscious that it was his own—and perhaps he was conscious too that he was himself the man who "can find satisfaction only in some conspirational activity of the mind perpetually plotting the disintegration of whatever at any moment exists." He had begun with a statement of his own torturing anxieties for the fate of Germany, only to return to them when he discussed the fourth group. It was all gratuitous: none of these portraits had any relevance to the theme of the blood bath. They were part of the smoke screen, part of his own secret homage to himself. The psychiatrist is trained to see significance in the gratuitous offerings of his patient, and here—more clearly than in Hermann Rauschning's *Voice of Destruction*—in a speech delivered six years before the outbreak of the war, Hitler announced, as publicly as any man can, that he was plotting the disintegration of existence, the destruction of the whole world. Why? The core of the answer lies perhaps in a strange phrase embedded in a speech he made in Munich in 1923. "If a people is to become free," he declared, "it needs pride, and will-power, defiance, hate, hate, and once again hate. . . ."[3] There were other answers, and these were provided by "the four faces of nothingness," that strange and clearly defined portrait—which was only a sketch for the larger portrait that came later when he drew it

[2] *My New Order*, pp. 257-260.
[3] *My New Order*, p. 49.

across the face of Europe—a portrait done in deceit, horror, poison, torture, the expiation of sins, suffering, and terror and endless delusions—and all the time his mind was rotting under the weight of visions of total destruction. From the beginning he had been, consciously or not, the apt pupil of Nechayev.

The specter of nihilism did not die with Hitler. It still survives in Soviet Russia where the same revolutionary purposes of destruction and the same methods, derived directly from Nechayev, receive official encouragement. The Cominform is full of Nechayev's doctrine, and the Russian secret police obediently follows out the principles of *The Revolutionary Catechism*.

The authentic tones of revolutionary nihilism are rare; nowadays they are too often disguised. They were heard, however, in July 1949 in a Paris courtroom. White-haired and pale after a long imprisonment, Otto Abetz, former Nazi ambassador to France, faced his accusers. The French prosecutor, holding up some documents bearing the signature of Abetz, asked how it had come about that he, who so often protested his love for France, had signed so many death warrants, collected so great a treasure from the French Jews, and had ordered the execution of so many hostages and former members of the French Government. For a while Abetz looked dazed. Up to this moment he had answered all questions politely and in perfect French, but when he answered the prosecutor's question his voice rose hysterically—*J'ai proposé des choses atrocement irréalisables pour éviter des choses atroces réalisables.* "I proposed things atrociously unrealizable to avoid things which were atrociously realizable."

The courtroom was stunned; there was a long gasp of astonishment; and when everyone began shouting, the judge hammered on his desk with his gavel. "What you call atrociously unrealizable," he said, "happened every day in occupied France."

Otto Abetz was not sentenced to death, but to thirty years imprisonment with hard labor. There were extenuating circumstances for his behavior, and the terrible phrase was, in some instances, no more than the truth. Like Albert Speer, and with the same coldly analytical mind, he played the nihilist game against the nihilists. He forgot that for Hitler there could be no real difference between "atrociously unrealizable" and "atrociously realizable," for in both these regions he was at home. On that hot summer's day the phrase of Otto Abetz sounded like the voice of Nechayev.

IV.
The Fault in the Culture

IN Nechayev's character there was a fatal flaw which split his mind wide apart. Determined upon revolution for the best of reasons—the autocracy of the Tsars had long outlived its usefulness—he was prepared to employ universal destruction for the worst of reasons, for reasons which went beyond all logic. He did not defend universal destruction. He simply stated that this was the end in view, and in no other way could the autocracy be destroyed; and in this he was prophetic; for in a very real sense Tsardom was abolished only when Russia was destroyed at the roots, only when— as he had prophesied—the peasants had taken to the shelter of the forests, disrupted communications, sabotaged all industry, and a revolutionary society had "used all its resources to increase and intensify the evils and miseries of the people, believing that at last their patience will be exhausted, and they can be incited to a revolutionary *levée-en-masse*." With the Russian Revolution the dream of Nechayev came true. The technique of revolution by destruction, faithfully copied by Lenin, proved so alarmingly successful that in the first days of power Lenin said, "I could not have guessed that it was as easy as setting fire to an old tree." But it was Nechayev who first said that everything, not only some part of the social order, should go up in flames.

ZERO

Nechayev was also the first to codify nihilism, and this he did in the twenty-six paragraphs of the catechism, as though providing a new alphabet for a new kind of man. The catechism is confused—it would have been more impressive if it had been half the length—but it gave concrete expression to a prevalent attitude of mind: the attitude of mind which appears at various times in history and says at moments of failure, "Burn everything! Who cares?" It was not therefore an unusual attitude. What was unusual was the intensity and passion with which it was expressed, and the ruthlessness of the revolutionary means—means which we now know only too well, because *The Revolutionary Catechism* has left its imprint on the whole world, so that even if we have never heard of Nechayev, we find ourselves contending with him; it is almost as though he is in the air we breathe.

Nechayev was the child of his time; the split in his mind was not only in his mind; it was in the whole culture of his period—that confused and dying culture of Russian orthodoxy battling against orthodoxy, religion split by schism, the waning power of the monarchy, alternately buttressed on ferocity, and on sudden, unexpected acts of mercy. The serfs had been freed, but for how long? They were quietly arming, afraid of being flung back into slavery again; and as always in Russian history since the days of the Stenka Razin revolt and the attack on the Solovetsky Monastery, the schismatic priests were preaching the gospel of revolt, some kind of unexplained revolt against the social order, their minds moving to the same music as the revolutionaries—for both desired vengeance more than they desired power, and both hated Tsarism, not so much for the evils which the Tsar inflicted on them, as for the frustrations they felt when they thought of the hundreds of years during which they had never possessed power. When the serfs were freed, their bitterness continued and even grew

THE FAULT IN THE CULTURE

greater, just as the Irish add fuel to their bitterness against the English, though they have received their independence. The emergence of an industrial proletariat only increased the strains that already existed. The workers, miserably underpaid and exhorbitantly overworked, were taking the place of the serfs in the Russian economy. There was no peace. Small revolts were continual; they were suppressed savagely.

From his childhood Nechayev saw the world through the eyes of his father, a schismatic village priest. From him he learned the legends of the schismatics, how Father Nikhon had thrown religion into a ferment by misspelling the name of Jesus, and how Archpriest Avvakum had said, in defiance of unorthodoxy: "Let us be monsters for the sake of Christ! All things are permitted to us if we destroy this Anti-Christ who has come among us!" One of Avvakum's followers declared:

> I wish that every man, woman and child of this town would come to the banks of the Volga, throw themselves into the waters, and sink to the bottom so that the temptations of the world would not attract them. And what is even better: that I might set fire to, and burn down the entire city; what joy if it were to burn from end to end destroying all the aged and infants, so that none would receive the stamp of Antichrist.[1]

The same follower went on to describe his greater joy if it could come about that the whole world would dissolve in the flames. He summoned the faithful in words of wild, discordant poetry. Remembering the parable of the tares—"*The harvest is the end of the world; and the reapers are the angels*"—and the incident of the Gadarene swine—"*It hath cast him into the fire, and into the waters to destroy him*"—he yearned for the time when all the souls under Christ would only be

[1] Paul Miliukov, *Religion and the Church*, Philadelphia, 1942, p. 57.

small flames in the greater flame of God. He was not alone. Hundreds of wandering priests brought these doctrines to the remotest parts of Russia, especially to the remotest parts, for they were themselves in continual danger of martyrdom. They called upon everybody to believe that the signs of Antichrist hung around the world "like a scarf round the neck." Fire alone, absolute destruction, absolved:

> To await this end in worldly surroundings is impossible, for these are evil days; if not burned alive, how could one be rescued from the Dragon? But when reduced to ashes, that is the end of everything. In fire you will find the direct way to paradise, for fire purges all sins. And there is no chance of escaping it, for with the end of the world a river of flames will flow engulfing everything. Even the Apostles must pass through that ordeal; but those burning themselves alive will be spared a second ordeal.[2]

They cited the examples of the saints who had sacrificed themselves in the flames; they spoke of a peasant from the White Sea littoral who had seen the vision of the flaming souls, saints whose heads were surrounded with halos; and even the children repeated after their priestly teacher, "Let us go into the flames, for in the other world our shirts will be of gold, our boots of red leather, and there will be plenty of honey, nuts and apples. It is better to burn than serve Antichrist."

The fury of the schismatics could not be maintained, but the spirit remained, and traces of the ordeal by fire and water survive among the Dukhobors. There were schisms within the schism. Some refused to face the ordeal by fire, and maintained that it was preferable to die of starvation, of cold, or

---

[2] I owe this quotation, too, to Paul Miliukov's scholarly book. A generally accurate account of the mass suicides of the schismatics is given in Merezhkovski's *Peter and Paul*, particularly in the terrifying tenth chapter.

THE FAULT IN THE CULTURE

by hanging. The ingenuity of the schismatics led them to invent even stranger and more horrible deaths, so that, as one historian wrote, "you would think that everybody is thinking how to kill himself, and take the rest of the world with him, for the glory of Christ." From the schismatics came the Wanderers, who erected their churches in the Arctic; the Society of the Castrated, who took literally a sentence from the Pauline epistles; the Shore-dwellers, the Brotherhoods of Fire, though these worshipped only the spiritual fire of Christianity. The Great Schism was like a blunt edged spear which dragged a great wound into the flesh of Russian history, and nearly everyone was affected. By 1750 most of the original violence had disappeared; but the wound did not heal, and at any moment one could expect a resurgence of this frenzy. Doom, destruction, the end of the world, were still commonplaces in the sermons of the village priests; and Nechayev's revolt had its origins in an ancient theological despair. He took the visions of the schismatics and sometimes the words, and translated them into modern revolutionary terms.

All this, then, was the common property of the Russians of the time. It was to Nechayev's dubious credit that he could think of *concrete destruction*, where Bakhunin rarely progressed beyond a *mythological destruction*. In his conversations with Richard Wagner, Bakhunin went to some pains to convince the musician in the powers of fire—Dresden must be fired, it was the only way in which the revolution could be accomplished. Remembering these conversations years afterwards, Wagner seems to remember even the emphases, the particular turns of phrase, as Bakhunin spoke of "the delight, at once child-like and demoniac, of the Russian people in fire, on which Rostopchin had reckoned in his strategic burning of Moscow." We hear the authentic tones of Bakhunin as

ZERO

Wagner describes him launching into a disquisition on mythological destruction. Said Bakhunin:

> All that is necessary to set in motion a world-wide movement was to convince the Russian peasant—in whom the natural goodness of oppressed human nature had maintained itself in its most childlike form—that the burning of their lords' castles, with everything that was in and about them, was completely right in itself and pleasing in the sight of God; from this there must result the destruction of everything which, rightly considered, must appear, even to the most philosophical thinkers of civilised Europe, the real source of all the misery of the modern world. To set this annihilating force in motion seemed to him to be the only worthy activity for any man.[3]

The vision, which Nechayev and Bakhunin shared with the schismatics, of some total destruction, some terrible dark power which destroyed the world in flame, was not only a vision; something very similar had actually happened exactly three hundred years before *The Revolutionary Catechism* was published. In the winter of 1569, Ivan the Terrible had decided that the city of Novgorod was in treacherous allegiance with Poland. He therefore set out with the Tsarevich and the hooded *Opritchina* to exact vengeance, even though he must have known that the accusation of treachery was unfounded. A tramp had brought the rumor to Moscow; this was enough. Ivan needed to demonstrate his power. How better could he demonstrate it than by destroying the richest city in Russia and murdering every inhabitant? Arriving at Novgorod, he built a huge wooden wall round the city, so that none should escape. Then he proceeded to the cathedral, prayed devoutly and took his meal in the archbishop's palace. Half-way

[3] Ernest Newman, *The Life of Richard Wagner*, II, 49.

THE FAULT IN THE CULTURE

through the meal he ordered the archbishop to be flung into a dungeon. The murder of the inhabitants began the next day and lasted for five weeks. Whole families were thrown into the river. The *Opritchina*, in rowing boats, pushed them under with iron crowbars. There were mass tortures; husbands and wives were killed slowly before each others' eyes, or flogged to death, or roasted over slow fires; there were other, more horrible punishments invented by Ivan on the spur of the moment. The thin ice on the river was stained with blood from bank to bank. Ivan took part in all the tortures, and punished those who were not sufficiently adept in inventing new ones. On February 12, 1570, he summoned the city elders and a few crazed survivors into his presence, showed them the smoking corpses and shouted, "People of Novgorod still living! Pray God to bless our sovereign imperial power, and for victory over all visible and invisible foes!"

The invisible foes were probably more real to Ivan than the visible ones, for he had killed sixty thousand innocent people by burning, frying, drowning, stabbing, torture and repeated blows—it was observed that he struck at defenseless people again and again long after they were dead, thus providing some clue to Hitler's order that the Jews should be annihilated again and again—and Kurbsky says that on a single day fifteen thousand died, and the Tsar witnessed each murder, or at least saw the greater part of them. Nothing quite like this massacre had occurred since the Tartar devastation of 1237 to 1239. Since there were only a few hundred people still living in Novgorod, Ivan felt that his power had been secured, placed one of the *Opritchina* in command of the city, and rode off to the city of Pskof, where he intended to repeat the performance. His parting words were, "May the wailing and crying cease in the city. Forget your wrongs! Live and prosper! I say to you all, go in peace to your homes!" Arrived at Pskof, he seems to have wearied of blood. He had intended to kill them all, for were they not all traitors? Awakened at midnight by the tolling of the church-bells, he murmured, "Listen, they are all praying to be saved from the Tsar's wrath," and in the morning, while the whole population knelt before him, he decided that they could be spared. For the rest of his life he continued to murder violently, but he never again put a whole city to the sword. To the end he was always strangely like Hitler in his rages, his sudden flaring denunciations, his belief in astrologers, his contempt for the living; he believed in the magic inherent in precious stones, and collected spiders which he placed in circles. If they died in the circle he became afraid for his own life. More revealing of the workings of his nihilist mind was his belief in the power of the dead; they alone were powerful, and their brooding presences were always beside him. He lived among these ghosts, and asked questions of the people he had murdered. He died screaming in a fit of rage because the king he was trying to put on the chessboard would not stand upright. "Thereupon there came," wrote a contemporary historian, "a great storm from afar, a storm which broke the repose of his good heart, so that he became a rebel in his own realm." From the very beginning the Emperor had been "a rebel in his own realm," never really desiring kingship, always at odds with himself and the world, hating with a malignant hatred, because there was no other way to show his rebellion.

This ancestor of Nechayev, the man who hated the living and consoled himself with the dead, was not wholly guilty of the crimes he committed. Crime was in the air. It was a time of desperate strategems, a time when the Last Judgment seemed very near, and the spectacle of terrible disasters was almost continual. Huge floods drowned whole provinces;

THE FAULT IN THE CULTURE

plague choked the roadways; armies spawned everywhere; the *Opritchina* massacred for the sake of massacre, but they were no worse than the Tartar Horde. The harm done by Ivan the Terrible on Novgorod was small compared with the harm done on Moscow by the Khan of the Crimean Tartars in the following year. He did not sack the city; he simply surprised it and put it to the flame. Ivan escaped, but upwards of half a million perished in the flames; a sober report, found in the Elizabethan state papers, speaks of "the people smothered and burnt ten thick, one lying upon another." It was the most terrible disaster that had ever fallen on Moscow, for all the wooden buildings were burned to the ground; no more than a handful of inhabitants survived. There was no looting. The Khan of the Crimean Tartars advanced slowly up to the huge city, six times as great as London, and fired it; then he returned quietly to the rich, safe corn lands of the Crimea, without fighting, without receiving envoys, like something that came out of the night. The plague followed.

The dream of world destruction, therefore, was not only a dream; it was something the Russians had seen, or almost seen; a commonplace of their talk, the familiar substance of sermons and priestly prophecies. As time went on, they forgot the details and even the name of the Tartar Khan, but they remembered the huge flames, those flames sent by God to destroy them.

Nechayev growing up in the small parochial circle of a village priest could not help but be aware of these events, which had left a scar on the Russian mind, never to be forgotten, and when he spoke of "terrible, total, inexorable and universal destruction," he was speaking of something familiar to Russians, though it was considerably less familiar to the West. But the famous destruction of Moscow was essentially meaningless. The Khan of the Crimean Tartars gained nothing except the satisfaction of seeing the flames. He took little treasure, he did not follow up his successes, and seems to have been himself terrified of the havoc he had caused. He had made a gesture of defiance in honor of Islam, but he left untouched and unburnt the Red Square, where the Russian archers remained at their posts, and the cathedrals survived, their tiled roofs reflecting the glare. Two cultures—Islam and Russian Orthodoxy—had met. Neither had consciously sought advantages from each other; neither sought to impose its will on the other; but the result of their short contact was a holocaust. A "meaningless sacrifice" had come into being.

It may be that whenever two diverse cultures meet, there is always danger of the "meaningless sacrifice." Something comparable to the meaningless destruction of Moscow in the late spring of 1570, occurred during the processional triumph of a Roman conqueror, as he rode to the Temple of Jupiter Capitolinus to offer up the emblems of his victory.

The Roman conqueror, returning from abroad, received the highest honors that the state could offer him. He rode in a triumphal chariot inlaid with ivory and garlanded with laurel leaves; the chariot was drawn by four pure white horses. Superbly confident, wearing clothes which no one else was allowed to wear—even his shoes were latched in a way allowed at no other time—he was the personification of Roman victory and the Roman genius, and he was attended by an enormous procession. This procession was most carefully arranged. The *triumphator* did not ride at the head of the procession; this honor was reserved for the Roman senators. After them came the trumpeters with the spoils of war, carriages piled high with glittering gold vessels, precious cloths and stones, seeming, as Josephus said, "more like a river than ornaments." Then came the gold and silver crowns traditionally offered by the townships through which the *triumphator* had passed

THE FAULT IN THE CULTURE

on his return to Rome. Then came the white bulls of sacrifice with gilded horns. Immediately after the bulls came the prisoners, yoked together, and after the prisoners came the lictors in blood-red tunics, followed by a band of musicians. It was at this point, near the end of the procession, that the *triumphator* rode in his chariot, and behind him came his army. When the procession had driven through the streets of Rome the white oxen were led up the steps of the Capitoline, and there they were sacrificed in sight of the Emperor, the nobility, the priesthood, and all the senators. There followed magnificent entertainments, feasts, games in the arenas; and late at night or early the next morning the *triumphator* was escorted by musicians and dancing-girls to his house. By this time, everyone had forgotten that the prisoners had been quietly murdered, usually by strangulation, in a small white-washed prison at the foot of the Capitoline Hill. They were hurriedly removed from triumphal procession when they were still far from the sacred heights. The entire families of the kings, princes, and generals who had fought against Rome disappeared, leaving no trace, their bodies thrown into a well. They could have been kept as hostages or sold as slaves, but nothing of the kind happened. Not the prisoners, but the white oxen were publicly sacrificed; and this might have been put down to the peculiar Roman blood lust, their delight in killing secretly, if it was not that in the early days of the history of Rome the prisoners were the center of the triumphal procession, they were given high honors and they were brought to the Capitoline Hill only to receive the freedom of the city. Why had there been this change? Why, in fact, had there been a "meaningless sacrifice"?

Discovering the reasons for this is like seeking the clues in a detective story. The change did not come about suddenly. The story of the prisoners begins shortly after the foundation of Rome and the rape of the Sabine women. A local chieftain called Acron, "a man of high spirits and grave prowess," ordered Romulus to surrender the Sabine women. Romulus refused. At first Acron decided to wage war against the Romans; relenting, he offered to fight Romulus in single combat, and so decide whether the Sabine women should be returned to their husbands. Romulus accepted the offer, and while the two armies looked on, the two kings stripped for combat. Romulus succeeded in killing Acron; Acron's army took to flight, and the Roman army went in pursuit, not to kill, but to capture the enemy. They were then formed into a solemn procession, and at the head of this procession marched Romulus, having cut down an oak tree and trimmed it so that it could hold the armor of his defeated foe. "Then girding his clothes about him and crowning his head with a laurel garland, his hair gracefully flowing, Romulus held the trophy erect on his right shoulder, and so marched, singing songs of triumph, while the whole army followed after, the citizens receiving him with acclamations of joy and wonder." The prisoners, by taking part in the procession, also became part of the Roman army, and once they had reached Rome, they were feasted and offered the privileges of Roman citizenship. Plutarch, writing at a time when the triumphal procession had become codified, with every detail carefully rehearsed, the senators, the lictors, the musicians, the prisoners and the *triumphator* in their proper places, says significantly, "The procession held by Romulus on this day was the origin and model for all future triumphs."

So it was, but a vast change had taken place. There is almost no obvious connection between the original triumph and the tremendous concourse which wound its way down the Via Sacra in the days of the Empire. There was a gradual

THE FAULT IN THE CULTURE

development from the elevation and worship of the prisoners to a quick, ruthless massacre.

We cannot follow every change in the ceremony. Occasionally the curtain lifts, and then it falls again. We know that the white horses and the chariot were introduced in 369 B.C. by Marcus Furius Camillus, who received a triumph after the destruction of Veii. The horses and the chariot were regarded as a detestable sign of pride by the Roman citizens, and of this triumph Livy records, "He was the cynosure of all eyes as he rode into the city with his team of horses—a thing deemed by the republic unbecoming even for a mortal man, let alone for a Roman citizen. They saw with superstitious alarm the dictator rivalling Jupiter and Sol in his equipage; and the result was that his triumph was marked rather by brilliance than by popularity." [4] Gradually, over the years, the procession is becoming more formal. Then in 181 B.C., in the period of exhaustion following the Punic wars, there was introduced into Rome the cult of the divine Dionysus. Livy records the horror with which the new cult was received by the senators, who passed stringent laws against the devotees. But the triumph of Dionysus had come to stay, and underneath the trappings of the Roman triumph can be seen the Greek bacchanalia. The strange rite of the bacchanalia was not only performed in honor of wine and fertility; there was conflict within the rite itself, and in the *Bacchae* of Euripides there can be watched the conflict between Dionysus as the hilarious wine god, accompanied by all the symbols of sexual license, and the other Dionysus, a terrible and irresistible god who unseats the reason, and whose *oestrus* can only be appeased by absolute obedience to his commands, a god who comes by remote ways from India, and who bears the marks of Siva the Destroyer. Three or four archaic and conflicting

[4] Livy, *History of Rome*, V, 23.

ceremonials have joined.[5] There is now no place for the prisoners, who are quietly murdered, because it is inconceivable that they can be put to any further use in the confused ceremonial procession. In one of his notebooks Franz Kafka wrote: "Leopards break into the temple, and drink the sacrificial vessels dry; this occurs repeatedly, again and again; finally it can be reckoned on beforehand and becomes a part of the ceremony." In the end, the meaningless sacrifice of the prisoners had become part of the ceremony.

What is at first surprising is that the prisoners are the chief evidence of the general's triumph. Walking in chains, showing their wounds and sometimes appealing for mercy—nearly every Roman observer has mentioned the pity they inspired—they were the living and tangible proof of conquests, the former owners of the great shimmering mass of gold and silver vessels paraded in the carts, the central objects of display. Once they had been greeted with open arms; now they were silently killed. Over them there had triumphed, not the *triumphator*, but the decaying forms of ancient cultural patterns. Occasionally, but very rarely, it happened that the prisoners were not murdered. Augustus pardoned Selene Cleopatra, and Aurelian pardoned Zenobia, but these pardons were dictated by the power politics of the age. In general, and over a long period of time, the fate of the prisoners was an absurd and meaningless death deemed necessary, not by men, but by the huge, mechanical and impersonal forces of ceremony.

[5] Very little has been said here about Etruscan or Egyptian influences, though these were strong. The red-robed lictors, with their bundles of twelve rods, were originally Etruscan, so too were the chariot, the heavy gold crown and the *bulla aurea*, the gold breastplate worn by the *triumphator* round his neck. The even greater influence of the Egyptian celebration, deriving from the triumphs of Alexander, can be seen by referring to the extraordinarily colorful description by Athenaeus of the procession held by Ptolemy II Philadelphus, on his accession at Alexandria in 285 B.C.

THE FAULT IN THE CULTURE

In the Roman triumph the whole *ethos* of the nation was expressed. During this solemn ceremony it was believed that the nation renewed its strength. The procession endured for a prodigious number of years. From the foundations of Rome in 753 B.C. to the fourth century A.D., there were these triumphs, not every year but whenever there were victories, or even, as sometimes happened, imaginary victories.[6] For roughly half this period, the ceremony celebrated the lives of the prisoners. Around 150 B.C. the whole purpose of the triumph changed; it celebrated only the fame of the conqueror, the glory of Rome and the guilt of power. For guilt there was; all these accretions to the ceremony could have no other purpose than to hide something which disturbed and terrified the Romans to the depths of their souls. From this period there dates the peculiar violence of Roman poetry; the surviving fragments of the tragic poet Ennius, for example, show an obsession with bloodshed and brooding shame. The *Aeneid*, too, is full of a sense of guilt, of some expiation to be performed to keep the nameless terrors at bay. The epic begins in a tempest, traverses whole seas of blood, and arrives at last in a staggering description of a world in flames, everything at the mercy of blind destructive forces. Almost certainly this sense of guilt arose from the horror with which the Romans regarded their own destruction of Carthage in 146 B.C., and Virgil hints as much in the *Aeneid* as he retraces, with extraordinary awe and depth of feeling, that other burning of Carthage which occurred when Dido was queen.

In 149 B.C. the Roman Senate, urged on by Cato the Younger, decreed that Rome's chief commercial enemy and

---

[6] Appian, in *The Illyrian Wars*, 73, mentions the example of Caecilius Metellus who declared war on the Dalmatians, spent a winter peacefully with them in their capital, and was rewarded with a triumph on his return to Rome, though no fighting had taken place.

rival in imperialism must be razed to the ground. For years, with neurotic repetition, Cato had been crying from the tribune, *Delenda est Carthago:* Carthage must be destroyed, deleted from the map. By treachery the Romans induced the Carthaginians to surrender first their youths, then their ships, then their weapons; then they massed their armies, and hoped to take Carthage by storm. Carthage held out for three years, and the people were still fighting when the whole city was in flames. For seventeen days the city burned. A population of half a million was reduced to a bare fifty thousand; but the rage of the Romans was equal to their treachery. Remembering the former power of the city, afraid that it would rise phoenix-like from the ashes, they were not content until there was a five-fold destruction. The survivors were exiled, the walls left standing were burned or reduced to rubble, the earth was plowed up, it was sown with salt and it was solemnly cursed. As he watched the flames, Scipio turned to his friend Polybius, the historian, and said: "It is a wonderful sight, but I know not how, I feel a terror and dread lest someone should one day give the same order about my own city."[7]

The terror and dread remained. Carthage still haunted the Romans. Uprooted and despoiled, she was more to be feared than when her fleet sailed from the harbor towards Sicily. There was nothing, Polybius relates, except a pasturage and a few shepherd boys; no sign of any walls, no palaces, no royal dockyards. With mechanical efficiency, the Roman soldiers had carried out Cato's order; Carthage must be destroyed; but the ghosts remained.

From this period there begins the Roman preoccupation with death and destruction, just as in Russia it emerges at the time of Ivan the Terrible. Up to this time the prisoners in the

---

[7] Polybius, *Histories*, xxxix, 5.

THE FAULT IN THE CULTURE

triumph were mostly spared; from now on they were relentlessly and meaninglessly strangled in the small prison erected for them at the foot of the sacred Capitoline. "Why," asks Lucretius, "are we always speaking of death and terror?" He brooded over volcanic eruptions, but Rome herself had produced mindless volcanoes. In the end he came to regard willful acts of destruction as an elemental law of nature, the *natura rerum*:

> .... *Natura nec ullam*
> *Rem gigni patitur, nisi morte adjuta aliena.*[8]

The formula went some way to solve the Roman dilemma, but it explained nothing. It was untrue. Life comes from life, and death cannot be explained away so easily.

With Carthage destroyed, and the ghosts flocking in towards the Capitol, the only resource lay in a blind exertion of the will, to keep the ghosts away. The ancient loyalties were losing their validity. Twenty religions took the place of the simple *pietas* of Aeneas. Troy and Carthage had perished in the flames; there was a twice uttered warning. It was an age when men had lost all beliefs, but fear was everywhere. By the time of Augustus, it was observed that the augurs were smirking when they examined the auspices; they no longer believed in the old ceremonies. From this time onwards, irresponsibility became the curse of the Romans; and the Caesars, not knowing what to do with their power, waged war on phantoms, went mad or committed suicide. The *History* of Tacitus provides a whole series of portraits of Nechayev monsters; on another plane the great series of descriptions of volcanic outbursts in Lucretius and Virgil describes the same phenomenon of the undifferentiated will.

---

[8] Nature does not suffer one thing to be born, unless aided by another's death.

ZERO

Nations like individuals suffer from traumas; the unhealed wounds remain to plague the generations, and in China, for example, we can trace through two thousand years the memory of the great blood-letting which occurred at the end of the Han Dynasty. Until the present century, Chinese poets were employing the same images which obsessed the Han poets and filled the poetry of the Tang period—five hundred years after the Hans had perished. Once the barbarians had thrust across the frontiers. They were to keep on forcing their way across the frontiers, but the memory of the original shock remained, and so too did the memory of the uncounted millions who went through the Yumen Pass to defend China. Li Po, writing in the Tang Dynasty, speaks of the dead Han soldiers as though they had been killed only yesterday; and it is significant that Taoism, which in its political aspect introduced a form of pure nihilism, came into political prominence during the time of the barbarian invasions. It was Taoism, too, which provided the excuse for the unprincipled violence of the Japanese *samurai*, though by this time the Japanese were Buddhists; yet Zen Buddhism was so deeply penetrated with Taoist thought that there was little difference between them. "Destroy to the uttermost," was the cry of the privileged gangsters of the shogunate, but this cry would have been impossible without the ultimate Taoist belief in the meaninglessness of things and the importance of doing nothing. "*Wu wei*," says the author of the Taoist canon. "Do nothing, because heaven does all things." It follows that men survive only by the utmost passivity or the utmost violence.

The character of the Chinese Taoist is so close to the character of the revolutionary nihilist that it is worth a more formal comparison. We have seen how General Chang Hsien-chung murdered the inhabitants of the vast province of Szechuan, and placed a memorial stone on the walls of

THE FAULT IN THE CULTURE

Chengtu which bears, except for the last line, a purely Taoist inscription. The last line merely draws the logical conclusion. For the Taoist there are no laws, no *natura rerum*. Heaven rules everything with complete impersonality. There is only the majesty of the visible earth and the idiocy of death, and the Way of Heaven is beyond anyone's understanding. The Taoist therefore immerses himself in himself, finding his refuge in his own loneliness; inevitably there comes to him at intervals the hysteria which is brought on partly by loneliness and partly by the terrible insecurity of life in China. Sometimes he becomes preoccupied with his own hysteria, and at such moments he falls into a rage and destroys everything in sight. The Chinese scholar, Lin Tung-chi, has drawn the classic portrait of the Taoist:

> Taoism may be defined as romantic individualism. It is the natural and necessary counterpart to the complacent and yielding gregariousness of Confucianism. Come what may, the first prompting of a Taoist is to "debunk," so much folly and bad taste does he see in this all-too-human world.
> One can best describe the workings of his mentality in terms of a curve.
> It begins with an ascending movement, whereby the discharging energy of debunking is directed outward to the external world until it reaches a point where the fire of debunking turns into a white flame of defiance. It is the moment most supercharged with possibility of action, the juncture at which a Chinese intellectual may most readily turn into a revolutionary if ever his defying mood finds its way to combine with the popular discontent of the age.
> A typical Taoist nature does not, however, become a revolutionary as a rule. He does not actually mix with the populace. A proud artist, he stands alone, contemplating no comrades. He, predestinedly, sees a war of one against all and

one against everything. And a more exalted and tense frame of mind cannot be imagined.

Yet there is no vent. Totally unable to view the impending battle in terms of practical interests and concrete issues, he is at a loss as to where and to whom to deal his blows. The intensity of his charged feeling, thus blocked, soon recoils upon itself. A mental crisis develops when an involuntary repression compresses the rising temper, which, foundering at this tremulous height, turns quickly into a state of Dionysian drunkenness. The Taoist revolt, at this stage, takes on the character of emotional self-abandonment. He gives himself up to himself. He no longer defies, he simply disregards. A sort of ecstacy takes place, in which the half-conscious bitterness and the half-felt rapture combine to produce a vent peculiarly Taoist—the devastating laugh of the intoxicated. But this blessed stage cannot last long. A mental numbness born of helpless desperation is foredoomed to come to a *dénouement*—the beginning of the descending curve.

As the effects of intoxication clear away, the last possibility of action disappears. He cannot but question now the worth of it all. "Why excitement and fury?" asks the erstwhile rebel. And he begins to debunk *himself*. With a chuckle he drops the gauntlet and retires into the mountains. The boisterous rebel becomes the saintly recluse. After the tempest the serene sunset.[9]

This portrait of the Taoist should be placed beside the portraits of Nechayev's revolutionary nihilist and Hitler's "four faces of nothingness." Very little distinguishes the Taoist from the nihilist who desires the destruction of the world, but this little is significant. The Chinese Taoist is happy enough to know that the destruction of the world is impossible, and a reasonable man may contemplate a sunset and see in it all the destruction he could ever desire. But in him the same intel-

[9] Lin Tung-Chi, *The Other China*, 1944, pp. 6-7.

THE FAULT IN THE CULTURE

lectual processes were at work; he too suffers from an exaltation of the will, and is totally unable to view the battle in terms of human issues, he must exalt himself at whatever the cost and defy the universe, and perform the meaningless act of destructive violence; and he fails to do these things only because he is conscious that they are ridiculous, at the last moment, when it is almost too late. But in Chinese history General Chang Hsien-chung was not the only nihilist who was prepared to massacre a whole people. There was the last emperor of the Liao dynasty who, for no reason that anyone has ever been able to fathom, threw himself, his concubines, his works of art, the servants of his palace, and even his animals, onto a bonfire, crying: "Let all things perish with me, the last Emperor of my dynasty." At the time of the Warring Dynasties, and the Three Kingdoms, there were the same violent and purposeless massacres, and it is significant that in our own time the Chinese Communist leader, Mao Tse-tung, has passed through a period of revolutionary anarchism and read deeply among the Taoist philosophers.

Taoism became, in time, an extremely complex philosophy, though never becoming entirely removed from the simple nihilism of the *Tao Teh Ching*. Since, except for rare intervals, the religion was officially prescribed, the Taoist priest became a wanderer who fought a continual Fabian battle against dogmatic Confucianism; he followed the schismatic command to go out into the desert, and between the *raskolniki* and the wandering Taoist monks there are remarkable similarities. There is no evidence of Taoist influence on Russia until 1863, when the *Tao Teh Ching* was first adequately translated into the Russian language. Both Tolstoy and Dostoyevsky read this translation and the commentaries written upon it; and so, during a time of revolutionary upheaval, Chinese and Russian nihilism met. "Destroy knowledge and wisdom, then there will no longer be brigands. Throw away all valuable objects; then there will be no more thieves. Burn contracts and agreements; the people will revert to their sturdy barbarity. Destroy weighing scales and measuring-rods; the people will no longer fight among themselves for what they receive . . . Offer the entire world to the good; and threaten the wicked with the destruction of the world; they cannot be reformed . . . Let every man act alone; if he sees with his own eyes, the world will not go up in flames. If he hears with his own ears, the world will not be confused. If he thinks only with his own mind, the world will not be snared." This is not the voice of Nechayev. It is Chuangtse, the Taoist philosopher, writing a commentary on a famous poem in the *Tao Teh Ching*. The commentary, which was written about 300 B.C., is entitled *A Protest against this Age and Time*.

Something of the same unbridled nihilistic violence occurred in mediaeval Germany. Once again it had its roots in schism—in the confused German desire to throw off the yoke of the Catholic Church. Luther, the schismatic, faced with the refusal of the peasants to enter his newly founded church, cursed them with the same fury that the *raskolniki* enjoyed as they raged against the orthodox. It is not Nechayev or Avvakum, but Luther who cried, "Whoever can should smite, strangle, or stab, secretly or publicly. Therefore, dear gentlemen, hearken here, save there, smite, stab, strangle at will these murderous and rebellious peasants." The atrocious words, addressed to the temporal and ecclesiastical princes in 1525, coming in a pamphlet simply entitled *Against the Robbing and Murderous Gangs of Peasants*, meant only that Luther had surrendered to the split in his soul, felt no loyalty to men, and considered all except the princes beneath contempt. Over two hundred thousand peasants were tortured and killed during the peasant war.

THE FAULT IN THE CULTURE

The causes of the war were partly political and partly theological, the Holy Roman Empire was breaking up, and those who defended it did so with the knowledge that they were already defeated men. But in Germany there were no religious foundations for peace. The Catholic Church was splitting wide open. "The elaborately woven structure of Christian theology," wrote Hegel, "was being entirely pulled to pieces, because men wished to bring Christianity back to the simple ways of the Word of God." The schism therefore, though it preceded the Russian schism, was of the same order, came about as the result of the same causes, and had the same effects. The schism remains. "In our minds," wrote Hermann Hesse, "we look down from both sides at the abyss within us," and not only Thomas Mann has called the Germans *die Herren der Gegensätze,* "the lords of contraries." There was a tendency towards nihilism among the Germans long before Hitler. The Protestant north and the Catholic south fought out their battles in many German minds, and the unification of Germany never solved the most pressing problem of all—in what shall we believe? Inevitably, with the two cultures overlapping, fighting a confused battle in the darkness of the mind, there came a time when the Germans went in search of "the prisoners of the triumph." Not even Kant, reviving the moral categories, stemming the romantic tide of willfulness, could prevent the Germans from the consequences of schism.

The general pattern by which nihilism evolves, now becomes clear. Whenever diverse cultures meet and overlap, there is the everpresent danger of the meaningless ceremony. There is a point where loyalties are confused, or cancel each other out, a wasteland where no god, no authority, no sense of human values remains; at such times men say, "It is a good idea to level the hills." We can represent the meeting of two cultures by two circles overlapping:

ZERO

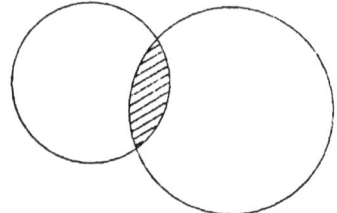

The dark space represents the "dead land," the home of the nihilist, the man who has freed himself from responsibility to all things, behaving like Stavrogin of whom Dostoyevsky wrote, "The prince has no ideas. He has only an aversion to his contemporaries. He does not believe in God, and he has lost the distinction between good and evil because he has ceased to know people. And so he can kill, whenever he chooses to kill." The "dead land" also represents the moment when "the prisoners of the triumph" may be carelessly sacrificed.

Generally, cultures do not overlap according to so simple a pattern. Usually three or four cultures meet at the same time, with widely different powers. There are then "regions of comparative deadness," and other regions where the "deadness" is absolute:

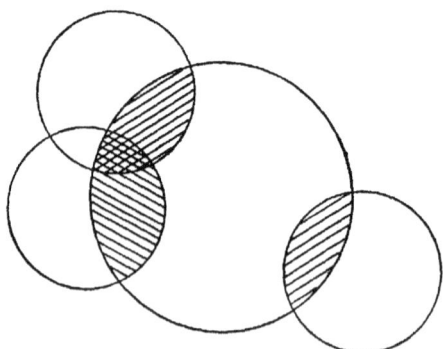

THE FAULT IN THE CULTURE

There may, of course, be more complex forms. The Roman Triumph represents the meeting of Etruscan, Greek, Phrygian, Egyptian and Latin cultures, and some of these—perhaps all of them—affected Rome in successive waves. It is also misleading to represent the converging cultures by circles; it would be more useful, but more complicated, to show them by wedges of greater or lesser penetration. That these "dead lands" must exist is not difficult to prove; for every culture introduces its own complex system of loyalties and duties, and the sheer complexity of these loyalties and duties makes it impossible for a real fusion of cultures ever to come about. Cultures may, and often do, become richer by fusion, but wherever there is fusion there must for a while be an unsettled period while the loyalties and duties are redefined; and they may never be completely defined. The laws in particular must suffer vast strains when cultures meet. If the various strands of law are continued without any deliberate effort to make a new integration from a multitude of laws deriving from different sources—as happened in Anglo-Saxon England, where three different codes representing three different Kingdoms were in use, and each code was hedged around with other codes—there comes a time when they are almost arbitrarily fused together; one code survives, but it contains the doctrines of separate codes; others are added in time, with the result that half the laws in the present British code are meaningless. Something of the same thing occurs with the convergence of cultures.

We cannot define the convergence with complete accuracy at any stage. All we can see is a general law, repeated in many civilizations. This law can be stated briefly: *When cultures converge and suffer a traumatic shock, there follows a meaningless sacrifice and a reign of nihilism.*

ZERO

Far from being a rare phenomenon, nihilism is a nearly inevitable phenomenon in the development of all cultures.

The table opposite makes no claim to completeness. In rough outline it sketches out the emergence of nihilism in nine cultures. In Germany, for example, the traumatic shock was far more complicated than hinted at here; there was the initial shock of 1918, followed by the general bankruptcy eleven years later, the vast wave of unemployment, the desolate fear of Communism, and a fear of nihilism so intense that it brought nihilism in its train.[10] An intense fear of nihilism may be almost as dangerous as nihilism itself and may have the same consequences, for both are flights from terror into an unreal world of nebulous power. The phrase "suicide by conquest" similarly needs definition, and the Jews were, of course, not the only victims in the "meaningless sacrifice." Moreover, it might have been more simple to describe all the forms of nihilism merely as "anguished pain," for nihilism represents the cry of horror which comes over wounded people, when nothing can be done except to rage against a pain too great to be borne. "Annihilation," said that strange genius Otto Weininger, "is only the intellectual equivalent of pain." It is difficult to believe that anyone has ever said anything wiser on the subject of nihilism.

If the Traumatic Law of Cultures is true, the possibility of an emergence of nihilism in America becomes all the more likely. The ferocious reign of individualism in the last cen-

[10] The fear of nihilism was exceptionally great in Germany in 1920. It is only necessary to refer to a passage in Hermann Hesse's book, *Blick ins Chaos*, which appeared in 1919. "Already half of Europe, already at least half of Eastern Europe, is on the way to chaos, travelling drunkenly in an illusion of holy ecstasy along the edge of the abyss, and celebrates this by singing drunken hymns, as Dmitri Karamazov sang. Over these songs the insulted *bourgeois* laugh; the saint and the seer hear them with tears." The passage is quoted with approval by T. S. Eliot in his notes to *The Waste Land*.

THE FAULT IN THE CULTURE

The Pattern of Nihilism

Nation	Converging Cultures	Traumatic Shock	Form taken by 'meaningless sacrifice'	Form of Nihilism
Rome	Etruscan Greek Egyptian etc.	Exhaustion following Punic Wars	Burning of Carthage; murder of prisoners	Caesarism
Greece	Ionian Scythian, etc.	Plague of 430 B.C.	Destruction of Melos; suicidal attack on Syracuse	Flight from terror
China	Split between northern and southern dynasties; barbarian invasions	Exhaustion following Warring Dynasties	Permanent civil war	Taoism
Japan	Ainu Chinese	Volcanic eruptions	Meaningless murders by Samurai	Zen Buddhism
Aztec	Maya Spanish	Prophecy concerning coming of white conquerors	Meaningless sacrifices	Religious nihilism
Russia I	Schism; Tartar invasions	Burning of Moscow in 1570 A.D.	Murders by Ivan the Terrible; suicides of raskolniki	Belief in the living dead; visionary nihilism
Russia II	French culture Modern industrialism	Burning of Moscow in 1812 A.D.	Government by assassination	Revolutionary nihilism
Germany I	Schism	Thirty Years War	Murder of peasants	Religious nihilism
Germany II	Breakdown of all converging cultures	Defeat of 1918	Murder of Jews; suicide by conquest	Revolutionary nihilism: most recent phase.

tury, the immense powers wielded by individuals, and the influence of the German transcendentalist philosophy on so many Americans would suggest that there is a basis for the unscrupulous use of power as it was wielded by the Caesars. It is possible that the explosion of the atom bomb over Hiroshima represents exactly the same phenomenon as the destruction of Carthage by fire in 146 B.C., and that in the column in the table reserved for "Form of Nihilism" opposite America there might, at some future date, be placed the words "anarchic royalism." It is, however, unlikely. America is too large, too wealthy, and too industrious ever again to suffer the kind of traumatic shock which occurred in 1939. Yet there are "faults in the culture," unresolved strains of the most dangerous kind, and a kind of neurosis which tends easily to panic; Orson Welles' broadcast of the invasion of the Martians showed only one aspect of a general problem. In America the converging cultures are not yet fused together, and the death-wish hovers near, or else the New York evening papers, or the sadism of so many Hollywood films are not representative of popular taste. The increasing number of "meaningless" or "unmotivated" crimes committed by Americans might also be thought to demonstrate the emergence of a kind of nihilism. The truth is, however, that America is so huge, rests so heavily upon a healthy agricultural population and has such vast resources that it can probably absorb these strains. If so, it will be the first civilization to have contended with all the forces that make for nihilism and the nihilist crackup, and emerged victorious.

Meanwhile, as long as cultures remain unstable, the danger of the nihilist nightmare—where there are no laws, where everything is permitted, where the strong and the cruel are allowed free scope for their strength and their cruelty, and the wildest plans of irresponsible destruction are carried through—remains. It is a permanent danger, and must be faced permanently; for the consequences of failure are too horrible to contemplate. Everything is within the power of the nihilist once he has attained power. Slowly, undramatically, he annihilates man. He is not a rare phenomenon. Millions upon millions of nihilists survive in the world, in Soviet Russia, and Germany; there are others nearer home. He is not a phenomenon of our age, but his powers are greater in our age than ever before. There are no resting places for civilizations; the war against nihilism is as eternal as the war fought by the stars against the dark spaces of the heavens.

Today, civilization is like a thin sheeting of ice; underneath the ice, always waiting to break through, are the black waters of the nihilist chaos. Every crack in the ice, every flaw, or scratch on the surface, only brings the day of dissolution nearer.

But the day of dissolution is not inevitable. It is not in the least necessary that men should surrender to the nihilist nightmare, the drugged neurotic stare, and the wild destructive flaying of the arms. Two things are necessary. We should make our civilization as firm and vigorous as ever, and we should come to understand the workings of the nihilist mind: why he destroys, and why his chief delight is the annihilation of man.

V.
Man=Zero

WHEN a Chinese was led out to execution under the rule of the Kuomintang, it would sometimes happen that the police dressed the condemned man in clown's clothes, paraded him squatting in a cart through the streets, wrote on his paper hat a list of his crimes and splashed red and white paint on his cheeks. Often a dance band accompanied the procession which wound its way towards the burial mounds outside the city gate, and sometimes the cart was drawn by a gaily decorated pony. Accompanied by the jeers and laughter of the crowd, the condemned man was slowly drawn through the streets, until the moment came when he stepped off the cart, knelt down, and was shot through the back of the head.

The formula of ridicule was based on a profound psychological insight. By making the prisoner ridiculous, the police removed him from the sympathy of the crowd. He could not beg for mercy. If he did, he would look even more ridiculous. He could not defend himself, or protest against his execution, because the crowd had no respect for him and would refuse to believe him even if it listened to him. He could not proclaim his innocence—if he were innocent—because it was ridiculous that a clown should be either guilty or innocent. By making him a clown, the police had removed him from the common humanness of the crowd, had made him unreal, and his death was unreal, and therefore of little importance. He squatted on a low stool on the cart, his arms were tied behind his back, he jolted absurdly with every jolt of the cart, and he could only seek to save his face by laughter, the one human emotion he could share with the crowd. In the ordered hierarchy of Chinese face, he had reached bottom; he had no face and had become zero; and for him there was no court of appeal, no justification for existence, and no need of repentence. Long before his death he had been reduced to insignificance, annihilated.

It was not always so in China. In 1935, the great short-story writer, Lu Hsun, wrote an essay called *The Dark Night*, in which he described at some length and with unusual penetration the changes which had come over China in his lifetime. He found himself thinking of an execution he had witnessed during the Ch'ing Dynasty, which came to an end in 1911. "At that time," he wrote, "there was a certain grace in life, and men were possessed of extraordinary courage. Not so long ago, when a prisoner was condemned to death, he was led through the busy highway, and was allowed to protest with the loudest voice his condemnation. He would say vile things about his judges. He could tell the story of his brave deeds and demonstrate his courage in the face of death, and at the moment when he was about to be executed the spectators would applaud him. When I was young, I thought this practice barbarous and cruel. As I grow older, it seems to me that our rulers in the past were superbly conscious of their power if they permitted these things to happen, and they were showing their kindness and even their benevolence to the condemned man. But nowadays this no longer happens."

In the interval between the end of the Ch'ing Dynasty and the coming to power of the Kuomintang, something had happened to abase man. Lu Hsun was conscious of the change.

ZERO

He suggests that it came about because men no longer possessed any clearly defined relationship to each other, for when the imperial system crumbled, no valid system came to take its place.

Death by ridicule and shooting was the method of the Kuomintang, just as death by ridicule and crucifixion was the method of the Romans in Jerusalem. The mockery of Jesus by the soldiers was part of the deliberate effort to reduce him to insignificance;[1] the mockery of the Jews by the Nazi Storm Troopers was of the same nature. But ridicule is only one way in which men can be reduced to insignificance. There exist countless other ways short of murder by which men can be made into shambling, mechanical, fear-ridden caricatures of themselves; and the gravest tragedy of our time is that there are increasingly efficient mechanical means available for this purpose. Men can be reduced to insignificance by torture, by drugs, by terror, by giving them nothing to live for, by making them cogs in industrial machines, by making them lose their identity in a formless and barren concept of the state, by giving them a place in a meaningless mythology, by the destruction of their memory or their traditions, by throwing them into a trance or a stupor. All that is human in man can be removed from him by the simplest means. His will and his

---

[1] It would appear that at one time there was a carefully elaborated ceremony of ridicule leading up to Crucifixion among the Romans. Pliny records a story which suggests curious parallels with the death of Christ. Pliny says that when Agrippa, the grandson of Herod, passed through Alexandria, after receiving the crown of Judaea from Caligula in Rome, a harmless lunatic called Carabas, who roamed the streets stark naked, was set up in a public place; he was robed in sack-cloth; a paper cap was clapped on his head, and with a broken reed placed in his hand by way of a sceptre, he was led through the streets, while the bystanders mocked him with cries of "Marin." Sir James Frazer has observed that this ceremony of ridicule and death may have been the pattern according to which Jesus was crucified, and Carabas may have been Pliny's natural mistake for the name "Barabbas," meaning "the son of the Father."

common humanity can be destroyed by threats, by silence, by the fear of unimaginable consequences, and by all that we mean by "terror." Men can be made irresponsible, or they can be made responsible only to the orders of a hypnotist. They can be twisted into almost any shape, and they can be warped either temporarily or for long periods. The machinery by which men can be reduced to insignificance lies all around us. Roughly, these machines are of two kinds, and following the terminology invented by Hitler—perhaps from his readings in theology—they can be called the instruments of spiritual terror, and the instruments of physical terror. They overlap. They are not equal in their effects; but all are deadly.

This chapter will be concerned with spiritual terrors, dominations, and powers. They are not happy terms, but that can hardly be helped; they are not happy subjects, nor are they amenable to complete analysis, for they lie on the borderregions of the human spirit, and it is not pleasant to observe the human spirit cracking under their thrusts. In these matters Nechayev was an amateur. He could understand dimly the employment of massive spiritual terrors, but the greater part of *The Revolutionary Catechism* is concerned with terrorizing the government; the terror which strikes at whole peoples is mentioned only incidentally and perfunctorily. It was left to Hitler, the pure engineer of terror, and to Trotsky—an able mechanic—to enunciate the theorems of pure terror with convincing force; and both, but in different ways, derived their terminology from the Jesuits and the Inquisition. Almost at the very beginning of *Mein Kampf*, Hitler states the basic axioms of terrorism as he had discovered them:

> The psyche of the great masses is not receptive to half measures or weakness.
>
> The great masses neither realize the impudence with which they are spiritually terrorized, nor the outrageous curtailment

of their human liberties, for in no way does the delusion of the doctrine (of terror) dawn on them. Thus they see only the inconsiderate force, the brutality and the aim of its manifestations, to which they submit.

I came to understand the infamous terror of the mind which the Social Democrats exercised on the people who, neither morally nor psychically, could resist their attacks. At a given signal Social Democracy directs a bombardment of lies and calumnies at the adversary who seemed most dangerous, till finally the nerves of those who had been attacked gave out and they, for the sake of peace, bow down to the hated enemy. But even then they find no peace. For these futile people the drama is continually resumed, till the fear of the mad dog paralyzes them by suggestion.

These tactics are based upon an exact calculation of human weaknesses; their results must lead to success with almost mathematical certainty, unless the other side also learns to fight poison gas with poison gas.

Weak natures have to be told that it simply means "to be or not to be."

The importance of physical terror against the individual and the masses also became clarified in my mind, and here too an exact calculation of the psychological effect is possible.

The terror in the workshops, in the factory, in the assembly hall and on occasions of mass demonstrations will always be accompanied by success as long as it is not met by an equally great force of terror.[2]

Nearly at the end of *Mein Kampf*, Hitler reverted once more to the basic assumptions of terrorism, but this time the thought is expressed without the previous fire, as he plays with the idea of a "Christian terror" which forced itself upon a free pagan world:

[2] *Mein Kampf* (American edition), pp. 56-57.

MAN = ZERO

A view of life, filled with infernal intolerance, will be broken only by a new idea driven forward in a similar spirit of frenzy, fought for with the same strong will, but pure and genuine throughout.

The individual may bitterly regret today that, with the appearance of Christianity, there came the first spiritual terror upon the more liberty-loving ancient world; even so, he may not deny that the world has been dominated by compulsions ever since, and compulsion is broken only by compulsion, and terror by terror.[3]

These are simple theses, but they had never before been enunciated so forcefully. To strike the larger enemy, not the least; to confuse by deliberate lies; to break terror with terror; to recognize the almost infinite capacity of the people for doses of terror, as though terror were a liquid which could be absorbed indefinitely—all this had been dimly recognized before, but never so objectively or coldly stated. He was to understand later the delicate niceties of terror, but already in 1924 he was marking out the roles which terror could play, and evaluating their consequences "with mathematical precision."

There seems to have been a time when he was even a little surprised at the ease with which terror could be employed; it was so much easier than he had thought. He saw that terror, once employed, perpetuates itself. All that was necessary was to set the machine in motion. It would never end. He made, however, certain important omissions in his calculations. He forgot that the machinery of terror is so all-embracing that inevitably it comes to terrorize everyone, even the leaders of the State. Also, the efficiency of terror is limited by the efficiency of its operatives, the mindless and inefficient secret police. So they too must be terrorized. There must be coils

[3] *Mein Kampf*, p. 676.

upon coils of terror, and every leader must set terrorists to watch every other leader. Ivanov had been high in the counsels of Nechayev. He had offered his entire wealth to the revolutionary cause, but in the end he had to be tortured into submission, or killed. No one could be trusted, once terrorism ruled, and the revolutionary leader could survive only by a delicate balance of power. The army must be set against the praetorian guard, there must be two seconds-in-command, so that they can be set against one another, and the least important spies must be surrounded with nets of spies. Perhaps the greatest of Hitler's mistakes was that he forgot that in the world of terror, nothing is ever learned from the past.

Having enunciated his aphorisms and given them the appearance of axioms, he was now determined to carry them through. They were not pretty. They were not intended to be. He was a desperate man. If he failed on this venture, he would die in a cellar in Vienna, poverty-stricken, a derelict like all the other derelicts he had known in Vienna before the war. The task was to find the vulnerable places. Wherever men are weakest, he would insert the knife. He would map out the human *psyche*; it was not necessary to know all the vulnerable places: a few were enough. On these few, and at the same time, he would exert the utmost pressure, and at the moment when the victim squealed, he would dig deeper, for it was not enough that the victim should be weak; *he must be made conscious of his weakness*. Therefore, to the German people thirsting for strength, he proclaimed their weakness. Thirsting for *Lebensraum*, they were reminded *ad nauseam* of the imprisoning frontiers. They thirsted for vengeance—at this point the knife was twisted in the wound—and he repeated every single one of their ignominious defeats. It was in these regions that he was most successful and most uncompromising. He knew and made use of a remarkable knowledge of the processes of the human *psyche*, derived more from Jung than from Freud, for Jung acknowledged the power-principle and recognized the hollowness of the pleasure-principle. He used these simple rough-shod methods with calculated effect, and if they seem as cheapjack as the methods of the Rosicrucians with their appeal to harness the mind to the universal mind, they were nevertheless more successful. Hitler realized to an unprecedented degree the weaknesses of the Germans. He knew, because he shared them, their day-dreams; knew that in every German there lurked a small Nechayev monster who only desired to be infinitely great. This last desire he refused them. Only he would be great, sent by God to resurrect an abstraction called the "German nation."

But this was only one part of the terrorist's aims. The final aim was the complete destruction of the human will of the German people. Therefore one part of the human *psyche* must be set against another; loyalties must be divided; consciences stilled. They were not asked to have loyalty to the National Socialist tradition; for there was no tradition; they must be loyal only to the huge dream-like figure who towered over them, remote even from the movement he controlled. The method was simple; all that was necessary was to press hard on all the vulnerable places, and then show them, as from a great distance, the figure of the divine rescuer who would save them out of his mercy. The rule was strict, undeviating, and bitter—too bitter for most men. So they were allowed a small private field of irresponsibility; they were allowed to attack the Jews. But even this relief was conditional; by committing crimes against the Jews they bound themselves closer to Hitler, and could be more easily blackmailed. It was a trick Nechayev played to bind his friends to him. Hitler played it with the whole German people. They were all guilty, and all knew they were guilty, and the more crimes they committed the more they were at his mercy, the more they would obey him, the more they felt it necessary that they should sink or swim together. The process of dividing the German mind was accomplished with diabolical ingenuity. By accident and by design it came about that the terror waged by the Nazis against the German people became a terror waged within the confines of the German soul, and each man terrified himself and defended himself against terror, and rebelled against himself, and cried for mercy, and was thrown down by something within himself, till at last he was listless, defeated by himself. Then he would do what he was told.

It could hardly be otherwise. All the mechanical and psychological resources of modern times were at the hands of the terrorists. They could awaken compulsive neuroses, compel the neuroses to follow appointed paths. Their aim was to deaden the soul and the will, and in the Germany of the twenties and thirties, there were few who could hold out against them. What the Germans call the *Grundlage* was already formed; the consciousness of deep-seated guilt and defeat was already there. It was only necessary that guilt and defeat should be completely acknowledged. They wanted to make men into *zombies*, and men were only too delighted to perform the mindless gyrations demanded of them. Not power, but irresponsibility ruled; and since everyone was enabled to play within the small field of irresponsibility allotted to him, the ordinary human desire to possess some authority, however little, was easily satisfied. At the head of this anarchic State only one figure was vested with effective authority and responsibility; and he was an irresponsible maniac.

The machinery of terror grew slowly. Hitler's original statements on the nature of terror only sketched out the outlines. By 1939 the machinery of terror had become, in Hitler's words, "a superb instrument of annihilation." The statement was true, much truer than foreigners thought, for the secrets of the concentration camps were still piously preserved by the faithful. Those vast, carefully calculated, supremely bureaucratic machines of destruction grew out of humble origins. The terror began with street brawls. As early as 1923, Hitler sent the brown-clad Storm Troopers out on the streets with specific instructions. These were, "You are to use frightful methods in order to attract attention." He was employing the psychology of the crowd that hurries around after every motor-crash. But terror was also an advertisement. The circus had come to town. There was the parade of the Storm Troopers, but who would remember this parade unless someone's skull was split open? *Flowing blood is memorable.* This simple discovery was perhaps the Nazis' greatest and most diabolical achievement. They could use this discovery in whatever way they desired; as threat, as punishment, as sensation. It was not an accident that three-quarters of the Nazi banner was the color of fresh blood.

The technique of the deliberate street-brawl paid handsome dividends. It did not matter who was struck down. What was wanted was blood, and the Storm Troopers passing unscathed through the murder. The mere sight of the blood they had shed showed they were powerful. These street-brawl parades inspired the requisite terror because no one could be certain he would not be caught up in them; it was hazardous even to go on a shopping expedition unless you wore the swastika arm-band, and half the people who wore them at the beginning of the movement, wore them as an emblem of their fear. Afraid to cross a street, they were compelled to pretend to a trust in the *Führer.* Then, too, the quite arbitrary way in which the Storm Troopers committed their arrests and murders was calculated to inspire terror. The blow might fall anywhere: there was no escape; it was best, after all, to spend 10 marks on a Nazi arm-band and swear allegiance to an incomprehensible *Führer*. Soon there was passive consent, and from passive consent to active participation there was only a hairbreadth.

Hitler had calculated exactly, "with mathematical precision." He was beginning to find and to evaluate the vulnerable places, and to employ the theorem that the greater terror defeats the lesser. He would play on men's fears. It was a game he played to the end, but it began one day in Munich when he discovered that by giving young men guns and arm-bands, he could make it impossible for anyone to cross a street without demanding his permission. The battle was half-won. After a while it was no longer necessary for the Storm Troopers to swarm the streets; the threat of them was enough. Nor does the terrorist machine necessarily need physical force to support it. Because the fear of pain is often more sharply conceived than pain itself, all he need do is to awaken fears, conjure up threats, and play one against another, till the crazed population, weary of the frenzied excitement, surrenders its will to the master, as a lion surrenders its will to the lion-tamer, who no longer has to protect himself with a barbed baton, but controls the defeated animal with a look or a shake of the finger. The atmosphere of fear was easy to maintain, for no one knew where the blow would fall next; and as Jack the Ripper subtly terrorized the whole of London, Hitler terrorized Munich, and from Munich he went on to terrorize the whole globe. And as the people surrendered their will, so the stature of Hitler increased. It was Hitler's genius that he could play this dangerous game of the will, but it is conceivable that the same game could be played without Hitler and without Storm Troopers. It is conceivable, under certain conditions, that terror can generate itself—by rumor.

There were, of course, some people who were immune to the reign of terror, but they were very few. Hitler had guessed correctly. The human crowd, caught in a net of fear, behaves less courageously than individuals. It has its own psychology. There is a moment, not too difficult to calculate, when it stampedes under the impulsion of intolerable fear. It is the crowd rather than the individual which is entranced by the sight of blood. Lost within the crowd, the individual performs actions he would not dream of committing among his intimate friends. The crowd is a hiding-place, not very different to the place where a man lives when he is most alone. In the crowd he has no moral scruples, and can shamelessly give way to his fears. Simultaneously with the march of the Storm Troopers, there came into existence the deliberate manipulation by the Nazis of the crowd's fears.

In the middle pages of *Mein Kampf*, Hitler has expounded at length on the manner in which he manipulated crowds, intoxicated them, frightened them, raised them to a pitch of fury, played on them as an artist might play on a musical instrument. He could evoke from them any reaction he desired. He deliberately kept a crowd in a beerhall waiting for as long as eighteen hours, till they were almost dead with exhaustion and expectancy. He discovered that a crowd that was hungry, impatient, and excited by Wagnerian music played without any pause possessed no restraint, and without knowing what they were doing, the crowd could be hypnotized into making the required responses. It was not a difficult accomplishment, but he was the first to seize upon the advantage. The crowd was in precisely the same position as the man who is put into a trance and then ordered to perform some ridiculous action. At a given time, the weak-willed man performs that action. Hitler had as yet no desire that they should perform any actions;

all that he demanded of them was that they should hate. He succeeded beyond all expectations, until the time came when they could hate Jews, Communists, gypsies, Jehovah's Witnesses, Freemasons, and all foreigners in a single breath. Once he had played upon their fears with threats. Now, almost casually, if they hated sufficiently, and if they followed him, he offered them the whole world.

Such a technique is familiar within a pressure cooker. He had placed them under terrible strains, then suddenly reduced the pressure and channelized the explosion; the mindless automata were given an aim—the conquest of the whole world. It was an aim which no reasonable man would have believed in, but the Germans were no longer reasonable people. The Nechayev monster had been awakened, but he was not a monster of the will; he was a monster of irresponsible destruction. The same process was repeated at intervals. They would be threatened, made submissive, then once again offered the vision of conquest—that dazzling justification for their sufferings. It was heady wine, and nearly every German got drunk.

Hitler has observed in *Mein Kampf* the incomparable advantages which radio offers to a dictatorship. The beerhall technique, which involved the suspension of the will and judgment of his audience, could be employed more subtly through the microphone. Because it was more impersonal, it was more powerful. Impossible to reject the voice that came so menacingly and so sternly from the neutral machine; the machine could not be turned off; the law and public opinion demanded that everyone should listen, but they were allowed to listen only to him. The German people possessed inexhaustible patience: he manipulated their patience. He had raised their hopes; now he studied the saturation points of hope, the curves of fear, and the moments when the greatest desire for vengeance fuses with the greatest hate. The dizzy pace was kept up, and on the nerves of an exhausted people, Hitler played his exquisite game of hope, and abandonment of hope, and then hope again, until it seemed that the people he had terrorized would die of excitement. Hans Bernd Gisevius had shown in his admirable book *To the Bitter End* how the masses of the German people hoped desperately for peace till the very last moment, believing against all belief that Hitler was too clever to lead them to war, but their will, snapped by the constant state of tension, their memories weakened by the constant changes of direction—the new and blinding emphases given to every new problem, so that the problem of a week before seemed to have happened weeks, and even years, and perhaps centuries previously—they were in no state to fight against the terror he had imposed on them. He had induced a new and vertiginous time factor into their lives, and they suffered in the mass the same kind of hallucinations as individuals injected with scopolamine, a drug which depresses the motor areas of the brain, affects the will and the memory, and leaves the patient in a heavy trance-like state, from which he can only be aroused by bright colors, piercing sounds or extreme pain. Such a patient, sunk in a torpor, oppressed by a sense of guilt and a vague memory of former triumphs, obeys orders instantly, signs confessions unread, repeats accurately any words which are slowly spoken to him and tells lies, while being completely unaware that he is doing any of these things.

By the time the war broke out, Hitler had accomplished his purpose; he had reduced the German nation to a state of mindless mechanical obedience. He had used all available weapons; the most terrifying of all had been silence. When he was silent there was terror, for no one knew where the blow would fall next. When he spoke, and something entirely unsuspected came from him, all directions were reversed;

there was to be peace, or there was to be war; there were to be campaigns against the Sudetenland, Teschen, Poland, Austria, Czechoslovakia or the whole world; an ever-changing conspiracy was in the air. But silence was the more efficient weapon, and after the frenzy of speech-making before the war, he deliberately spoke rarely when the war was on. Long ago Houston Stewart Chamberlain had written: "Only let the *Volk* speak, and it will speak thus perceptibly." When Hitler was silent, he was more compelling than when he used the most menacing words.

Perhaps it should not surprise us. The Chinese and Indians have known for centuries that silence, darkness and emptiness were the most provocative, and the most efficient weapons of torture; they could kill, and they could also be employed to create a dream-like atmosphere where the will was held in suspense, and they could also cause the most excruciating agony. But though silence is often effective, it is sometimes a two-edged weapon. In the most completely silent room suspended on a vacuum, where the walls are thick with felt and rubber, a man standing in the center hears the roaring of waves louder than he has ever heard them before—the loud, ominous beating of his own heart.

Hitler did his best. He drowned out, wherever it was possible, the sound of the human heartbeat. He did not always succeed, but he had succeeded on so wide a plane that he could overlook the small failures. He had drugged the mind of a whole nation, and with a pharmaceutist's ingenuity he had increased the doses at the appropriate times. There are limits to the amount of drug a man may take without achieving immunity, but Hitler had stepped up the doses, and sometimes he disintoxicated the Germans only to provide them with a whole new regimen of drugs immediately. The radio blared—it was nearly all confusion, and the only unconfusing thing hammered into the brain of the Germans was that he was there, a god-like figure controlling them from the heights of his boundless authority. The hugeness of the man dominated. It was not necessary that he should be seen or heard—the portrait was enough, and the accusing portrait with the glazed eyes and the look of stupor glared down from every wall. Having once brought them into his power, he could hardly fail. To the end of his life, and even beyond, he could have maneuvered them according to his will, if only he had acted a little more carefully. His greatest mistake was that he did not face the consequences of the "reign of stupor" he had himself created.

Stupor is endemic. Anyone, for example, who finds himself walking among catatonics, finds himself in danger of falling under their mindless spell; and so at last Hitler's mind, never very sharp, became as stupified as the rest. He had produced on the masses the dreaded disease of *Angst*. Then he, too, dreaded whatever might come to pass, and unlike the German people, he had no one to whom to turn. The incident in the bunker when—while the Russian armies were converging on Berlin—he simply surrendered all his authority, could, I think, have been prophesied from his former actions. It had never weighed heavily on him, he was never really interested in the fate of Germany, it was all a kind of dream, and he waved it away with a shrug of the shoulders, to the horror of his generals, who thought that the greatest crime of a German officer was to dispose gratuitously of his authority.

Until 1941, when the first cracks appeared, he maneuvered his forces with skill and ingenuity. His chief creation, endlessly elaborated, was a myth—the myth of his own supremacy. It was unnecessary for this myth to be either comprehensive or clearly expressed; the myth could change in its details, and did change; a confused, wandering and distorted myth was discovered to be more enervating than one which possessed elements of verisimilitude. He had said once that the masses could only believe big lies; he had invented lies so big that no one could possibly believe them, yet everyone went through the processes of registering belief, for if they refused to accept this myth in its entirety, unknown punishments lay in store for them. On those who refused to accept the myth, he cast a terror so complete that it sometimes happened that people even welcomed being arrested, being tortured, being put to death. Those who were on the black-lists simply waited. They dared not hide, for they knew that their wives and children would be arrested. They dared not leave the house, or cross the street, for they knew they would incriminate everyone they met. They dared not telephone for the same reason. They dared not commit suicide, for then their insurance automatically ceased, and their families would be left unprovided for. While they waited for the *SS*, they hoped that the hammer beats on the door would come soon. There were many people on the black-lists who telephoned the Gestapo and said, "Come and arrest me."

This huge terror was not entirely the work of one man, though he continually directed it and took pains to make it more efficient. To control the almost uncontrollable secret police, he possessed only two weapons: 1) He mapped out fields of irresponsibility, assigned them to various organizations, and so cunningly were these fields of irresponsibility interwoven that the friction between them would absorb what energies remained from their work of terror. 2) He demanded and enforced an oath of loyalty to himself as the supreme leader of the nation.

It was all dangerous, ghostly ground; he walked on knife-edges, but he walked carefully. Both methods involved fear, and he was a past master at manipulating fear. To control the terrorists, all that was necessary was to terrorize them. Often they were the ones who were the most completely terrorized of all. In his axioms he spoke of setting the greater terror against the lesser; in his own party he applied the same formula. When the praetorian guard grew too powerful he destroyed it ruthlessly, and brought into being the more mechanical instrument of the SS (*Schutzstaffel*), but within the SS there was another terrorist organization, the SD (*Sicherheitsdienst*), and running beside the SS, watching over it continually, possessed of weapons which gave it the semblance of a smaller *Wehrmacht,* there was the SS-in-arms (*Waffen-SS*). Besides all these there was the Gestapo. These rival organizations, and there were many others, continually fought for position among themselves. He encouraged their rivalries, and sometimes deliberately set them at each other's throats.

The oath of loyalty was one of his chief instruments of terror. From the very beginning of the organization of the National Socialist party he had insisted, against all opposition, that the will of the leader should be the ultimate source of party rule; all parties must bow to Munich, and all Munich must bow to the leader. He had demanded an oath of loyalty to the party in the early days of the movement; as soon as he was let out of prison he demanded, and received, the oath of loyalty to his own person. Tacitus has related the power of the oath taken by the early Germans to their elected leaders; it was an oath they kept to the death. Hitler asked for more; he asked that the oath should be kept even after death, and on the graves of Germans killed in Russia there was sometimes inscribed the motto, "Beyond death he keeps his oath to Hitler and the Reich."

Hitler had destroyed the law, and put his own will in its place. One by one he stripped from the Germans their protective clothing, till at last they were naked and defenseless.

ZERO

From the moment when Goering, with Hitler's approval, gave the Gestapo blank warrants for murder, the terror could only move in one direction; these naked and defenseless people were to be thrown to the mercy of the terrorists. Old customary laws survived; people went through the motions of obedience to a law which no longer possessed any significance; the only Law was the law of terror. Law was an illusion, incarnated only in the lawless figures of Hitler and his terrorists; and when Frick put his signature to the Reich law which declared the events of June 30, 1934 legal, he was only approving a law to declare Law itself illegal.

Hitler had abrogated Law to himself; so had all those who wore the Nazi arm-band. The state was cut cleanly into two; those who possessed mastery, and those who had surrendered; yet the dividing line was unreal, for all in their different fashions had surrendered. Only by this surrender could the secret police be confirmed in their powers, and only by surrender could the common people live at all.

It was not only that the secret police obeyed no laws, but there could be no laws; if there had been Law, they could not have continued their practice of lawlessness. They might arrest whom they would, punish whom they wished, hold secret trials, fake evidence, and torture; they were bound by no statutes; their excesses were pardoned as "overzealousness in the cause of the state"; and though every excess necessarily drew in its wake a new excess, they survived because there is no limit to man's desire to be lawless, once it is awakened. The highest honors of the state were showered on murderers, and simply by giving them the most magnificent uniforms and the most high-sounding titles, Hitler was able to destroy at the source any natural shame they might have had in carrying out the murderous reign of lawlessness.

In an extraordinary passage of *Les Soirées de St Péters-*

bourg, Joseph de Maistre said that when the executioner is removed from the scene, at that moment all order will give way to chaos, the thrones will totter and society will perish. But he is puzzled why it should be so, and describes the perplexities of the executioner himself. The executioner is living quietly with his wife and children in some backwater of the city, then a messenger comes with the invitation to execute a criminal in the public square. The executioner embraces his wife, and hurries to the scene of execution. The public square is filled with a huge, palpitating crowd of observers. The criminal is presented to him. He hardly pays the criminal a glance, because he is so busy adjusting him to the wheel. The bones are smashed, the blood flows, the last cries of the condemned man are drowned in the sound of horror coming from the audience. "The executioner has finished, his heart beats with joy, he applauds himself, and he says to himself, 'No one breaks a man on a wheel better than I.' Thereupon he climbs down from his platform, stretches out his hands which are still red with blood—and then walks through a double line of men who start back in horror at the sight of the executioner." [4] Why? The question absorbs him, and because there is no answer he is nearly driven mad. He is performing a useful function, perhaps the most useful function the state has to offer any man. Is he not the final court of justice, the final court of law? What would happen if he refused to practice his sacramental office? The criminals would be overjoyed, the reign of terror would be introduced, law would be derided. Baudelaire read Joseph de Maistre carefully, but came to entirely contrary conclusions. In a curious passage of his diary he denies that the executioner performs a useful function, because there is no equation between the

---

[4] Joseph de Maistre, *Les Soirées de St Pétersbourg*, I, 31.

physical means and the spiritual ends; the punishment is appropriate only when the victim joyfully assents to his own torture and execution. "The sacrifice is not complete without the willing assent of the victim." [5] He adds that the proof of the perfect sacrifice would only occur when the victim, freed by the people, returns to offer himself gladly to the executioner. As for the desire to torture, he regards it as a symptom of sexual repression, and returns to his old thesis that cruelty and sexual enjoyment are identical sensations—like extreme cold and extreme heat.

It is probable that Joseph de Maistre was much nearer the heart of the matter than Baudelaire. He described the enjoyment of the executioner in his technical skill, his sense of fulfilling a useful public service, and his feeling that he is himself the judge and the protector of society, whatever society it has pleased God to install. Though puzzled by the horror he inspires, he continues to perform his function whenever he is ordered to, and we are left with the prospect that there will always be executioners as long as there are men interested in the mechanics of killing and able to convince themselves that they are the appointed judges of others. Perhaps it was Otto Weininger who was most nearly successful in answering the executioner's question. In the notes left at his death, collected together under the title *Concerning the Ultimate Things*, he wrote, "Who judges another goes seldom into himself. Every judge has within him much of the hangman, and it is because he is enraged with himself that he behaves fiercely towards others." [6] Jean-Paul Sartre perhaps completed the picture when he suggested that "the moment of pleasure for the executioner occurs when the victim denies his crime and hu-

---
[5] Charles Baudelaire, *Mon Coeur mis à Nu*, XXI.
[6] Otto Weininger, *Über die letzten Dinge*, Wien, 1907, pp. 58-59.

miliates himself."[7] Above all, it was humiliation which Hitler, as the self-appointed executioner, desired. He could never rest content until he had humiliated everybody else; and terror was the instrument by which men were humiliated; that is, they were reduced to insignificance and made conscious of their insignificance in relation to himself. To degrade men completely in their own eyes, to make them perform a long expiatory sacrifice, to humiliate them as they had never been humiliated before—these aims he succeeded in accomplishing, and he behaved towards the German people, and towards the Jews in the concentration camps with the same instruments of terror, and in the same way; the only difference lay in the fact that the terror waged against the Jews led to a different death.

The terror of the concentration camps differed only in degree from the terror inflicted on the German people. It was made of the same cloth, and it was instituted for precisely similar ends. The whole of Germany had become a concentration camp; inside this camp there were smaller camps, where the techniques of terror could be tried out in complete freedom from interference, and the results of these experiments performed on a relatively small scale could later be applied to whole nations, and perhaps whole continents.

One of the most profound accounts of the concentration camps, and of the mentality which inspired them, is given by the French novelist David Rousset, who was for three years a prisoner. He showed that the real aim of the camps went far beyond the extermination of the prisoners, or their employment as slaves. They were singled out for a slow, relentless, expiatory destruction while remaining still alive, and it is significant that up to the present time not one word exists by

[7] Jean-Paul Sartre, *L'Etre et le Néant*, Paris, 1946, p. 473.

ZERO

which this ghastly process can be described. In the confused minds of Hitler and the Nazi leaders, the prisoners, whether they were Communists, Socialists, Liberals, Jehovah's Witnesses, Jews, Freemasons or gypsies—were all regarded as sub-human, and active agents of the evil principle. The task of the concentration camps was to grant them a vivid awareness of their sin, to make them beg for pardon and desire *not* to die. Writing immediately after his release, David Rousset said:

> It is not necessary that a Jew or a Pole should have taken part in the fight against National Socialism. They were by birth predestined heretics, who could never be assimilated and were therefore dedicated to apocalyptic fire. Death was an insufficient punishment for them. Only expiation satisfied the demands of their lords. The concentration camps, therefore, assumed the shape of engines of expiation, extraordinary and complex machines, which ground out death slowly, and with calculated abandon in order that the moral and physical fall from grace should take place only by degrees, making them conscious of being damned, expressions of the evil principle rather than men.
>
> This is the only philosophy which explains the extraordinary *development* of these tortures, their complexity and their subtlety, exquisitely designed to be prolonged in time, and the manner in which the camp was industrialized. The presence of criminals, the brutal mixture of all nationalities, so that every kind of understanding among the prisoners was made impossible, the calculated mingling of the social classes, and of the aged with the young, the relentless famine, the permanent fear in men's minds, the blows—all these are factors which tend towards a single objective aim—the total disintegration of the individual, which is also the total expression of expiation.

In these camps, death inspired very little horror. The long silent avenues of hanged people had only a mediocre power to haunt our minds. The permanent rule of torture became at last a natural condition of being, and this produced endless depths of fear. The concentration camps by their existence involved society in the destructive nightmare eternally present, and eternally within reach. Death vanishes; torture triumphs, always active and alive, springing like an arch over the affairs of men. It is not a question any longer of reducing and paralyzing an opposition, but these weapons acquire a singularly greater aim; the concentration camps are the instruments for chastising free minds.[8]

This is brilliant writing, but also accurate writing, and the evidence of other prisoners confirms that the concentration camps were not simply prisons run by over-bearing and unusually brutal prison guards. An obscure purpose informed the concentration camps: to disintegrate men by a process of sacrificial expiation. An old and primitive rite had been resurrected. The prisoners were laid on the altar, and there they struggled, the knife poised above them, to the end of time. If they were killed, their deaths were arbitrary and accidental. Death, certainly, had little to do with the purposes of the rite, for it was not their deaths, but their agony which was welcome to the new god. To "kill" men by keeping them alive was not new, and the English jurist, Blackstone, quotes from the German *Golden Bull of Rimini*—published to the world in 1226—the punishment for the sons of traitors, which reads as though it might refer to the prisoners in the concentration camps. They were to be deprived of all their effects and rights and ecclesiastical and civil honors, "to the end that, being always poor and necessitous, they may forever be accompanied by the infamy of the father; may languish in continual

[8] David Rousset, *L'Univers Concentrationnaire*, Paris, 1946, p. 109.

indigence; and may find (says this merciless edict) their punishment in living, and their relief in dying." [9]

This was not, of course, always the case. There were times when the knife was allowed to descend, when huge massacres were ordered, when a defeat in Russia could be answered only by a holocaust of Jews in Poland. Even then, they must not simply die; they must die in agony. In Warsaw, in 1942, Himmler stated that "in accord with the will of the *Führer*, a simple decision had been made, and our decision is that the Jew must die in agony." The laboratories of the concentration camps were searched for a suitable instrument which would produce an agonizing death, and it was decided that the prisoners should be thrown into freight cars of which the floors were coated with dehydrated calcium oxide—quicklime. The moist flesh coming into contact with the quicklime produced searing burns, but death came slowly; it was estimated that it took four days for the prisoners to die, and for the whole of that time the freight cars were allowed to rest in some forgotten siding. "Then nothing at all would happen. The train would stand stock-still, patiently waiting while death penetrated into every corner of its interior." [10] All over Eastern Europe there were these lost trains with their sealed compartments, the people slowly dying of burns and asphyxiation, so that the lonely train stationed quietly in a deserted field became almost a symbol of modern mechanization gone wrong, for the only purpose of the train was to take the prisoners to a place where their death-cries could not be heard. Nearly always in the concentration camps, death took place in enclosed spaces—in poison vans, gas chambers, sealed freight cars, concrete cells. Why? Because then the slowness or quickness of death could be regulated. In all this, the guards

---

[9] Sir William Blackstone, *Commentaries on the Laws of England*, IV, 383.
[10] Jan Karski, *Story of a Secret State*, New York, 1944, p. 350.

of the concentration camps differed from the soldiers of the *Wehrmacht*, who were not interested in torture, punishment or expiation. They were not concerned with regulating death, but with the complete and merciless destruction of the enemy. For the Nazis there must be enough life, a marginal life, sufficient for its punishment.

But the Army, like the pure nihilists, set no value to human life, and in a sense they were more nihilistic than the Nazis. In an order published on September 16, 1941, shortly after the invasion of the Soviet Union, Field Marshal Keitel said, "It should be remembered that a human life in unsettled countries counts for nothing, and a deterrent effect can be obtained by unusual severity."[11] The statement was characteristic of Nazi leaders, but it was not characteristic of German generals, brought up on the *Ten Commandments for the Conduct of the German Soldier in War*, a once-sacred document pasted on the first sheet of every German soldier's paybook. The sixth commandment stated that the Red Cross was inviolable, and wounded enemies were to be humanely treated, the seventh stated that "the civilian population is inviolable" and "the soldier must not plunder or wantonly destroy." These were, at least, the professed commands of the old German Army, deriving from the knightly codes of honor of the Middle Ages. Since the invasion of Poland they had lost all meaning. Keitel meant precisely what he said, and in later orders only repeated, with minor modifications, the same meaningless nihilistic creed. "It is useless to take prisoners," he said. "Kill them, it is useful for the fertility of the earth." He seems never to have been conscience-striken by the enormity of the crime. One order, found among his papers, even deliberately included women and children among those whose lives counted for nothing.

[11] *Nuremberg Trials*, Judgment, p. 49.

ZERO

This irresponsible order read, "You are authorized to take any measures without restriction, even against women and children, in order to achieve success." General Rudenko, the Soviet prosecutor at Nuremberg, asked the former Field Marshal whether he seriously considered that such an order was a just one. Keitel explained that he had not given instructions to murder women and children, he had simply suggested that they should be removed from the scene of operations. "But removal means murder," General Rudenko objected. "Tell me if you believe this order is a just one." There was a long pause. Faced with the incriminating document bearing his signature, that terrible signature where the "K" resembled barbed wire, Keitel replied, "I consider this order to be just, and as such I admit it—but not measures to kill. That would be a crime. No German soldier ever thought of killing women and children." [12] It was a strange answer, for he more than anyone except Hitler was responsible for the killing of noncombatants as the German Army swept across Russia; and if the SS was responsible for the murder by machine-gunning of the inhabitants of Lidice, it was the German Army which machine-gunned and burned to death the inhabitants of Oradour-sur-Glane, where only eight villagers survived out of eight hundred former inhabitants, and countless other peaceful civilians fell to German arms. It was total war, and Keitel believed in total massacre. "No," he said, "I never meant to harm peaceful civilians, and no German would ever think of harming women and children. What a ridiculous idea! Of course, sometimes it may have happened, on distant battlefronts, but I couldn't be everywhere."

The judges at Nuremberg refused to believe in these protestations of innocence. He had stated the nihilist philosophy

[12] *Nuremberg Trials*, XI, 72-73.

MAN = ZERO

more succinctly than Nechayev or Hitler. *A human life in unsettled countries counts for nothing.* He had condemned all life, everywhere, for there is no country where life is settled. The exchange between General Rudenko and Field Marshal Keitel should be read in full, not only because it was one of the most tragic revelations of the Nuremberg Trial, but because it is one of the most critical documents in European history. In the somber recital of an unheard-of crime, in the hesitancies and self-commiserations of the Chief of the Combined General Staff we are enabled to see how the valuelessness of life had become an axiom, one of the basic assumptions concerning which no one need argue; and in Nuremberg, Keitel was faced with the consequences of his own nihilism. He recoils in assumed horror, pretends to be tragically unaware of the consequences of the order he had himself signed with a flourish, and almost jumps out of his skin in his eagerness to explain that in no manner whatsoever could "removal" mean "murder." There was nothing in the least elegant in his shambling defense; he was trying to explain—as Hitler might have tried to explain if he had been brought up to trial—that when he issued these commands he did not know what he was saying.

Keitel was a symbol of the times. Together with Albert Speer he represented the technician placed at the service of destruction, the laboratory scientist in command of the relentless machine of the German Army. He was disinterested in life, and there was always something completely inhuman in the frozen Prussian face which looked out on a world he vaguely condemned. He had lost his sons in the wars; he might therefore have been expected to know the value of human life. As he stepped out of the dock at Nuremberg with tears in his eyes, he said, "You cannot accuse me of cowardice, or dishonor, or faithlessness." The judges properly condemned him to death for these three crimes against humanity, of which to the very end he regarded himself as innocent, perhaps because he also regarded them as irrelevant.

The German Army under Keitel invented the "traffic desert." It destroyed blindly everything that lay in its path. For the enemy it reserved only one fate—complete extinction. It was prepared to follow Hitler's order to destroy thirty-six million Slavs. This number, which represented roughly half of the Slav population west of the Urals, had been chosen blindly. There was no reason why Hitler should not have said seventy million, or even ten times as many, for the figures possessed no meaning, no relation to life. Whatever the number, the Army would have attempted to murder them with the same mechanical efficiency. Placing no valuation on the lives of foreigners, the Army found it difficult to place a valuation on the lives of its own soldiers. At the beginning of the war, for the death of every German officer, ten hostages were shot. Afterwards the figure varied between wide limits, the number arbitrarily selected to suit the convenience or the rage of the local commanders. In such cases, a German life was evaluated in terms of a number of foreign lives, but in the concentration camps it was impossible to give any human value to the marginal lives of the prisoners, for they were no longer regarded as human. We do, however, know the value they possessed in German eyes. The market-price of the prisoners is found by weighing one prisoner's life against another. For how much money would one prisoner execute another under the command of the Nazis? We know that in the spring of 1942, they were paid five *Reichsmarks* for each execution, but on June 27, 1942, General Gluke issued from the Gestapo headquarters an order to the commandants of all concentration camps to reduce the honorarium to three cigarettes. I can find no evidence of the market-price during the rest of the year. After a while the fee may have been two cigarettes, then one, then half a cigarette, till finally it was only a puff of a cigarette, and even this on special occasions may not have been allowed to the executioner; it seems possible that sometimes the honorarium may have consisted only of the hope of a cigarette or the hope of a speedy death.

In *Crime and Punishment* Dostoyevsky puts into the mouth of Marmeladov the words, "The true evil is when men no longer know where they are going." Neither the German Army nor the Gestapo knew where it was going. Hitler, firmly rooted in a faith of nihilism, did know, and did not care. The holocausts were immaterial to him; he could not feel the suffering on his own flesh; he was concerned only with the anguish in his own mind, an anguish he often spoke about and paraded in his speeches, saying that he was not thrown into these depths of spiritual torture for his own sake, but for the sake of the German people. His anguish appears to have been real, but it was noticed that there were long periods when he suffered from apathy; and it is one of the characteristics of terror that beyond a certain point it is no longer effective, for the mind and the senses rebel, and something like unconsciousness ensues. Hitler, waging terror against the world, combatting phantoms, and whatever is real with the same wild blows, sometimes waged terror against himself. The result was inevitable; he, too, sank into a stupor.

Hitler was perfectly conscious of the dangers of too much terror. It was a thing that had to be used "with mathematical precision." One must calculate minutely the time and place where it can be applied, then relieve the victim, then bring down the terror again. He despised the terroristic method of the Bolsheviks. There were, he said, better methods, and he explained them:

ZERO

Unless you are prepared to be pitiless, you will get nowhere. Our opponents are not prepared for it, not because they are humane or anything of the sort, but because they are too weak. Dominion is never founded on humanity, but, regarded from the narrow civilian angle, on crime. Terrorism is absolutely indispensable in every case of the founding of a new power. The Bolsheviks applied it in the old style; they killed off the whole of the former ruling class. That is the ancient, classic method. To the best of my memory it is recommended by Machiavelli; or, at least, he recommends extending good will only to the second stratum, those who were immediately below the ruling class. I go further. I make use of members of the old ruling class itself. I keep them in fear and dependance. I am confident that I have no more willing helpers. And if they become refractory, I can always return to the ancient, classic method.[13]

It was immediately after this attack on Bolshevik methods, that Hitler said, "Too much frightfulness does harm. It produces apathy," and he went on to explain that terror had become finally unnecessary, for the radio was at his command. But in fact, as we know, it was the radio which remained to the very end the chief instrument of the spiritual terror he waged against the Germans. To this instrument he brought vast skill, and understanding which amounted to genius. He did not always scream. He could be gentle and insistent; and his gentleness could be more terrifying than his fury. At such times his voice could be rather feminine, faintly insolent, and entirely captivating to the Germans—who remembered that only a week before he had thundered at them in the manner reserved, in our own time, only for the Chinese Emperors, who also assumed the necessity of speaking to their subjects in a deep, throaty and menacing voice. But Hitler's sweet

---

[13] Hermann Rauschning, *The Voice of Destruction*, p. 282.

voice—the famous *süsse Stimme*—was a reality, and by playing terror against relief from terror, by speaking in blood-curdling tones one week, and then most softly the next, he held his audience to him; they could not escape; they were fascinated not only by the man, but by the thought that "tomorrow he will speak to us softly, and all will be forgiven." It was the ancient technique of the master with the slave, and Hitler performed it admirably. There may, however, have been moments when he remembered that he had warned against the use of radio in *Mein Kampf*: "The receptivity of the great masses is small, their understanding is limited, but their forgetfulness is great." And with forgetfulness, there was once again the danger of apathy.

Terror can be made so overwhelming that there are only a few instances where it fails. It fails when it produces apathy. It fails when its victims of their own accord regard their trials as an expiation of their sins, for then terror seems to them predestined and they welcome it openly. Occasionally, it happened that the most religious people in the concentration camps were the least affected; the Jews, the Jehovah's Witnesses, and the devout Christians found themselves able to withdraw into the castles within themselves, and even if the enemy broke through the walls, they were still immune, because the interior castle contained yet another castle within it, and however much the enemy destroyed, there remained somewhere a place of refuge. There were many too who, without the comfort of religion, were immune from terror because they retained under all circumstances a sense of their human dignity. Possessed of a rock-like human integrity they resisted to the end, knowing that terror is not infallible, and consists of so many deceits, and is so ignoble, that it can always be successfully opposed. Even in the concentration camps and in the slaughter pits, the machinery of total terror fails against man's total dignity.

Hitler chose to wage war on the Jews, to terrify them, to make them perform an act of expiation. He did not always succeed; for he had chosen as his enemies the people who were most accustomed to terror and were therefore to some extent immune from it. Fortified by their faith, they often died with extraordinary dignity. The classic text, which is also the most terrifying of the documents produced at the Nuremberg Trial, concerns the fate of the Jews in the small industrial town of Dubno in the Ukraine. The German engineer, Hermann Graebe, described how the Jews were taken to the slaughter-pits:

> Without screaming or weeping these people undressed, stood around in family groups, kissed each other, said farewells, and waited for the sign from the SS man who stood beside the pit with a whip in his hand. During the 15 minutes I stood near, I heard no complaint or plea for mercy. I watched a family of about eight persons, a man and a woman both of about fifty, with their children of about twenty to twenty-four, and two grown-up daughters about twenty-eight or twenty-nine. An old woman with snow-white hair was holding a one-year old child in her arms and singing to it, tickling it. The child was cooing with delight. The couple were looking on with tears in their eyes. The father was holding the hand of a boy about ten years old and speaking to him softly; the boy was fighting his tears. The father pointed to the sky, stroked his head and seemed to explain something to him.
>
> At that moment the SS man at the pit shouted something to his comrade. The latter counted off about twenty persons and instructed them to go behind the earthmound. Among them was the family I have just mentioned. I well remember a girl, slim and with black hair, who, as she passed me, pointed

MAN = ZERO

to herself and said, "Twenty-three." I walked around the mound and stood in front of a tremendous grave. People were closely wedged together and lying on top of each other so that only their heads were visible. Nearly all had blood running over their shoulders from their heads. Some of the people shot were still moving. Some were lifting their arms and turning their heads to show that they were still alive. The pit was already two-thirds full. I estimated that it already contained about a thousand people. I looked for the man who did the shooting. He was an SS man who sat at the edge of the narrow end of the pit, his feet dangling into the pit. He had a tommy-gun on his knees and was smoking a cigarette. The people, completely naked, went down some steps which were cut in the clay wall of the pit and clambered over the heads of the people lying there, to the place to which the SS man directed them; some caressed those who were still alive and spoke to them in low voices.[14]

I know no other account which shows so well how the Jews quietly resisted the terror. It is true that the terror was not prolonged; they had not time to become dehumanized, as men so often became dehumanized in the concentration camps, but their remarkable fortitude was a sign that the terror had failed; they did not perform any expiatory rite, nor did they die willingly; but to the last moment they showed their natural human dignity. Hitler's own death could not have been more different from this.

Towards the end of the long reign of terror which Hitler waged against the world, the apathy became greatest. The most terrible threats could be made, but defeat was so inevitable that the threats no longer moved men. So far he had spoken of *certain* terrors, destruction on terms, at a given rhythm and falling at a given time; now there emerged a new

[14] *Nuremberg Trial*, Judgment, p. 52.

conception of terror—much vaster, more comprehensive but less defined. Whole peoples were to disappear, leaving no trace. It was not destruction he wanted, but annihilation. People, he said, must become mist, *vernebelt*. It was at this time that there emerged the theory which lies behind the *Nacht und Nebel* Decree. People would disappear; nothing would be left of them; their names would be taken from them; they would be removed into solitary confinement; and there, though they were still allowed to live, all their identity would be lost. The decree was signed by Keitel, but originated in Hitler's fertile mind. The fate of the prisoners was to be "night and mist."

Something very similar to this had come into being as soon as the first gas-chambers were erected in 1941. Hitler luxuriated in the thought that his enemies would become smoke, but smoke was too heavy a thing—it was almost tangible, and Hitler desired to reduce his enemies to something more ghostly. He wanted them to leave as little trace as the morning mist. Mythology was beginning to rule him, and like so many of the expressions to which he gave utterance during the days when the Nazi regime was crumbling, the *Nacht und Nebel* Decree derived straight from ancient legends. The *Nibelungenlied* is the story of the "mist-men," and Siegfried, on whom Hitler attempted to model himself, wore the *Tarnkappe*, the ghostly helmet, which made him invisible. There had been degrees of nihilism; now at last he had come to the very end; a little puff of smoke and all the comedy would be over, but the smoke must be as thin as mist or darkness. Once long before, the poet Ludwig Schemann had cried, "The Teuton or the Night!" Now the night was coming, and this was the last threat of all.

During the course of his dictatorship, Hitler had used up, one by one, all the instruments of spiritual terror, and with them alone it might have been possible for him to enslave the world. He had not taken into account what might be called man's ultimate resistance to terror. Men do not break unless both the weapons of spiritual and physical are employed. He had learned in a hard school, discovered that he had not terrified sufficiently, or that it was impossible to terrify sufficiently, but he had attempted, with all the weapons at his command, to introduce the perpetual terror to the world. He nearly succeeded. When he discovered that he had failed, there was only one alternative: he made himself into *Nacht und Nebel,* leaving no trace at all.

Through the whole history of Hitler's use of terror, one thing has been left unsaid. The terrorist, when he reaches a certain pitch of frenzy, no longer believes in the efficacy of terror on others, for he no longer believes in the existence of others; what he is trying to do is to terrorize himself. In this, Hitler succeeded beyond his expectations. There is a sense in which he resembles the man who reads a mystery story in bed and when he is sufficiently thrilled, he calmly turns off the light. All that had happened was a horrible game played in his lunatic mind, and he may have been almost unconscious of the real suffering involved.

Where he had failed was in making terror *pay*. The Russians have made it pay by instituting slave camps. Until nearly the end of the war, Hitler used the concentration camps only as places where mythological experiments could be performed. He was a past master at the art of terrorizing for no purpose at all, or rather he terrified in order to experience the thrill, to feel himself superior, so that he could pay homage to his own divine powers; and all this was utterly useless for Germany. He read Machiavelli often—for long periods *Il Principe* lay under his pillow—but he had never understood what he was reading. In the *Discorsi* Machiavelli speaks of the tyrant who uproots everything; officials, institutions, titles, even the location of cities, moving the inhabitants from one province to another "as shepherds drive their flocks from place to place." Such a tyrant, says Machiavelli wisely, will never know tranquillity; those tyrants who desire to be tranquil should change as little as possible. Hitler had no desire for tranquillity, and so far he read accurately; it was when he came to perform terrible things that he misread Machiavelli. In the chapter of *The Prince* called "Concerning those who have obtained a Principality by Wickedness" Machiavelli says blunt things about the use of terror (*crudeltà*):

> Hence it is to be remarked that, in seizing a state, the usurper ought to examine closely into all those injuries which it is necessary for him to inflict, and to do them all at one stroke so as not to have to repeat them daily; and thus by not unsettling men he will be able to reassure them, and win them to himself by benefits. He who does otherwise, either by timidity or evil advice, is always compelled to take the knife in his hands; neither can he rely on his subjects, nor can they attach themselves to him, owing to their continued and repeated wrongs.

In the end, Hitler having brought into being the "continued and repeated" terror paid the forfeit, but he failed only because our armed forces destroyed his armies. In another sense he succeeded; the terrors he invented did not die, but remain in the spiritual atmosphere we breathe, and may be more dangerous now that he is not alive. We have not finished with him. Rings upon rings of terror came from him, and they are still pulsating; only after the lapse of a long time can we be made immune from them. The explanation was provided by Hitler. "For most people, words are more real than things, and the terrible word is the most real," and in another place he wrote, "They will never realize the impudence with which they are spiritually terrorized, nor the outrageous curtailment of their personal liberties, for in no way does the delusion of the doctrine (of terror) dawn on them." [15]

It was the summary of all his fatal judgments on men, a judgment which becomes all the more terrible when we realize that on the whole it has been proved true. Against this judgment, men of this generation must work to the end of their days, and perhaps we must work against it to the end of the world.

[15] *Mein Kampf* (American edition), p. 56.

VI.
The Nihilists in the Camps

WHEN the Allied troops advancing through Bavaria rode down the winding road, shaded by lindens, which branches to the left from the main highway between Augsburg and Munich, they found near the village of Dachau a high-walled camp inhabited largely by dead and dying prisoners. They learned that in these marshy plains three hundred thousand prisoners had been put to death. For the first time, reports which had been coming out of Russia began to seem credible; there had been vast murder factories in the Reich—how vast they really were we shall never know.

Dachau, however, was a comparatively small camp. At Auschwitz over four million naked human beings had been murdered over a period of only two years. The prisoners were compelled to murder each other; the execution squads were changed every three months, the new squad gassing the old. Nothing comparable to this had occurred before; even the great Mayan sacrifices—at which, according to Torquemada, seventy-five thousand prisoners were once killed over a period of four days—were small in comparison with this terrible holocaust. Why did it happen? This, too, we may never know for certain. All we can attempt to do is to examine the workings and the history of the concentration camps, and try to discover what aims were expressed.

THE NIHILISTS IN THE CAMPS

German concentration camps were usually situated in marshy land, in the neighborhood of obscure villages, remote from industrial cities; occasionally they were near cliff quarries. They had wooden walls; and sometimes ditches were dug round the camp; and along these ditches the guards went on patrol, only their heads visible, so that they offered no target to the prisoners. The ditches, however, offered refuge to the prisoners when, as sometimes happened, they escaped. Occasionally the camps were surrounded with high tension wires, or more often, with barbed wire. Each guard post was usually provided with two machine-gunners, one directed upon the camp, and the other along the roads leading to the camp; and to these guard posts stretched telephone wires. From high pillars along the walls of the camp, and down the main avenues hung floodlights, and at night the camp was usually flood-lit. The light was very hard, a "white purplish blue" according to many prisoners, and at night especially, the camps possessed the look of hard unreality which otherwise survives only in films. These lights had the effect of making the camp seem desolately unreal, and everyone threw down a confusing number of shadows.

By day, however, the camp resembled a hastily erected village with the huts arranged in perfect alignment. At one extremity lay the gas-chamber and the incinerator. The gas-chamber was of brick or concrete, as far as possible away from the main entrance. Near the entrance were the offices, guards' quarters, hospitals, kitchens and clothes' stores. They were separated from the rest of the camp by heavily guarded wire fences. There was nothing remarkable about the prisoners' huts except that they were rarely provided with windows; they resembled cattle sheds. There were often no lavatories for the prisoners, who washed in pails outside their huts. Near the offices, also made of concrete, were cells, for there were varying degrees of imprisonment; in the cells the prisoners could be tortured, but since tortures were inflicted openly, their purpose always remained insufficiently explained. The huts set apart for the prisoners' brothels did not differ from the huts they inhabited; the huts set apart for the guards' brothels were usually brightly painted. In general, the guards' huts were painted green, and had carefully arranged flower-beds in front; the prisoners' huts were not painted, and the huts themselves, like the prisoners, were left to rot. The lamp-posts in the camps served a double purpose; they were also used as gallows.

The general plan of the camp helps to suggest its purpose. Seen from above, it resembled a curious intermingling of the plan of a mediaeval moated city, and the plan of a cathedral, the incinerator and the gas-chamber taking the place of the altar. In fact, the camp *was* a feudal city, the nobility residing in a small battlemented corner, and they were served by the disenfranchised workers living and dying in a world of their own. The workers belonged to guilds, and were given privileges; the executioners, the cooks, the tailors, and the nurses in the camp hospital possessing distinct privileges denied to the rest. They performed the *bourgeois* duties of the camp, and these they shared with the *kapos,* the hut-commanders, who were chosen to keep order in the huts. Gradually, as the concentration camps evolved, power leaked increasingly from the hands of the nobles into the hands of the camp *bourgeoisie.* In a place apart, even more powerful than the feudal baron, was the chief doctor; on him rested the selection of the prisoners who were to die, and in mediaeval terms he represented the *inquisitor,* a profane priest who chose the sacrificial victims for the fire. The camp was also a cathedral with its own sacred ritual, a ritual which had not developed spontaneously but grew slowly, though the final act of worship was always

THE NIHILISTS IN THE CAMPS

the same; the offering of the blood. The concentration camp, then, was a feudal city where the lords possessed power of life and death over their subjects and ruled with arbitrary power, though their power was sometimes modified by the presence of the emerging *bourgeoisie;* it was also a place where a pagan worship was performed, and the culminating act of the worship was the procession of the prisoners to the gas-chamber, and we shall see later that this procession possessed a curious resemblance to the Roman Triumph.

The feudal and "religious" elements in the concentration camp served different purposes, for generally the feudal baron enjoyed his power over the living and the *inquisitor* enjoyed the power to kill. All the problems of feudal city life were repeated. There were quarrels between the "clergy" and the nobility, for they served different masters, or rather the different preoccupations of the same master. The baron, owing allegiance to the emperor, Hitler, could be confirmed in his powers only by mandate from the seat of authority; the *inquisitor* normally carried out his orders, but he could, and did, exceed or change them, and his authority was infinitely more capricious; he was not in the least concerned with the *normal* working of the camp, but with a purely arbitrary selection. He was the engineer of the destructive process, with powers to determine who were the predestined victims; and it should not be forgotten that in this ritual predestination played a great part. There were variations in the way the procession was formed, in the details of the worship of the incinerator, and in the preparation of the prisoners for the sacrifice, but there were no variations in the continual process of dehumanization demanded by the ceremony. The processes of dehumanization were largely in the hands of the camp guards.

Two culture complexes met in the concentration camps:

the feudal city and the pagan worship of blood. They were joined by a third: modern industrial technique. With immense care and elaboration, mechanization was introduced. In this way, the prisoners could be destroyed doubly; they could be bureaucratized as numbers and they could be dehumanized by being treated as slags of metal on a conveyor belt, punched into the required shape, indexed, catalogued, weighed, spun round on a lathe. The general name for them was "canned goods" and each was given a number, while the statistical department entered the details in double-entry bookkeeping. Bureaucracy went hand in hand with industrialization. The most minute details concerning the prisoners were kept. But the conveyor belt did not lead to the open market; it led to the gas-chamber and the cloud of thick purple smoke which, in many camps, hovered above the incinerator all day and all night. Here, too, obscure mythological purposes were at work. It would have been comparatively simple to "reduce" the smoke in the manner commonly employed by smoke-abatement engineers in German factories; they chose not to, and they seem to have delighted in the idea of humiliating the Jews with the sight of "the pillar of cloud by day and the pillar of fire by night." The fourth culture complex was a kind of inverse Judaism, and throughout the history of the concentration camp there are strange efforts to turn Jewish ritual upside down. Ultimately, the sacrifice of the victims seems to have been based on the memory of the stories published by Julius Streicher in *Der Stürmer* on the blood-sacrifices supposed to have been performed by the Jews on Christians.

At least four culture complexes were inextricably involved in the functioning of the concentration camp. None of these culture complexes was assimilable by any others. Each had originally possessed aims which denied the aims of the others,

THE NIHILISTS IN THE CAMPS

and they could only be made to give the appearance of being assimilated by overwhelming force. The guards and the prisoners were rarely conscious of the confused historical and mythological forces at work, and the prisoners could hardly have recognized in the guards the relics of feudal powers, or in the doctor the representative of the feudal *inquisitor*, but these were in fact what the guards and the doctor represented; they were both performing tasks which in our own time have no validity. Three putrescent culture practices survived; to them was added modern mechanization. The result, which we have seen before, was the "meaningless sacrifice," for there was no room in the sacrifice for the living prisoners.

This is not, of course, the whole story, for a nihilist rage against life in all its forms was present in the mind of the man who was emperor and chief inquisitor at the same time, the man who claimed, like some of the early Holy Roman Emperors, complete spiritual and temporal powers over the world. But the pure nihilist—and Hitler was almost certainly a pure nihilist—is not interested in the processes of expiation, the long drawn out agonies and the almost religious sacrifice of prisoners. Having made a pact with destruction, he is content to destroy. But the concentration camps were not content to destroy, and the complex ritual derives from ancient cultural forces which, having decayed, seem to regain their strength only during periods of exhaustion; then they emerge to confront an exhausted civilization, themselves hideously distorted. The "meaningless sacrifice" occurs only when different cultures meet. There was no purpose to these sacrifices. The concentration camps were costly, and impeded the German war effort, continually draining resources in wood, iron, chemicals, building materials, and transportation from the army, and they employed thousands of guards who could have been employed at the front. They used up spades, whitewash, paint, enamel, drains, uniforms, and weapons on a preposterous scale; and all these things were devoted to useless and inefficient ends, to the dehumanization of the prisoners, to the expiation of their sins, and to their final ascension in a cloud of fire. The Jews could have been quietly shot out of hand or freed on condition that they left all their possessions in Germany. Instead, at immense cost, and with the inauguration of an enormous bureaucracy, they were imprisoned, and sacrificially murdered.

The practice of the concentration camps in 1941 to 1945 was the result of a long process of development. There were not always the clouds of purple smoke. The original concentration camps were small cellars in the workers' quarters of Munich. Here, in dark rooms, the windows plugged with mattresses, the first Storm Troopers tortured their enemies. They had two purposes; to strike fear into the hearts of peaceful citizens, and to extort money. They were out for loot and pillage. Sometimes they tortured prisoners to death, and this happened most frequently when the prisoners were Communists. The Communists were poor, and were not expected to possess large sums of money; but they had memories. They were forced to reveal the names of the party members, with addresses. The Communists themselves had done the same. It was civil war fought out by arrest, torture, and war in the cellars. From the *bourgeoisie*, the Storm Troopers demanded only loot; they were ordered to sign checks in favor of the Storm Troopers against their bank-accounts. These Storm Troopers were privileged gangsters, with connections with the police. They grew more daring. By 1930, with money extorted from the rich, they began to take over unoccupied factories and disused warehouses, and it was then for the first time that they employed the term "concentration camp." Between 1930 and 1933 the techniques for the future concen-

THE NIHILISTS IN THE CAMPS

tration camps were worked out. The arrest was made at night, the guards deliberately smashing all the furniture in the prisoner's house; then a long period of quiet in the car which drove him to the prison; then a severe beating; then another long period of quiet, or else a whole series of minor beatings. Nothing was explained. He would be punished suddenly and mercilessly for no reason whatsoever; the Storm Troopers were employing the technique of the Sergeant-major, who punishes because a button has not been polished. If a coat was undone, the prisoner would be told that it showed signs of disrespect, though the guard may himself have torn off the buttons; if the bed covering was wrinkled, the prisoner would be told that it showed signs of slovenliness, though the guard just that moment may have jumped on the bed. The knowledge of the effects of perpetual terror increased, and was elaborated. The feudal city was gradually emerging. In the warehouses there were well appointed apartments belonging to the guards; the prisoners lived in huge dormitories. There was no *habeas corpus*. The prisoners did not know what had happened to their families, and because they lived together in the dormitories, they were reduced to a state of collective hysteria. They were deliberately encouraged to talk with one another, so sharpening each other's fears; and every kind of prisoner from every kind of political party, the old and the young, the poor and the rich were thrown together. Executions were infrequent within the warehouses, though innumerable murders took place outside. An unprincipled feudalism ruled, but there was as yet no sign of the sacrificial offering of the Jews. Hitler had not yet decided what to do with them. Even in 1933, when the first concentration camp at Dachau was opened, the prisoners largely consisted of Communists, members of the Center Party, and officials of the former Bavarian Government. By the time of the *Macht-*

ergreifung there was no longer any need for looting individuals, for the whole of Germany could be looted at will. This looting was done on high financial levels; the Storm Troopers gained nothing for themselves. More disastrously, the Storm Troopers had been buoyed up by the sensation of power which came to them when they tortured in the cellars and warehouses; now, even this was taken from them.

In order to recompense the Storm Troopers for their assistance, they were given powers over political prisoners, and funds were set aside for them to construct concentration camps. It was decided that they would receive no loot; a separate department was created for the organization of loot, and the Storm Troopers were allowed only to organize the prisoners. Four concentration camps were then begun; they were the parents of the thousands which, shown in dark specks on a map of Germany and Eastern Europe at the Nuremberg Trials, seemed to cover the country like a dark cloud. Dachau near Munich was immediately enlarged, and they began work at Oranienburg near Berlin, at Duerrgoy near Breslau and at Boergermoor in northwestern Germany. The theme was now plain torture. The utmost ingenuity was employed to make these camps torture machines. It was not only that prisoners were flogged, pummelled, burnt, and had their testicles twisted; they invented revolving cages, upright coffin-shaped concrete cupboards, cells with steep sloping or jagged floors. It was a reign of pure bestiality, which continued to the end, though the concentration camps of 1941 to 1945 bore only the remotest relation to the original. The penalty of execution-by-hanging for light offenses was also introduced at this time, designated as a disciplinary measure. This, too, continued to the end, and in the war concentration camps the guards still hanged prisoners, though the purpose of the camp had subtly changed, and those who were not

THE NIHILISTS IN THE CAMPS

hanged died in the gas-chamber. It was death either way, but one death derived from the cellars of the dispossessed Storm Troopers, and the other from the *inquisitor*. It was a time of experiment. They discovered that prisoners made to stand out in the sun for long periods, erect and motionless, suffered unmitigated torture—this was new to them. They knew already that prisoners compelled to face overpowering bright lights could be tortured to the extent that they would go insane. They invented the "concrete-mixture" death. A prisoner would simply be thrown into a concrete-mixer in full sight of all the other prisoners, till his flesh and bones were crushed to powder. Prisoners were thrown into drains, tied to electric generators so that their bodies were flung around in circles or they were cut in two by heavy steel cutting machines. Some of this they may have learned during the warehouse period, but in general it was new. There was new territory to be explored; they explored it thoroughly; but they were still far away from the gradual, deliberate, and remorseless process of dehumanization which characterized the war camps.

The change came with the passage of the "Nuremberg Laws" by the Reichstag on September 15, 1935. The Jews began to be rounded up in larger numbers. They possessed no civil rights whatsoever; anything could be done with them. They were now no longer given over to the Storm Troopers; the SS was expanding prodigiously, though Himmler still claimed that there were only six concentration camps in the whole of Germany. There were at least 457. There may have been more. All this was the work of two years. But though the camps had grown, no one had yet decided what was to be done with the Jews, or the other prisoners. Racked by doubts, at the mercy of continual changes in the political weather, which he seemed to dominate but secretly feared, Hitler re-

ZERO

fused to make the decision; the prisoners were being held, but no one had decided yet who was going to pay the ransom. Meanwhile, although the Storm Troopers guarded the concentration camps, the SS took over the control of the camps, and there began to appear, in the role of an adviser in mufti, the ancestor of the *inquisitor*, the *private* representative of Himmler within the camps. At the same time, in despair of ever discovering what useful purpose could be served by the camps, orders were given that the prisoners should perform useless work. They should quarry stone, let it roll down the hill, then carefully replace it; they should push heavily loaded wheelbarrows through loose gravel; they should carry loads backwards and forwards across the camp. The impetus for this decision came from the "Nuremberg Laws"; deprived of all rights, the prisoners must appear inhuman. In fact, this process had been gradually developing, and there were seeds of it in the warehouses. Now it had crystallized into a rigid rule. The death sentences were not yet entirely arbitrary. The *inquisitor* still sought for a valid excuse for killing.

There were many changes later, but in November 1938 came the most important of all. Following the murder by Herschel Grynszpan of Ernst vom Rath, third counsellor in the German Embassy in Paris, the die was cast, the Jews were rounded up in greater numbers than ever before, and for the first time there were mass executions in the camps. The death of vom Rath was the excuse for a murder terror which until that moment had been held to some extent in reserve. From that moment Hitler refused to consider any means by which the Jews would be allowed to emigrate *en masse*, and in any case, following the weakness of Great Britain and France at Munich, he had decided upon war. The preliminary to war was the mass executions of the Jews, resembling the sacrificial

THE NIHILISTS IN THE CAMPS

offerings of enemy soldiers which the Greeks and the Romans occasionally made before a coming war.

From those winter decisions there was never any retreat. Hitler had sealed the fate of Austria and Spain; there remained Czechoslovakia, then the rest of the world. In this conquered world—for Hitler had already conquered it in his imagination —there was no place for the Jews; and while people waited breathlessly to know the fate of the Spanish Republic, there was occurring in Germany a reign of unparalleled slaughter. It was small by comparison with the massacres which came later: in the winter of 1938 to 1939 a hundred and fifty thousand Jews were murdered.

From this point on, the concentration camps were looking for some simple method of killing great numbers of men. There were complaints that mass executions by clubbing or shooting were unnerving the guards; the bodies could not be buried sufficiently quickly; it was thought that disease would inevitably spread, when there were so many unburied bodies in the camps. The same kind of complaints were made in the Revolutionary Tribunal in Paris during the early stages of the Terror; these complaints led to the invention of the guillotine. In Germany they led to the gas-wagon, which appeared first in the spring of 1940, and to the gas-chamber which followed in the summer of 1941. In the early stages, the gas-wagon was filled with its human cargo and then the truck was ordered to go some distance out of the camp. The truck drivers protested against unloading the prisoners, who had turned bright red, with bloated faces, the blood and *faeces* all over the floor. Later, special squads of Jews and political prisoners were made to clean out the trucks. This became dangerous: they might seize the trucks and use them against their captors. It was decided to keep the truck stationary, at the rear entrance of a house. The prisoners were made to undress in the house, and then ordered to enter the truck; the bodies could be burned nearby. The combination of the gas-chamber and the incinerator was apparently decided upon after the prolonged mass murders which took place in Helmno in Estonia.

The process of destruction in this initial stage followed a pattern which, with some slight changes, continued to the end. No one assents to his own murder; he must therefore be deceived into thinking that something entirely pleasant is about to happen to him. At Helmno a large mansion surrounded by woodlands was chosen as the place where the prisoners were received. As the trucks unloaded, a representative of the Sonderkommando made a short speech, promising good treatment and adequate food. "You must not be afraid of us; we have your interests at heart." They were then reminded that they were dirty after a long journey, and told to take a bath while their clothes were disinfected. The rooms on the first floor of the mansion, where they were taken, were made pleasantly warm. Half an hour later, wearing only their underclothes, they were led downstairs along corridors where signs read *To the Medical Officer* and *To the Bath*. The arrow beneath the words *To the Bath* pointed to a door, and beyond the door lay the gas-wagon. Guards were waiting just outside to club the prisoners who refused to enter the wagon. Three hundred forty thousand men, women, and children were exterminated at Helmno.[1]

The necessity of deceit remained, long after the prisoners knew their fate; it was as though deceitfulness dogged the Gestapo to the end. At Auschwitz, though the purple plume of smoke rose from the incinerator, the gas-chamber continued to be covered with inscriptions in several languages

[1] *Nuremberg Trials*, VIII, 20.

THE NIHILISTS IN THE CAMPS

explaining that the prisoners would first be deloused and then taken into a shower. Afterwards, when the signs finally failed to be credible to anyone, the prisoners were whipped or bludgeoned into the gas-chambers. Occasionally the deceit took on vast proportions; Potemkin villages were erected; the prisoners were asked to believe that they had come to a village especially built and planned for their occupation. At Treblinka, a railway station was erected. Near the station-master's office could be seen posters showing the train schedules to and from Grodno, Vienna, Berlin; the prisoners were not expected to know that there was no railway line further than Treblinka. They were taken to a barracks—the barracks was actually a clothing store—and here again there were more Potemkin signs, reading, *Restaurant*, *Ticket-Office*, *Telegraph*, and *Telephone*. There was no restaurant or ticket-office; the telegraph was in direct communication with Berlin. Once the prisoners entered the barracks there was no further effort to deceive. With machine-guns directed on them, they were ordered to undress, sprayed with warm water, and led down the road to their deaths. For some inexplicable reason the road was called *Himmelfahrt*—the Way to Heaven—and they were not gassed, but burned in pits. Burning, however, was becoming increasingly rare. Too many escaped under cover of the flames.

With the invention of an efficient incinerator, there came about the final development of the pattern which had taken hardly more than eight years to evolve. There had been a kind of residual humanity in the mass-executions beside the open graves of Poland and the Ukraine; the prisoners still retained their human dignity, could still comfort one another; now they were killed mechanically, obscurely, by an intricate machine. The machine was efficient and infallible, and its waste products could be used, if necessary, to grease the wheels.

The machine solved many problems: it saved bullets; it saved the nerves of the guards (for they saw nothing); it saved money, and it could be manipulated by the prisoners themselves, not in large numbers, but in such small numbers that they could be easily guarded. It was at this point that the *inquisitor* stepped into prominence. Previously, all the prisoners were killed; now some were preserved so that the concentration camp itself should run smoothly, and others were preserved simply because it was in the interests of Hitler that they should perform the rites of expiation; still others were preserved because no one had decided what to do with them. The *inquisitor* was a law to himself. Usually a doctor with Gestapo connections, he chose those who were to die, sometimes as they entered the camp, more often whenever it occurred to him that the machine demanded to be fed. He selected the prisoners according to his private whim. As they passed in front of him, he jerked his thumb up; they were to die, or jerked it down; they were to live. There was no appeal. Usually the weak, the sick, the haggard, the ill-clothed, the children, and the old were summarily ordered to the gas-chamber. He represented the center of nihilist power, and of all the men in the camp he was the most to be feared.

The *inquisitor* was not, however, the only nihilist in the camp. There remained the *Kommandant*, the guards and the bureaucracy. They, too, demanded to be amused, and invented tortures and maintained a reign of terror, but the *inquisitor's* terror was separate from theirs. One terror had its source in the desire for loot and excitement, and derived from the time when the Storm Troopers were in power; the other stemmed more directly from the diseased brain of Hitler. There were still other minor centers radiating terror.

THE NIHILISTS IN THE CAMPS

The criminals who found their way into the camp exploited and terrorized the rest. The Communists, a close-knit group among the prisoners, plotted against the prisoners from their center, and would use their influence with the *inquisitor* to have other prisoners placed on the death-lists. The thieves and murderers were as dangerous as the others. By stealing a coat they could make it certain that a prisoner would die of influenza, or, because he looked half-dressed and ragged, he would be chosen by the *inquisitor* during his periodical inspections. The war raged in the concentration camps was atrociously bitter for those who were weakest—women, children, the very old. More women than men were murdered; fewer women survived. The children and the old were usually not taken to the gas-chamber: they were clubbed, or murdered in other ways. At the Lvov camp, children were seized by the feet and torn apart, then thrown into the flames. At Yanov no ammunition was wasted on them; they were sliced in half with rusty saws. At Rostov-on-the-Don, a child was trampled to death because it kept pigeons. Children at Auschwitz received no better treatment; bonfires were built and they were thrown into them in front of their mothers. The old, living in a world of their own, driven to madness by the crimes taking place all round them, were done to death in the same manner; no one cared whether they lived, they fulfilled no purpose within the camp, and so it sometimes happened that they were allowed to wander away into the nearby fields, to die of hunger. The records of the camp generally omitted the names of people over seventy, though hundreds of thousands of aged people were imprisoned.

The sick, too, were treated in the same way. To be sick was to know that death was almost inevitable. The *inquisitor* was sometimes prepared to put the name of a sick person on the death-list in substitution for someone relatively healthy.

ZERO

The sick were as defenseless as women, children, and the old against the guards. Hitler, himself a permanent invalid, raged against sickness everywhere. On September 1, 1939—the date is significant—he signed an order empowering a certain Dr. Brandt to kill off by "mercy-death" all those suffering from incurable diseases. The order was inferred to grant immunity to doctors who killed the insane, and death came about by a hypodermic injection of air in the veins.

This order set the stage for what followed; an incredible mercilessness ruled. Hitler envisaged a world of young, vigorous, and obedient boys and girls. Age, even middle-age, was suspect. Physical weakness of any kind was derided. It followed that children, women, and the old could seek no protection anywhere. To exist, the prisoners had to fight for privileges; those who were most innocent, most incapable of discovering a privileged place went to the wall. Usually, they were not sufficiently privileged to be allowed to expiate their sins; they were more often tortured to death by the guards.

To support the vast network of concentration camps stretching from France deep into Russia, a huge, top-heavy bureaucracy ruled. No bureaucracy like this had ever existed before. Normally, bureaucracy can afford to be reckless of human material; this bureaucracy was *absolutely* reckless. Yet it was demonstrably a bureaucracy, and anyone looking at the clerks poring over their ledgers might have thought it was a quiet government office. The most minute details of the running of the camp were kept by the clerks. They obeyed a complicated pattern of laws, the forms of law remaining, though the Gestapo had destroyed Law at its source. In terrible black-bound ledgers the executions were meticulously recorded under eight headings, and according to Heydrich's Order Number Eight any other procedure, any deviation

THE NIHILISTS IN THE CAMPS

from the rules to be obeyed by the clerks would be severely punished. The eight headings were (1) serial number, (2) surname and last name, (3) date and place of birth, (4) profession, (5) last known place of domicile, (6) grounds for execution, (7) date and place of execution, (8) remarks.[2]

There were orders relating to the exact size, position, and depth of brand-marks; the exact shape and use of branding-irons. The instruments were supplied by headquarters; no other instruments were to be used. Penalties were attached to the misuse or loss of these instruments, and special training courses for branding were arranged. The branding was a sign that the machine was becoming a permanent institution, and that men were henceforth to be known only by their numbers. The prisoners were not the only people who were branded, or received tattoo marks. The SS themselves were stamped with numbers, as though they were automobile engines. The leading members of the SS had tattoo marks on the left ankle, while senior officers had them inside their thighs, and the *Liebstandart Adolf Hitler*, the personal guard of the *Führer*, had the letters *L.A.H.* tattooed behind their right ears, while on all SS guards there were blood-type marks in the armpit. Prisoners were generally branded on the left fore-arm, and children were branded on the thighs, apparently because the five figure numbers could not be written on their thin arms. In the case of Russian prisoners, no numbers were allotted. "The brand is to consist of an acute angle of about 45°, the long side one centimeter in length, and is to be marked on the tightly drawn skin of the left buttock at about a hand's breadth from the rectum."[3] It was emphasized that branding was a serious operation, and no one should take advantage of his position to make tattoo marks of a less mathe-

[2] *Nuremberg Trials*, XVII, 188.
[3] *Nuremberg Trials*, Judgment, 48.

matical character; only the simple brand was required, and by the brand the prisoners could be recognized.

A huge unwieldy bureaucratic machine had come into existence; it numbered and grouped the prisoners, recorded the time of their deaths to the exact minute, examined them while living as a mechanical punching machine will examine the strength of material, and presided over the collection of their remains. In still more ledgers there was recorded the weight of gold removed from the prisoners' mouths, and the weight of the hair shaved off women—the hair was used to make seamen's padded coats and to stuff chairs. The weight, number and sizes of clothes left outside the gas-chambers was also recorded. The time-hours of the guards, the exact minute at which they left their duties were recorded; the food supplies brought into the camp were carefully weighed for statistical purposes. New orders, new punishments, new torture devices came with every post, and graduated premiums were awarded to dutiful guards only after a careful examination of the statistics concerning them. Most of these statistics were kept by the prisoners, for they were enrolled into the bureaucracy of the camp. All these statistics were fundamentally useless. No one was ever to read these tragic ledgers in full, and anyone who did read them would be completely incapable of comprehending the suffering and misery they represented; they were facts; Himmler, unlike Hitler, liked facts.

These records were carried down almost to the day when the Allies entered the camps. Most of them survived. But in spite of a complete statistical record—as complete as one could ever expect it to be—we do not know even today how many people died in the concentration camps, for since the figures were purely mechanical they were easily faked. In some cases a reasonable guess can be made only because receipts from factories producing Cyclone B have survived. From the

THE NIHILISTS IN THE CAMPS

amount of poison it is possible to make a rough estimate of the number who were killed.

The bureaucracy of the concentration camps was the pattern of the bureaucracy of the German state, and there was the same division of labor between the *inquisitor* (Hitler), the mad doctor who arbitrarily chose his victims, and the *Kommandant*, (Himmler) who represented the slowly grinding destructive machine, where there was nothing arbitrary at all. The machine demanded to be fed; the *Kommandant* was empowered to feed it, but he was not himself the prime cause of the sacrificial offering; he resembled the feudal lords who looked on when the heretics were burnt, and helped to drown the cries of the victims with applause. He permitted and encouraged the *inquisitors* at their work, but the actual evil was done by these extraordinary doctors, who completely reversed the Hippocratic oath and committed all the sins which the Hippocratic oath was designed to prevent. Hippocrates had said that a good physician was the equal of a god; but these *inquisitors* were also god-like in their power to terrorize, and they were more feared than anyone in the camp; they rarely committed brutalities: they had only to point with their thumbs.

Meanwhile, though the greatest terror came from the *inquisitor*, the guards were instructed and encouraged to dehumanize the prisoners, and this slow, relentless, degrading terror continued on another plane, and with different objects from the other. The bureaucratic machine could absorb strains; the guards could not. The guards did not always torture because they were sadists, but because they were afraid and could not master the situation. By 1943 the original bloodlust had gone; the guards were already tired and sick of brutality, and they continued only because they were caught up in the inertia of the machine, or because they needed excitement to prevent them from dying of boredom. For four or five years they had been isolated from the world, condemned to live among tortured and burned bodies. The strain was beginning to tell. As the war drew to an end, their brutality increased, as the mechanical brutality of the gas-chamber increased. Their nerves were frayed. They murdered now more on impulse than on instruction. They often had the look of harassed old men, and were heard complaining bitterly of the rise in the cost of living.

It was excitement that kept them alive; they went in search of excitement with the same dread and terror with which the prisoners received their blows. They desired to be drugged, and they found the appropriate drug in brutality, and they found it also in speed. All prisoners have commented on their maniacal love of speed. They were always shouting "*'Raus*," and "*Schnell*." The first word meant "Come here as fast as lightning," and the second meant "Come with ferocious speed, be like us, drown yourself in speed—it is the best of all drugs." Their tortures and punishments were geared to speed. A Russian report quoted at Nuremberg spoke of one punishment which was characteristic of many:

> The person interrogated, with his hands tied behind his back, would be hoisted up to the ceiling, where he would be spun round and round. After having been rotated 200 times in one direction, the victim suspended on a cord would begin to turn in a mad speed in the other direction. At that particular moment the executioners would beat him on both sides with rubber truncheons. The man became unconscious both from the mad speed of the rotation and the beating.[4]

But they had other desires besides speed. They desired to be amused, and the prisoners offered them a field of irrespon-

[4] *Nuremberg Trials*, VII, 73.

THE NIHILISTS IN THE CAMPS

sible amusement. A tall and handsome woman would be ordered to couple with a dwarfish man; afterwards they would both be shot. Why? Because they had behaved unconventionally. Jews would be ordered to let their trousers down, and then they would be sent running across the camp; those who tried to keep their trousers up were of course shot. One says "of course" because there was a desperate logic in these charades. What was wanted was that one of the Jews should behave conventionally, because this too they hated. It is amusing to revolt against the conventions, but no one else must be permitted to be unconventional or conventional. People were shot for having blue eyes, because this was conventional; or for having brown eyes, because this was, in a sense, unconventional. Women were atrociously punished for bearing children in camp because it was a "conventional" thing to do, and if they aborted, they were punished for being "unconventional." The clown likes to break up the symmetry and order of a pattern—it is his source of amusement. The guards amused themselves in this way; they would go to the first man on parade and ask why he took precedence. He would be shot. Then the guard would move slowly down to the end of the line and shoot the last prisoner. In this way all could be killed with the argument that each had taken precedence. All that even faintly suggested the human, the normal, the genuine, was unbearably suspect, and so too was all that suggested extremes, either of beauty or talent. A beautiful woman would be gassed because she was beautiful. A good worker would be clubbed because he was better than other workers; but the mediocre worker and the normal worker were both clubbed as well. They had the best of both worlds. All that was good they detested, and all that was extreme they regarded as an affront against themselves.

Nothing so much approaches the atmosphere of a concentration camp as a fun-fair. There are the same shooting galleries, the same stupid pictures of men's faces on the bodies of women, the same desperate effort towards hilarity, speed, the dehumanization of the individual, the same smoke from the engines and the same screams—are they screams of joy or screams of horror? There are the tunnels with the ghostly skeletons, and the watershoots; old women tell fortunes and the skirts of pretty girls are thrown up above their waists by concealed airpipes, and you won the prize only by luck: skill was forfeit. Here everything was made ridiculous, including death. Life was forbidden—there were even posters reading *Alles verboten*, but it was not so. Some things were permitted; you were permitted to expiate your unknown sins. To look horrified was a crime; to have the impassivity of the clown was the only way to survive. And if it was absolutely forbidden to live, it was absolutely forbidden to die. Prisoners who fainted on the long march to the gas-chamber were awakened into consciousness by being splashed with water.

So many conflicting forces were working in the prison camp, there were so many directions from which punishment could come, there were so many conflicting regulations—if you did not wash, you could be shot; if you fetched water for washing, you could also be shot, because you were not expected to go near the pump—that the camps sometimes gave the appearance to the prisoners of being wholly unreal. It became simply impossible to believe that men behaved in this way. It was like a nightmare; if you waited patiently, you could shake off the memory of the thing. A British prisoner said: "It was so stunning that it was almost unreal, and I think probably when one has been back among civilized people for a while one just forgets it." Mme. Claude Vaillant-Couterier said at the end of her astonishingly brilliant summary of the conditions in the prison camps during the Nuremberg Trial,

THE NIHILISTS IN THE CAMPS

"If I was asked what was the worst of all, it would be impossible to answer, since everything was atrocious; it is atrocious to die of hunger, to die of thirst, to be ill, to see all one's companions dying around one, and to be unable to help them; it is atrocious to think of one's children and of one's country which one will never see again, and there are times when we asked if our life was not a living nightmare, so unreal did this life seem in all its horror."

This feeling was shared by nearly all the survivors from the camps. They had reckoned on real punishments, real torture, but it was so violent that it could sometimes have the effect of being unfelt—it was like a blow received in a dream. Everything became meaningless. Even the clothes they wore had meaningless symbols printed on them. Hundreds of thousands of prisoners wore clothes marked in large letters: *Mitwerda*, a word which has no meaning at all. Most meaningless of all was the solemn procession to the incinerator, the final mechanized form of the great Roman triumph. Then, walking like automatons, with black chalk crosses on their faces, shaven, wearing the clothes they had worn throughout their imprisonment, they were pummelled and beaten towards the iron doors. At this moment they had reached the utmost point of degradation. All the time the prison-guards, the *inquisitor*, the bureaucracy, and the National Socialist hierarchy had demanded that the prisoners should conform to their own nihilism; now at last they were to be annihilated physically.

There were ceremonies to be performed before the prisoners were murdered. They would be deliberately kept waiting outside the gas-chamber. They were lined up. Their crimes were usually explained to them. They were told they were about to take a bath, and the guard would point to the billowing purple smoke. They were examined for concealed weapons, and for signs that they would faint, and careful attention was paid to the chalk marks. These were usually on the forehead and near the cheekbone. The journey to the incinerator, therefore, possessed a remarkable similarity to the journey made by the prisoners of the Maya to the sacrificial stone, for these prisoners were also marked with chalk—the faces in white chalk with a black chalk ribbon over the eyes—and were also inhumanly degraded. It was the custom of the Mayas to take from their captives all that had given them dignity. They were allowed to retain their eagle feather headdresses, but their feathery loin-cloths, waistbands and collars were exchanged for paper ones; instead of feathery flags they carried paper flags; instead of a wooden shield ornamented with jewels, they were given bundles of reeds. They, too, were made to wait in line, as the Nazi prisoners were kept in line, to feel once more, for the last time, the blows and the sensation of brutal power flowing from the guards. Then they were rushed into the gas-chamber; small blue pastilles of cyanide of potassium in solution were rolled down a shoot, to explode in a small basin out of the prisoners' reach. They were allowed twenty minutes to die; then the bodies were collected and placed in the ovens. Almost to the very last moment their screams could be heard through the reinforced concrete walls.

The horror of the thing did not weigh on the Nazi guards; it had become a ritual, sanctified by forces beyond their control. It was observed that they behaved towards the dead as they would behave towards any mechanical instrument. They would sometimes break down when confronted with sickness in the prison hospitals; they did not break down in their dealings with the prisoners they led to the gas-chamber; nor were they unusually brutal at this point. The process had been codified and bureaucratized to the last detail. But the machine had failed in its purpose. It had desired that the prisoners

THE NIHILISTS IN THE CAMPS

should be killed quietly and painlessly, leaving no trace; there were no walls thick enough to prevent their screams, and the purple cloud was evidence of the crime. This could not be removed.

These huge engines of destruction, erected at great expense, with almost no profit to the state, were hopelessly inefficient; they failed to accomplish the purpose they were designed to accomplish. They murdered, but they could not remove the evidence of the crime. And their expensiveness shocked the National Socialist economists.

To keep these hundreds of concentration camps running experts were perpetually moving around the Reich, interminable wagon loads of prisoners were continually arriving, and whole industries were in full production. The Danzig firm which produced the electrically heated tank for the manufacture of soap out of human fat, the Erfurt firm which produced three-part cremation furnaces with electric elevators and complicated apparatus for removing the ashes, the Hamburg firm which produced Cyclone B, all these were working *against* the war economy. A thousand useless and tragic employments were being created; the organization of massacre within the Reich had become a vast industry which threw production out of line with the war effort.

Meanwhile, the camps continued, increased in numbers and became even more centralized. By the spring of 1943, it was beginning to be realized that war production was suffering from the industrial demands of the concentration camps, and by the summer of 1943, Hitler and Goebbels had agreed, partly as a result of Albert Speer's recommendations, to change their policy; they would make every effort to insure that the concentration camps served industry. Trainloads of prisoners left for the factories, and the factory managers were encouraged to treat the workers well, "Treat them well," says the proclamation issued at this time, "and then their reliability will be retained and expedited, and a rise in production will occur. Everyone, even the primitive man, has a fine conception of justice. Consequently every unjust treatment has a bad effect. Injustices, insults and trickery must cease." It was too late. The new edict, in any case, excluded the majority of the Jews. The machine of the Gestapo, solemn, menacing, moving faster as it moved downhill, continued to grind out death sentences, ferocious punishments, and incessant torture to the very end. The government had seen the dangers, but had been incapable of stopping the machine. "We could have employed uncounted millions of people," said Albert Speer, "but we—that is, Hitler and Goebbels—could never be convinced." With something of the same philosophy Margrave George wrote to his brother Casimer during the Peasant War: "If all the peasants are killed, where shall we get the peasants to make provision for us?"

All this terrible machinery had been the product of the nihilist mind, enforcing the law of nihilism, zero demanding that everything else should be zero. There were different degrees of zero; different punishments corresponded to different aspects of zero; but, in fact, each zero had been the same—annihilation for no reason at all. In all this absurd and terrible wantonness, the Nechayev monster can be seen working at the peak of his activity, mindless, almost catatonic, taking every conceivable advantage from the cultural breakdown which had already occurred. It is possible that the concentration camps would have spread over the whole world if the Nazis had been successful; Himmler, at least, promised that there would never be any change in the method—the bureaucratic engine could not come to a standstill of its own accord. The machine worked against a concept of freedom. In that sense it failed, because freedom remained; but it is significant

THE NIHILISTS IN THE CAMPS

that the gypsies, the most freedom loving of all, were the most to suffer, suffering even more than the Jews. In one camp in East Germany, of eight hundred gypsies, only three survived; all of them died shortly after they were released.

In the complex mechanism of the concentration camps, I have deliberately omitted one aspect to the end. It was a machine for producing a permanent rite of expiation and a permanent sacrifice, but it was also a machine for producing vast and inhuman satisfactions. No one will ever know Hitler's "joy" as he read through the methodical reports of the Gestapo, with their long columns of figures totalled, countersigned, each page bearing a rubber stamp. We do however know something about the satisfaction of one of the least known Nechayev monsters of our time. His name was Adolf Eichmann, who spoke Hebrew and seems to have been partly Jewish. He was director of the bureau within the Gestapo directly concerned with the liquidation of the Jews. In February 1945, realizing that defeat was inevitable, he said to a friend, "I will die leaping into my grave, laughing happily. To have had these five million Jews on my conscience is an extraordinary satisfaction."

The nihilists in the camps were generally men like Adolf Eichmann; they obtained their satisfactions from the contemplation of mechanical figures, long lists of death sentences; concerning real suffering, they had little knowledge. Even the guards seem to have lived in a kind of stupor, hardly knowing what was happening. They were ordinary men, and they had little in them of the dreaded Norse fighters, the Berserk, who went stubbornly mad in battle, fought naked, and possessed the strength of ten men, and when wounded, did not bleed. They were men very much like us as we take vicarious satisfaction from reading about crime in newspapers. It is true that their sensibilities were rotted by continual reading of *Der*

Stürmer, but it is debatable whether *Der Stürmer* has any worse effect on sensibilities than some New York evening papers. They were not necessarily compulsive neurotics; they were men who were fed on a machine they could hardly comprehend, and they could not have seen or guessed the intricacies of the machine. Just as a machine for producing women's stockings can be adapted overnight to producing trinitro-toluene, so this machine might easy have produced some other product than death; but it produced death well, and to some extent efficiently, and its very efficiency seemed proof of its validity. Into the making of the concentration camp went all the forces of modern civilization, subtly altered. Feudalism, the inquisitorial aspects of the church, propaganda, the conveyor belt, the theory of sacrifice, and the theory of the state, systems of bureaucracy and double-entry bookkeeping, all came together in these desolate camps; and by the fact that these things could have a place in the camps, their general validity becomes suspect.

If there is another war, we can expect to see the concentration camp revived, becoming even more bureaucratic, even more relentless. It will be employed, not against Jews only, but against whole nations. As a weapon of destruction it is infinitely superior—because it can be controlled—to the atomic bomb. To an even greater degree it will produce the same satisfactions, the same rites, the same deaths; it will be more fearful than the actual war. Once again, what we have to fear is the mindless figure of the Nechayev monster, and the plan of a concentration camp with the yawning mouth of the incinerator is as good a picture as any of the face of the Nechayev monster.

VII.
The Destruction of the World

NO one going through the urbane pages of David Hume's first *Treatise of Human Nature* expects to find there an analysis of the German concentration camps. The prose is cool, smooth and decisive. He writes of philosophical problems as Jane Austen writes of young spinsters. "The world," he says, "is very amusing, and the philosophers are the most amusing of all. They talk about passions, cause and effect, reason and self-love, and they have no idea what they are saying." And suddenly, quite quietly, allowing the words to flow from the argument, he begins to talk about the destruction of the world. There is no malice. He is simply describing things as they are. He writes, in the chapter describing the passions: "When I am angry, I am actually possessed with passion, and in that emotion have no more reference to any other object than when I am thirsty or sick, or more than five feet high. It is impossible, therefore, that this passion can be opposed by, or be contradictory to truth or reason." This is only the introduction. He has stated that passion and the reason belong to different categories. He then follows the statement to its logical conclusions, "Where a passion is neither founded on false suppositions nor chooses means insufficient for the end, the understanding can neither justify it nor condemn it. *'Tis not contrary to reason to prefer the destruction of the whole world to the scratching of my finger."* [1]

He had given the primacy to the passions, as Hitler was to do later. There was no turning back. Men would settle upon that page, and wonder precisely whether there existed means for this passionate end. His works were translated into Russian; there is a sense in which Nechayev merely refined the original impetus given by Hume's scepticism. He opened the gates. The straight line that passes through Hume and Nechayev ends with the concentration camps and the destruction of the world.

The phrase "the destruction of the world" had become, by 1920, almost a *cliché* in Germany. The rage of defeat, like the scratching of Hume's finger, was not contrary to reason; it was a real rage, and it had real consequences.

Men were perfectly conscious that the reign of nihilism in Germany was beginning. On June 24, 1922, Chancellor Wirth, of the Catholic Center Party, was informed in Berlin of the assassination of his friend Walter Rathenau. He addressed the Reichstag, facing the deputies of the Right, "Gentlemen, things cannot go on as they have done until now. There must be a thoroughgoing change. This growing terror, this nihilism which often hides under the cloak of patriotic sentiment, must no longer be treated with consideration. We shall act quickly." [2] He did not, of course, act quickly enough. The nihilist tide of fascism was already rising.

Ernst Röhm, in his autobiography *The Story of a Traitor*, wrote, "Europe and the entire world may perish in flames—it need not distress us. Germany must be free, whatever the cost." As one reads the novels that were written in Germany

[1] David Hume, *A Treatise of Human Nature*, II, part 3, section iii.
[2] Louis Fischer, *Men and Politics*, New York, 1941, p. 32.

THE DESTRUCTION OF THE WORLD

at the end of the last war, a clear picture emerges; the picture of the new Germany, stainless, shining white, against a background of perpetual flames. The destruction of the world is the price to be paid for German freedom. Destruction—eternal destruction—is the theme of Ernst von Salomon's novel *The Outlaws*, which borrows heavily from Dostoyevsky's *The Possessed*, but adds a German mysticism. The novel tells the story of the murder of Rathenau and describes with real names and apparently with inside knowledge the flight of Erwin Kern, the assassin, to the day of his final suicide. Kern is asked how, as an imperial officer, he survived the ninth of November, 1918. He replies:

> I did not survive it. As honor demanded it, on November 9, 1918, I blew out my brains. I am dead. What still survives is another thing. Since that day, I have lost my ego. But I will not be other than the two million who died. I died for the nation; and all that is surviving of me lives only for the nation. Were it otherwise, I could not bear it. I follow my star. I die daily, because I am mortal. While my actions are the sole motive force within me, everything I do is the expression of this force. This force is destructive—hence I destroy. Up to the present I have desired only destruction. Who sups with the devil must have a long spoon. I know that I shall perish in the moment in which this power no longer has any use for me. Nothing is left for me but to reconcile myself to the noble suffering imposed upon me by Fate.[3]

Destruction for the sake of destruction was the theme of the early Storm Troopers, who had come from the ranks of the separatist murderers; but it was not until Hitler came to power that the theme finally emerged in all its terrible symphonic force. In the last days of the German Reich the real destruction, not the music, was attempted.

[3] Ernst von Salomon, *The Outlaws*, London, 1928, p. 272.

ZERO

By the autumn of 1944 the German leaders realized that the war was lost. Only a miracle could save the war, and there were no signs of miracles. As winter set in, while the Russian armies rolled across the Vistula and the British and Americans lunged across the Rhine, Hitler began to speak again of the destruction of the whole world.

It was a plan which had been maturing for a long time, growing by slow accretions over the years. He despised men, therefore he would destroy them; the Germans especially, because they had not come up to his expectations, were to be destroyed. There would be one final burst of spiritual and physical terror. He would introduce the dreaded *Muspilli*, the fierce fire "that cometh in dark night, like a thief faring forth secretly and suddenly." [4] For many years of his novitiate Hitler had dealt in spiritual terrors, and now this magician was prepared to spirit Germany away into the primal chaos from which he may have felt he charmed it into existence. He had often spoke of complete destruction. Once, in *Mein Kampf*, he had even spelled out the Hebrew word for the primal chaos—*tohuwabohu*. In the spring of 1945, the reign of *tohuwabohu* was approaching. The court astrologer, Wulf, had seen it in the stars; Hitler knew it on his nerves, once finespun, now jaded by too much dismal excitement, and the poisons administered by his physicians.

During that spring he lived cooped up fifty feet below the ground in the bunkers of the Chancellery. He was a small, pale, shrunken man in ill-fitting clothes who suffered from palsy and looked through convex spectacles at a world no longer recognizable; observers saw a gray film over his eyes, and sometimes he slobbered. He gave orders, and knew that they were not always obeyed. He had lost touch with the real

[4] Joseph Grimm, *Teutonic Mythology*, II, 808.

world. Even after the first dramatic Russian victories, he kept on saying, "Russia does not exist." He meant, "Russia no longer exists in my mind—it is too dreadful to contemplate." He had never understood Russia, never felt that the Russians were people, never realized that they possessed muscles and a vigorous will to live. He had once ordered Leningrad to be razed to the ground "until not one stone lies upon another," and then, not knowing what to do with the desert he had created, he ordered that it should be given to the Finns who had not asked for it, and probably would not have wanted it. Moscow, too, was to become rubble. Again he employed the characteristic Nechayev language; the airplanes were to destroy the city "at one blow, at an appointed time." It was all on paper, seen in the abstract; he was destroying with complete finality things which had never come within his grasp. The greatest cities of the world were wiped from the map, new maps were drawn, and on these new maps he outlined new deserts, and so *ad infinitum*. It was the endless pursuit of nothing, the frenzy which comes over the nihilist mind when it sees the limitlessness of nothingness. There can never be any end; he must go on forever, destroying everything in his path, for only in this way can he be assured of his own existence, his own reality. We possess the stenographic reports of his speeches to his generals, those speeches which were delivered in a clipped nervous exultant voice in the high room at Berchtesgaden, where all one could see from the windows was the towering cliffs of the Austrian mountains, and the mists rolling beneath; he would reduce the whole world to a mist. Speaking to his generals on August 22, 1939, two weeks before the invasion of Poland, he said, "The aim is the elimination of the living forces, not the arrival at a certain line."

There was no "certain line," for there could be none; there was only the vastness of space, and all this must belong to him, and at the same time he wanted nothing of it. Like Ivan the Terrible he was "an enemy in his own realm." He did not dread the elimination of the living Germans. Once before, he had threatened to put the whole of Germany into a blood bath. He told Rauschning that he would have had no objections to letting the Storm Troopers loose on the streets. "It would be more wholesome for the people to endure a really bloody revolution for some weeks. I have refrained only out of consideration for them and their *bourgeois* love of comfort."[5] The threat of the blood bath for the Germans was one of his most consistent weapons.

Once again it is to Dostoyevsky that one must appeal for an explanation of the extraordinary behavior of nihilists. "A man who bows down to nothing can never bear the burden of himself," says Makar Dolgorusky in *A Raw Youth*. Hitler could not bear the burden of himself. He must kill himself, but like Shatov he must kill himself in a way which would leave a mark on the world; at the moment of his death, by some mystical process, he would feel that he had lived, that he had imposed his will upon the world, that he would be remembered and feared. He was growing old. He was fifty. Nearly all the great conquerors had been young men, and he was already twenty years older than Alexander had ever been. When he explained the basic reasons for his decision to make war, he used words that might have been used by a hero of Dostoyevsky:

> Essentially, it all depends on me, my existence, because of my political activity. No one will probably ever again have the confidence of the whole German people as I do. There will probably never again be a man in the future with more authority. My existence is therefore a factor of great value.[6]

[5] Hermann Rauschning, *The Voice of Destruction*, p. 94.
[6] *Nuremberg Trials*, I, 172.

THE DESTRUCTION OF THE WORLD

The repetitions, the inconsistencies, the extraordinary conclusion suggest a pride which was wearing thin; he was like a drug-addict, giving himself continually increasing doses because the excitement was wearing off. There was no longer now any survival of fascism, the rulership of the integrated *élite;* it was the maniac staring straight ahead and saying: "It would be a good idea if the mountains bowed down." But there must have been—it is inconceivable that there never occurred to him—the possibility that the mountains might stand up and fight.

His mind slowly decaying, his eyes fixed in a glassy stare, living only at night and fearing the sun, Hitler set out on his nihilistic campaign against mankind. With a maniac's cunning he chose the place and the time; autumn, in Poland, when the mist blows off the Vistula, that river which he once described as "an unruly stream or a dried-up bog," and beyond the Vistula lay the endless muddy fields stretching to Siberia. He hated the Poles with an obscure hatred. He did not hate the Czechs so much, though they were Slavs, because when he developed the *Heu Aktion*, the systematic capture of fair-haired children to be brought up within the German Reich to replenish the lost blood, he deliberately excluded the Poles, but admitted the Czechs, as he admitted the Dutch and the Scandinavians. Chiefly, he hated the Poles because they were in the way.

Even in the early days he was always thinking of annihilation. "The Poles must be exterminated," he screamed. He wheeled around and confronted the West, and for the first time he seems to have doubted; perhaps it would be the Germans who would be exterminated. "I realize," he said in the spring of 1940, "that this great struggle, if it continues, can only end with the complete annihilation of one or other of the adversaries." By July nineteenth the theme had assumed an even greater gravity in his mind, "The German people entered this war with the fanatical grimness of a nation aware of the fate which awaits it, should it be defeated." On September fourth he declared that "the hour will come when one of us will crack." He added that it would certainly not be Germany, but the air of intense conviction is absent. By December eighteenth, though Germany was still winning victories, and some of the greatest victories were to come, he returns to the thought of annihilation: "We know perfectly well that if we are defeated in this war, it will be the end of the German people as a whole. These are two worlds, and I grant that one of the two must succumb." As the war goes on, he keeps asking a peculiar question. "Does England think I have an inferiority complex regarding her?" The phrase is repeated seven or eight times in several speeches; that too is part of the atmosphere of doom he has created around himself. When he speaks of the possible annihilation of Germany, he is doing more than reminding the Germans of the issues at stake; he is reminding himself, and rejoicing in the inward excitement of the long balancing of terrible things. The tired voice grows shriller. Around the German state there is a vast and ever expanding rim of devastation where hatred and rebellion brewed, but he plunged on. Then came the mobilization of his armies against Soviet Russia, and the almost casual declaration of war against the United States.

Because nihilism survives, the processes of his mind are interesting and should be studied carefully. Here at last is the nihilist at the high pitch of nihilism. Like Ivan the Terrible he was "an enemy in his own realm," but we should be concerned with the precise definition of "enemy" and "realm." These are not things that we know normally; the fury of this enemy and the vastness of this realm, and its shoddiness, are such that they are difficult to visualize. If Hitler had not lived,

THE DESTRUCTION OF THE WORLD

no one would have been able to imagine him; it was beyond ordinary human credibility, because he lived in a realm where there was no need to think of ordinary human passions; it was a world where only the ideas of ruin, chaos, annihilation, destruction were commonplace, and all the rest was beyond his comprehension. Having plunged into nihilism, he did not know and perhaps never cared that he would be drowned in its nothingness.

Until the last moment Hitler never realized the futility of his nihilism fully. He seems to have realized it partially, in sudden flashes, and then immediately afterwards he would draw strength from the vision of futility. Ashen-gray with sleeplessness, his speech thickening, he paced up and down the carpet, now ordering a death-sentence, now obeying some obscure impulse to put order into the dream. He had said to Rauschning that there was a secret he could never tell, but Rauschning had guessed the secret easily. It was very simple: the Roman emperors had made no secret of the fact that they were gods and possessed of superhuman powers. But there were other dreams. Somewhere in the East lay the Garden of Eden. He thirsted for the vast spaces of Asia—he could not have told why, but it was so, and there was no reason for it, the myth demanded it and that was enough. He wanted space to move about in, and there were the Russian plains and all the manpower of Asia waiting for slavery. Hitler spoke often of the East; he did not mean Russia only. One day in 1943 he had explained to Himmler the grand policy; the whole of Europe would be hammered into a spear directed at Asia. Then the Germanic peoples, "numbering a total of six hundred to seven hundred millions" would launch an attack against Asia, and this time the slaves would be counted not in millions, but hundreds of millions. The final *Götterdämmerung* would take place in the fertile fields of Central China, but it was the Asiatic gods who would fall from grace; and afterwards the conquest of the world was easy. It was a dream-world, made out of zeros, full of intangible essences and dark forebodings, like one of those soap bubbles which still mirror placidly the surrounding world while black lines creep round it, a bubble so thin that it fades into nothing without warning. When he heard of local defeats, he would be buoyed up by the memory of the vast battles in Asia which would take place later, at another time and somewhere else. There were similar dreams among the Roman Emperors, who also doubted the reality of the world, sent expeditions on aimless wanderings through Asia, and were more concerned with their deification than their responsibility over the people they ruled. At the very end of his life, when he came to write his testament, Hitler wrote in obedience to the dream: "The destiny of the German people lies in the East, though this time we have failed to take possession of our destiny."

He was old and dying, and the East was still as far away as it had ever been. He detested the oriental, but except for giving orders that Russians with mongoloid faces were never to be captured, but slaughtered, he had little contact with orientals. He disliked the Japanese, and said so privately to his entourage; and perhaps he hated the Jews because they came from the East. The East was fabulous land, and he hated all fables except his own.

"The criminal," wrote Otto Weininger, "commits crimes out of his most fearful despair; it is his method of filling his own interior emptiness. If the criminal should desire to be a criminal no more, then he should do nothing, but then his life would be aimless; therefore he commits crimes." Hitler's rage for killing increased as his own life became more aimless. When he possessed almost no power at all, shut up in the Chancellery bunker, moving his armies across the map while

THE DESTRUCTION OF THE WORLD

knowing that no officers on the field obeyed him, he gave orders for the execution of the ex-jockey Fegelein, who by marrying Eva Braun's sister had become a close family connection; the ex-jockey was murdered simply because he had escaped from his cramped quarters in the bunker and was living in an apartment in Berlin, in ease and luxury, no longer within Hitler's immediate power. The restless desire to fill up his own emptiness went on to the end. He committed on paper or in his imagination more staggering crimes than he had ever committed before. He ordered that all the inhabitants of all the concentration camps should be poisoned, and that the whole of Germany should become a traffic desert; if it had been even remotely possible, he would have ordered the suicide of every German. Germany must become pure desert. Bridges, railways, locomotives, canals, ships, radio stations, post-offices—all were to be destroyed. No factory, no machinery, no building was to be spared. The war would come to an end in mountains of rubble, and the Nechayev dream would at last come to fulfillment. There was nothing surprising in this. He had spoken about defeat often enough, accepting its logical consequences. *Weltmacht oder Niedergang*—world power or ruin, the ego or chaos, absolute power or *tohuwabohu*. As early as 1934 he had told Rauschning: "Even if we could not conquer, we should drag half the world into destruction with us, and leave no one to triumph over Germany. There will not be another 1918. We shall not surrender." At another time he said: "We shall not capitulate—no, never! We may be destroyed, but if we are, we shall drag a world down with us—a world in flames." [7] Actually, he was not interested in killing people, but in the idea of killing; he was not interested in a world in flames, but in the idea of a

---
[7] Hermann Rauschning, *The Voice of Destruction*, p. 6.

world in flames; perhaps he was not interested in victory, but in the idea of being victorious. If he had been victorious, he would probably have become hysterically terrified and gone insane.

He was caught in a trap. He was in the position of a man who is held in a web of leather straps, so that the more he exerts himself, the more he suffers pain. Everything he did was a mistake. He could have gone to the Alpine redoubt, he chose not to. He could have perpetuated the legend of his physical courage by joining his soldiers; but he stayed in the comparative safety of the bunker. He could have ordered resistance on the model of the French and Polish underground; he ordered destruction instead—the easier way out. He did not care any longer either for Germany or himself, and it is possible that he had never cared; he had only played with the idea of Germany and the idea of his own ego; and so he put a bullet through his mouth.

But if he did not care, he still went through the processes of caring, of pretending to care. The blind death wish demanded to be fed. The brain's searchlight wheeled around, picked up stray fragments, lit upon the most secretly hidden things and then magnified them; these long forgotten, and often terrible impulses which had been concealed in the unconscious were suddenly revealed. Was there anything he could do that was greater than destroying the world? Was there some fabulous lever by which the whole universe could be thrown out of gear? The rage increased. There were times when overnight he seemed able to shake off the nightmare and deal with practical things. It did not last. He had said farewell to the world long ago, but now, as the Russian shells kept pouring over Berlin, he kept on making a mindless ceremony of farewell, repeatedly lining up the remnants of his General Staff, going down the line, and repeatedly shaking

THE DESTRUCTION OF THE WORLD

their hands. There were good reasons for this. In a mind given over to abstract images of life, only repetition gives events the appearance of reality. He must keep on making these mindless ceremonies, for the same reason that his lieutenant-governor in the east, Hans Frank, once wrote in an unguarded moment: "Everything revealing itself as a Polish power of leadership must be destroyed *again and again* with ruthless energy." Deaths, farewells, destructions, all must happen "again and again" before these monstrous minds are convinced of their reality. Hans Frank added, "This doesn't have to be shouted about; it will happen silently." So with Hitler there was only silence in the end.

He had built up a machine of terror, killed people on impulse, destroyed a whole national civilization, but when it came to his own death, he was to behave towards himself exactly as he had behaved towards the people he had imagined as his enemies. It was not that he had become his own enemy, but he did not know how to deal with things in any other way. The old patterns remained. He would kill himself. What then?

There occurred during the closing stages of the war one of those strangely revealing acts which light up the mythology of German conquest and German nihilism. The time had come to liquidate the terror. It was decided to destroy the concentration camps. Kaltenbrunner and Eichmann, the chief of the Jewish section of the Gestapo, were placed in charge of the destruction. The Jews must die, not as they had died before, in batches chosen by the bureaucratic machine, but in a final blaze of vengeance. Poison and fire—these were the weapons chosen by Hitler. The Jews were to be poisoned with arsenic and then their bodies and the whole camp were to be given over to the flames; when the Allies arrived, they would discover only the Viking funeral. For this action the code word was *Wolkenbrand*—the Cloud and the Fire, and if the code word had ever been received at Auschwitz (for some reason it was delayed), this would have been the fate of the Jews.

But why the Cloud and the Fire? It is not far to seek. We may expect to find it in ancient Teutonic mythology in some kind of relationship to the *Muspilli*, the World Destruction; and there, in fact, we do find it, for in the *Voluspa*, there is the description of the flames at the end of the world, "The sun begins to darken, the earth sinks into the sea, the bright stars vanish from heaven. Vapor and fire rage, the high flame licks the sky." [8]

But it was by poison and fire, the heroic death suffered by Beowulf, that Hitler chose to die with his mistress. So Eva Braun died of poison and was committed to the flames.

It is unlikely that Hitler shot himself without having a poison-pellet in his mouth, in case his hand failed him. The wheel had turned full circle; he died as his victims had died before him. Hans Frank observed to an American psychologist at Nuremberg that Hitler "must have foreseen his own death quite early, perhaps in the beginning of the war, and was determined to take the Jews with him." He had done all this; and when the Allied soldiers entered the bunker where he had shot himself, they found the poison-pellets strewn over the floor, and in the courtyard of the Chancellery were the shrapnel-riddled canisters which once had contained the petrol to be poured over his body. What is strange is that he seems to have died in exactly the same way as the Jews in the concentration camps. But the Jews had been martyrs, and there was nothing approaching martyrdom in Hitler's death; it was a very small death, and he had no control over it.

[8] *Voluspahin Skamma* in *Hyndluljódh*, 43.

THE DESTRUCTION OF THE WORLD

Death fascinated him, as it fascinates all nihilists. He had spoken about it often. Apparently, he did not fear death; he was like the "crowd man," who according to a famous phrase of Heidegger "suppresses within himself the courage to be afraid of death." [9] He had played with death, employed the threat of death always on individuals, but the crowd was immune to this fear. He said to Rauschning, "The most horrible warfare is the kindest. I shall spread terror by the surprise employment of all my measures. The important thing is the sudden shock of an overwhelming fear of death." It was simply not true. He had thought it out as a chess-player might think out some dramatic move; he had terrorized, but "the sudden shock of an overwhelming fear of death" is rare. He had forgotten that most men are less afraid of death than of the loss of their human dignity. It was terror they feared, not death, and Hitler's greatest success was that he was the world's greatest terrorist. He was more accurate when he said, speaking of the crowd, "The people need wholesome fear. They *want* to fear something. They want someone to frighten them and make them shudderingly submissive. Why babble about brutality and be indignant about tortures. The masses want that. They need something that will give them a thrill of horror." [10]

Death, however, was something that Hitler understood intimately, for the nihilist is closer to death than any other. Death was nothing, the final terror, the planet whirling through space empty of habitation. He said once, "If the Jew triumphs over the nations of the world, his crown will be the funeral wreath of humanity, and this planet will once more move through space as empty of human inhabitants as

[9] *Sein und Zeit*, I, 251. Heidegger, at this point in the argument, admits his debt to Tolstoy's extraordinary story *The Death of Ivan Ilyitch*.
[10] Hermann Rauschning, *The Voice of Destruction*, p. 83.

millions of years ago." Substitute for the word "Jew" the word "Hitler." The result is the same. This at least is what he desired: to be the instrument of divine vengeance against man. Perhaps, as Rauschning suggests, Hitler was himself partly Jewish, and there was an unconscious identification between the torturer and those he condemned. It has been remarked many times that there is a peculiarly Jewish cast to Hitler's thoughts; he will speak of the Jews as Isaiah spoke of the Babylonians, consigning them to Gehenna, a place where they lived obscure ghostly lives in eternal punishment, eternally damned. In Vienna he may have come upon the legend of the Golem. The Golem was a mechanical monster, made of clay, fashioned by a rabbi in Prague, and given all the endowments of man except the breath of a divine soul. The function of the Golem was to destroy all those who attacked the Jews. In one of the versions of the legend, the Golem kills its creator, then wanders out of the synagogue to disappear, but for the rest of time people are terrorized by the Golem, for they know it may reappear, a symbol of mechanical vengeance and man's power to destroy.

But if there was a prevailing Jewish caste to Hitler's thoughts concerning the Jews, there was also a purely Germanic caste to his thoughts concerning destruction, blood, vengeance, death by poison, and fire, and that other death by darkness, and mist, which so surprised the judges at Nuremberg. "I expect deadly fire, blast and poison," says the Germanic hero, Beowulf, when confronted by the Dragon who causes his death. In early German legends there is a story of creation, such a story as must have been imagined by cave-dwellers. In the beginning there was an abyss full of mist and poisonous vapors. Gradually, at the bottom of the abyss, there appeared a small spluttering white-hot spark of life. Three or four times the spark was put out, then at last it shot out of the earth and

THE DESTRUCTION OF THE WORLD

became the sun, and as it left the earth it left upon the walls of the abyss signs of abundant life, but all this life was doomed; there would come a time when the sun would explode and the whole earth would disappear in a sheet of flame. The dreaded *Muspilli*, the World Destruction, was written in the stars. The word comes frequently in Old High German, suggesting that even in the early Middle Ages men were tortured by the thought of a coming cataclysm. Poison, the abyss of nothingness, the whole world in flames—they are all there from the beginning; Hitler only borrowed them; or he rode on the mythological wave.

Perhaps he rode on the mythological wave because there was nothing else for him to ride. He had no real sympathy for people, no roots, no sense of history, almost no identity. He was the crowd speaking to the crowd, feeding on racial memories, and an obscure thirst for vengeance. There seems to have survived in him a "corpse of memory" from the past. Living on his nerves, remote from people, he possessed the strange power of being able to incarnate their nightmares; in him the berserk fury, which exists to a small degree in all men, came into its own. He seemed to be the strongest of the Germans when he was the weakest; he was simply a reflection of their wildest, unconscious desires.

When a man comes to murder, to a high impassioned pitch of murder, concentrating all his available senses on the person he is about to murder, it often happens that he is overcome by a kind of paralysis. He does not murder. At the very last moment he is held back, even though he might be able to accomplish the murder without any danger to himself. His human dignity, or a sense of morality restrains him. But Hitler could not think in terms of human dignity—like Himmler, he was continually saying that men were "like lice and offal," and the repetition itself suggests that he was hardly convinced of the axiom, and saw its dangers—and still less could he think in terms of a reasonable morality. He had known the extremes of suffering, and loneliness, and misery in Vienna, and never forgot them, and in the earliest pages of *Mein Kampf* he confesses unashamedly that pity had been destroyed in him. And because pity had gone, nothing was left to him but to insist upon his own supremacy, his own power, his own shattering triumph over other men. Like Nechayev he blackmailed, killed, tortured, employed all the weapons of deceit and cunning; unlike Nechayev, he lacked even an elementary human courage. To the very end he remained the little bourgeois in need of habitual comforts, and in his last testament he reveals that his final desire is that his relatives should be maintained "in a petty-bourgeois standard of living" and that his paintings, acquired by the rape of half the museums of Europe, should decorate the walls of his home-town of Linz on the Danube; a small grocer interested in pictures might have had similar aims in life and written a similar will. In the end, when all the veils were unloosed, he showed himself as a petty-bourgeois who had cut loose from the sanctions of petty-bourgeois morality only to return to them at the moment of his death. Hobbling across the small concrete cell in the bunker, livid with the fury of defeat, Hitler could realize at last that he was himself what he had hated most. He despised the bourgeois. There are at least fifty pages in *Mein Kampf* devoted to consistent attacks on bourgeois morality. And so, when he came to killing himself, he was only following out his own commands—*the bourgeois must be extinguished*.

But the matter is not so simple. The last hours of Hitler are of abiding significance to us, because from them we can learn something of the working-out of nihilism in our own time. The nihilist is an unrealist, and to him everything is possible. The destruction of the world is possible. Becoming

THE DESTRUCTION OF THE WORLD

a god is possible. But in the high regions of the possible where the nihilist dwells, the imagination has free course, and what is imagined is real, tangible, terrifyingly present to the mind's senses. In such regions, where contact with reality is rare, orders and commands have the effect of past events. He would say in a rage, his hands and legs shaking, "Shoot them all!" referring to separatists in Austria and Bavaria, to prisoners of war or Jews. It was observed that after having given these orders, there would appear on the once-frenzied man's face a look of calm and quiet satisfaction. The deed had been accomplished, the prisoners had been shot, there was nothing left to worry about; the actual shooting, when it occurred, had something of the appearance of an anti-climax, for in Hitler's mind they had been killed already. For him, as for *shamans* and some great poets, words were more real than the things they described. A child can sit in a corner and say "Tiger," and immediately there will appear within its field of vision a huge emblematic tiger which can be touched, seen and felt, and it can even be played with and become the companion of the child throughout its childhood. Hitler sat in a corner and said: "I am a god, I shall bring about the world destruction," and he played with these words, suddenly become real within a mechanical age, throughout his mature life.

The question remains: why he should have troubled himself to assume so great a burden? What compulsions were there, what swayed him to go craftily through so many dangers in order to acquire so small a prize? Partly it was vengeance against the human race. He did not really despise people; he hated them. He was determined that they should pay for the punishments they had inflicted upon him in Vienna, just as Nechayev was determined that mankind should pay for the fact that he was born in slavery, and spent the first fourteen years of his life a serf. Both counted men nothing, and still hated this nothingness. There were degrees of nothingness. They would set nothing against nothing, form equations of zeros and then strike through the equations. Even then, there was nothing, and they would begin again, covering more sheets of paper with zeros, blowing more smoke-rings, and though they were nihilists, they raged hopelessly against a world of zeros, for the nihilist hates zeros as much as any man. He sees the vacuum and demands that the vacuum should be filled. Though he seems to be, the nihilist is not a free agent. He is at the mercy of the vacuum which demands to be filled.

In the rarefied heights on which the nihilist moves, all things lose their significance, and only the putrefying "corpse of memory" has power to sway the workings of his mind. Old memories, rancors, odd fragments of disjointed knowledge, mythologies inherited from remote ancestors, all these may act on him with frightful force. The old Germanic legend of the *Muspilli* seems to have been one of the forces that swayed Hitler's mind. Indeed, half the old Germanic mythology appears to have flowered within him, and when defeat seemed certain, his mind went back to the legend of the Werewolves. This was the name he gave to the armed youths who were to fight the enemy, and at the same time reduce Germany to rubble. The Werewolves were two brothers, Sinfiotli and Sigmund. They wore the skins of wolves and they had a wolf-like ferocity, which went beyond all bounds. They fought one another to the death, and though Sigmund survived, he was lamed for life. Sinfiotli was cut up into small pieces. Years later his body came to life again when the magic spells were uttered and a green leaf was placed on his breast. But for Hitler there was no green leaf of life, no sense of ordinary human fecundity, ordinary human joys. He was like Melville's Pierre, who said: "Deprived of joy, I feel I would find cause for deadly feuds with things invisible."

Hitler found his joys, when he found them, in the contemplation of his will, in blood vengeance, and in a lust for annihilation. Even when he had grown prematurely old, as a result of Dr. Morell's injections of camphor, he was still at the mercy of the blind destructive forces of his own will, and of ancestral images; but as he grew older, he grew more bored. Boredom caught up with him. He needed greater and greater stimulants, and the only stimulant that remained was the stimulant of defeat. There is considerable evidence that he took a kind of joy in defeat; it was not a masochistic joy. It was simply that there was nothing else so calculated to enflame his over-stimulated mind. But boredom remained. Living in the small cellars beneath the crust of a Berlin slowly being pounded to rubble, he had all the appearance of the little brutal *SS* guards, bored with killing, bored with torturing, bored with the effrontery of his plan of destruction, bored with living in the realm of the impossible. Now at last for a brief while he would live in terms of reality, of fact, and the necessary fact consisted of a bourgeois marriage, followed by a reception with champagne and cream buns, then his own death. Concerning his marriage, nothing is so astonishing as his demand that it should take place legally and with all propriety, with a municipal inspector, Walter Wagner, officiating at the ceremony; the man who had denied all conventions of morality showed himself the most conformist of conformers. Concerning his death, it can be said that it took place much as one might have expected, in the bowels of the earth, away from the world of men and the sunlight, to the sound of the loud humming of electric ventilators and in the glare of electric lights.

It could hardly have been otherwise. Squalor had marked

ZERO

him; it would follow him to the end. He had pretended to cover up the squalid walls, but the whitewash had flaked away. There was nothing on the wall, only dirt and disease and the smears of blood left by previous tenants, and in the room there were only the memories of the people who had lived there, intangible and confused. He would erase the whole wall by an act of will; when he died it was only a little dirtier and more diseased than it had been before, because he himself had been there. He had killed millions of people, but to no purpose. He had defied the elements, defied God, defied the human condition, defied everything, but the result was the same; he died in a cellar. In one of his pregnant aphorisms Franz Kafka wrote, "Death is before us like the painting of Alexander fighting against Xerxes, which I saw in my schoolroom. In this life our task is to obscure or efface the picture by our actions." Hitler did not efface the picture. He did the opposite. He tried to become the picture, wove spells, and pretended to be a hero as great as Alexander, conquering the East and reducing it to his will. But it had never been more than a picture, a dead thing, a cheap engraving picked up somewhere in the rag-market. His heroic actions were no more than gestures, and his death too was no more than a gesture; to himself he had never been real.

It was a game which he played out to the end, spilling the bright counters haphazard, not knowing or caring where they landed, concerned only with the demonstration of his powers, though he was powerless. He liked to use words like "thorough," "frenzied," "unheard-of," "incalculable," "disaster," and "my inflexible will," but his habits—the only things that bound him to common humanity—were those of a small bourgeois: the cream buns, the desire for a fresh shirt every day, the luxury of a private cook, the thought of leaving a small collection of pictures to his native town so that he

THE DESTRUCTION OF THE WORLD

would be remembered. He read Nietzsche, and Nietzsche went to his head. He talked often of his own mysterious fate, and once, in the presence of Hermann Rauschning, he paraphrased a famous sentence of Nietzsche's in which the philosopher speaks of the great man of the future as some dreaded instrument of punishment, and if one saw him, one would be immediately struck dead; and Hitler quoted the phrase as though he himself had invented it, and was the first to see the relevance of the dreadful possibility to himself. But Nietzsche understood nihilism better than most men. He said once, "What does nihilism mean? It means that the supreme values devalue themselves. There is no goal and there is no answer to our questioning." Of the pure Machiavellianism which Hitler regarded as his private preserve, Nietzsche said categorically, "Machiavellianism *pur, sans melange, tout vert, dans toute sa force, dans tout aprêté* is superhuman, god-like, transcendental; it will never be attained by man, touched on at most." These statements occur in *The Will to Power*, which Hitler read avidly. It is unlikely that he ever read *The Twilight of the Idols*, which contains a half-mocking inquiry concerning reality, called "The History of an Error," which ends with the curious summary:

> We have suppressed the true world: what world survives? the apparent world perhaps? . . . Certainly not! *In abolishing the true world we have also abolished the world of appearance.*
> Noon: the moment of the shortest shadows; the end of the longest error; mankind's zenith; *Incipit Zarathustra.*

It was to this point that Hitler had come, by rugged and uncomfortable ways, denouncing both the true world and the world of appearance, lost in the maze and blinded by his own glory, without will, and without grace, determined to destroy the world, and give men such agony that, if any survived, they would remember him always; and in all this he nearly succeeded.

The terrifying thing, of course, is that he might well have succeeded. If he had had a little more stamina, if he had visited his astrologer Wulf a little less frequently, if he had realized that his aim of ultimate destruction involved an occasional pause in committing unnecessary murders, if he had understood human nature nearly as well as he understood the mentality of the crowd, he might have ruled the world. There were men around him who were clearer thinkers. Seyss-Inquart, Gauleiter of Austria and the Netherlands, had the same lust for power, the same lust for destruction. He was a cold and lonely man, whose upper lip trembled continually, and he looked at the world with a frosty stare of pride. Like Hitler and Nechayev, he liked to use the word "annihilation." He wrote to the leaders of the Dutch church, who courageously protested against the execution of hostages:

> It is unbearable to tolerate conspiracies, whose goal is to weaken the rear of the Eastern front. Whoever dares this must be annihilated. We must be severe and become even more severe against our opponents. This is the command of a relentless sequence of events, and for us, perhaps, inhumanly hard, but our holy duty. *We remain human because we do not torture our opponents. We must remain hard in annihilating them.*[11]

[11] *Nuremberg Trials*, IV, 326. The letter was written on January 29, 1943, at a time when the gravest defeats were taking place on the Eastern front. The complete identity between nihilist and Nazi judgments on humanity can be seen by comparing the letter of Seyss-Inquart with a passage from the nihilist philosopher Max Stirner's *The Ego and His Own*:
"I love men too—not merely individuals, but everyone, but I love them with the consciousness of egoism; I love them because love makes *me* happy, I love because loving is natural to me, because it pleases me. I know no 'commandment of love.' I have a *fellow-feeling* with every feeling be-

THE DESTRUCTION OF THE WORLD

For Seyss-Inquart, too, a massacre was an abstraction, something which happened somewhere else, on another plane, even in another dispensation of time and space. To kill, for Hitler, was like performing a magic spell; to saturate the earth with blood was only to ripen the earth. To kill, for Seyss-Inquart, was a far more cold-blooded and rational thing. There was only the intellectual problem: how to kill? There are moments when Seyss-Inquart appears far more terrifying than Hitler because he is far more rational. Hitler made mistake after mistake, because he depended upon forces over which he had no control; in his short career of crime there is no evidence that Seyss-Inquart ever made similar mistakes. In the future we shall still have to fear the emergence of the Nechayev monster, but our weapons are beginning to be sharpened against him. Against the ruthless and supremely intellectual Seyss-Inquarts we have not even begun to polish the proper weapons.

Among the hierarchy of Nazi leaders, there was one man who was potentially even more dangerous than Seyss-Inquart. His name was Albert Speer. He was tall, bald, immaculate in appearance, handsome, even if his brown eyes looked a little too prominent as he gazed behind thick spectacles. He was, in his way, an excellent architect, who took pleasure in designing the colossal marble halls which Hitler was continually erecting all over the Reich. Unknown until 1934, a casual meeting with Hitler at a time when he was works-manager for building the Chancellery in Berlin led to his appointment as Reich Minister of Armament and War Production in 1939. He was the architect of Germany's huge military machine. It was his technical ability which produced the armaments of destruction. Where Hitler was weakest, he was strongest, and where Hitler failed, Speer very nearly succeeded in saving the situa-

---

ing, and their torment torments me, and their refreshment refreshes me. *I can kill them, not torture them.*"

tion during those last frenzied months when he opened the prison camps and sent the unfortunate prisoners to the factories, so replenishing the depleted labor forces of the Reich. He supervised the construction of the V-bombs which the Germans, in their rage of despair, hurled on London. If Germany had won the war, he would have been the only man in the Nazi Party clear-sighted enough to manipulate the plunder, and make the technical plans for employing victory to suit German purposes. He complained in prison that he had looked forward at the end of the war to constructing, at the cost of two days' war-expenditure, a huge and grandiose capitol sufficiently imposing to house the master-race. He thought in terms of mastery. He was the pure scientific nihilist. Whatever the technical problem, he was prepared to solve it to the best of his ability, even if the problem was how to destroy the world. One day in 1944, Hitler summoned him to the bunker in the Chancellery. Hitler said, "If the war is to be lost, the nation also will perish. This fate is inevitable. There is no need to consider the basis even of the most primitive existence any longer. On the contrary, it is better to destroy even that, and to destroy it ourselves. The nation has proved itself weak, and the future belongs solely to the stronger Eastern nation. Besides, those who remain after the battle are of little value; for the good have fallen." [12] Speer rebelled. He had lived in a world where all the values were zero, he had been obedient to its commands, but now at last he realized that he was among those "who remain after the battle." He wanted to live, wanted to continue his technical experiments, employ his undoubted ability in works of monumental construction. He says (and there is no reason to disbelieve him) that as soon as he heard Hitler's statement, he

[12] H. R. Trevor-Roper, *The Last Days of Hitler*, p. 82.

decided to murder him. He thought of flooding the bunkers with poison gas, but this plan was later abandoned. He never came close to murdering Hitler, but he disobeyed Hitler's order that all the bridges in Berlin should be destroyed, and he prevented the wrecking of the factories. Meanwhile the preparation, construction and firing of V-bombs went on. He had no scruples. He had observed, despised, and in his own mind condemned the leaders of Nazi Germany, while observing that they themselves had come to power by despising men. He had seen the abyss of their nihilism, and recoiled in horror at the prospect of a Germany consigned to rubble. He had followed them at every move since the inception of the Nazi regime in 1933, and he had done nothing to prevent them from carrying out the consequences of their announced policy. He could quite easily set about solving the problem of how to destroy the world. Such a man can give all the appearance of being perfectly normal. He can lead a normal human life, have a wife and children whom he adores, take his dog for a walk every evening, and attend football matches on Saturday. The problem that obsesses him is inherently no more complicated than the problem: How to destroy rats. He succeeds in solving the problem, and offers it at a price to the chief of the bureau of inventions, and then goes and spends a weekend in the country, fishing or climbing mountains with his children, and when the destruction of a large part of the world is announced in the evening newspapers he is only faintly surprised; it is what he had half-expected. Closest of all to the pure scientist who regards the world as a problem in ballistics was the architect, Albert Speer, who amazingly was sent to prison by the judges at Nuremberg for only thirty years, and who was continually congratulated by his prosecutors on the clarity of his mind, the accuracy of his memory, and the brilliance of his deductions. He was the chief technical assistant to the planners of world destruction, and he belongs to a type which has only come into existence within our own time, but for the rest of time we must live in fear of him.

The pure scientist of our age, as soon as his mind turns towards the problem of how to destroy the world, finds himself on ground that has been thoroughly prepared. The weapons are at hand. It is not necessary to go to the immense pains of making hydrogen bombs; sufficient *psittacosis* bacteria solves the problem just as easily. He does not have to wade through blood and misery like Tamerlane, who cut off heads and stacked them into mounds of skulls. All that is necessary is that he should press a button. He is concerned with processes, not with human beings, and he possesses a sufficient neutrality towards the aspirations of humanity to be able to disregard their human existence. He can regard the nihilism of a Nechayev, a Lenin, or a Hitler as mischievous nonsense, the romantic prelude to his own calm assumption of authority. He does not deal with the possible, but with fact, the world as it is; and he makes no threats. Quietly, in some carefully arranged laboratory, he presses the button.

It seems, at this late date, that almost nothing can be done to prevent such a scientist from carrying out his experiment. The powers within his grasp are so overwhelmingly great; the calculated objectives are so easy to achieve—even without the assistance of great State-run laboratories and workshops—that all the advantages would appear to be on the side of the scientist, or even of the people who have access to his laboratories. No government regulations can prevent him from doing what he desires. After the bombing of Dresden, Goebbels had threatened to use the terrible poison gases *Tabun* and *Sarin;* both of these odorless gases, if left on the skin for ten minutes, are absorbed into the bloodstream in twenty-four hours, causing the most painful death. He had desisted, not because he knew that the formula, though invented in Germany, was already in the hands of American and British scientists, but because he hoped that the V-weapons would create even more destruction; they were more direct, and the Allies had no answer to them. There was no sufficient reason why he should not have directed the use of these poison gases; nor is there any sufficient reason why they should not be used in the future. Goebbels was in the position of the scientist who presses the button; he decided to press the button labelled V-bomb, but he might just as easily have pressed the button marked *Tabun-Sarin*.

The destruction of the world, planned by Hitler, failed. There is no adequate reason to suppose it might fail if there is ever a second attempt. "The revolution cannot be ended," said Hitler. "It can never be ended. We are motion itself, we are eternal revolution. We shall never allow ourselves to be held down to a permanent condition."[13] The revolution of destruction does not end; it will always be there; the forces of disruption and decay will always permit the nihilist revolutionary some leeway. A small crack in the dikes, and then the flood. All that we can oppose to the chaotic flood is the creative efforts of the people, and these, at the best of times, can only be just sufficient.

In the charred remains of the place from where Hitler had once commanded the destruction of the world, newspaper correspondents, coming shortly after the surrender, saw a strange sight. On one of the broken walls of the Chancellery there was written: *Das Jahr nul*—the year zero. Facing it, on the opposite wall, there was the rough drawing of a naked girl with the inscription *Vive Mistinguette!* The symbolism was superb, for over against the nihilism of the Nazis there had been placed the perpetual challenge to nihilism—the symbol of ordinary human creative life.

[13] Hermann Rauschning, *The Voice of Destruction*, p. 175.

VIII.
The Continuing Terror

IT sometimes happens in history that students of society are possessed with the gift of accurate prophecy. So Rousseau prophesied that out of Corsica there would come an emperor. Joseph de Maistre prophesied that out of the Russian universities there would come a nihilist with full power. The actual prophecy, made in *Les Soirées de St Pétersbourg*, reads, "I predict for Russia a Pugachev formed from the University." It was a startling prediction, but it was not quite accurate, for Nechayev never came to power, and though Lenin was partly a nihilist, he was as much a Marxian communist, and these two sides of his mind were held in uneasy balance through most of his life. A more terrifying prophecy was made by Hegel in the form of a blunt statement on the nature of the State. "The function of the state," he said, "is so to act that individuals do not exist."

As Hegel grew to middle age, the rot set in. He thought in terms of categories and the Prussian parade ground, and became increasingly divorced from men, sunk in a loneliness which was like a stupor. His brilliant mind reached out to embrace the whole universe; he would invent a system, like Kant, and find the secret of the universe. He never found the secret. He invented a curious concept of negative and positive forces, which he derived from his readings of Chinese philosophy. The *yang* and *yin* ruled everything, or rather they were eternally changing into one another or fusing together in a process called "synthesis." It had been known since the world began that there was diastole and systole, the rise and fall of the sun, but he was in love with his mechanical concepts, saw all history through them, and so he sacrificed man, almost in the same way as the captives were sacrificed in the mechanical pattern of the Roman triumph; there was no room left for them in his system. They do not obey the unchanging laws. The state, permanent, secure, completely furnished, must be erected over them, and this alone is "the real." He had not always believed this nonsense. In his early notes on *The Spirit of Christianity and Its Destiny*, written when he was still friendly with the poet Friedrich Hölderlin, he wrote, "In every man himself there is light and life, he is the property of light, but he is not illumined by light like a dark body which possesses only a reflected brilliance; man's own fuel is kindled, and he has a flame of his own."

When Hegel was old and famous, it was too late to change. He had never received the preferments he expected, his bitterness increased, he raged at men, and more and more he came to identify himself with the state, finding in the concept of the state the refuge for his brilliant imbecile mind. There it was—the pure efficiency of the Prussian state, the guards standing at attention, every order instantly obeyed; he must write upon the categories of obedience, the categories of command; men had disappeared, but their obedience remained. He would have been surprised to discover that all those efforts to wrest the secret of the universe, all those philosophic dissertations on the nature of reality, were no more in the end than a nihilist's confession of faith. From his system, Marx borrowed his method of analysis. Once again there is a nihilistic confession of faith, for into the *Communist Manifesto*, twenty years before *The Revolutionary Catechism*, he wrote, "When the proletariat proclaims the dissolution of the hitherto existing world order, then it is only suppressing the mystery of its own existence, for it is the actual dissolution of the world order."

It could hardly be stated more bluntly, though the terms were Hegelian terms; and implicit in the vision of the dissolving world order there was a vision of a dissolving universe, the destruction of all. Ill, neurotic, hating men—he complained in a letter, "they are always hedging me around"—he was fighting out a battle in his mind, huge shadowy forces were at work, he could not rest until he had laid these forces low. He, who had once commended the bourgeois for their skill and the greatness of their civilization, consigned them to extinction, and knowing nothing at all of the proletariat except what he had found in the British Museum statistics, elevated them to the role of permanent conquerors. It would be the last social revolution. Unthinkable that there would be any other. This vision was perhaps essentially Jewish, deriving from the rage of the Jews against the Assyrians, from Ezekiel's flames, and Isaiah's valley of bones; the Jews too had suffered, like the Romans and the Russians, from having seen too great a fire. But the statement of the vision remained in purely Hegelian terms. Hegel had no dread of the thought that the individual should disappear; he had simply stated the fact precisely, for the state was metaphysically superior. So Marx, playing with the same mindless categories, allowed the state to disappear; there was to be a dissolution of a whole world order. In his *Diary of a Writer*, Dostoyevsky speaks of a man who could say, "Let everything perish as long as I have my cup of tea." Both Marx and Hegel say, "Let everything perish as long as I have my metaphysics."

The matter is one of the utmost seriousness. Whole generations have been brought up to believe that the state alone exists; it was the teaching of Hitler, Marx and Lenin. Hegel's thesis was expressed quite candidly by Hitler: "To the Christian doctrine of the infinite significance of the human soul and of personal responsibility, I oppose with icy clarity the saving doctrine of the nothingness and insignificance of the individual, and of his continual existence in the visible immortality of the nation."[1] It is strange, and very revealing, how the mysterious word "existence" peers out of all these ghostly sentences. Marx's imaginary proletariat proclaiming "the dissolution of the hitherto *existing* world order" and "suppressing the mystery of its own *existence*"; Hitler's nihilist who finds "satisfaction in some conspiratorial activity of the mind perpetually plotting the disintegration of *whatever at any moment may exist*"; Hegel stating calmly, "The function of the state is so to act that individuals do not *exist*," all these spring from the same attitude of mind, a relentless nihilism. The mind's equations are worked out, and the result is zero. What is infinitely disturbing is that these zero philosophies have assumed tremendous importance in our own time, and not only the Nazis, but the Communists, have employed them to their own mechanical purposes of destruction.

For some time it has been the custom to regard Lenin as a great genius, the mechanic of a social revolution which embraced a sixth of the globe. He seemed to tower over other men. He was, we are told, very human in his dealings with his fellow-men, and all his hopes were centered about bringing to birth an empire in which each man had empire over himself, where there was no terror and the burdens of capitalism had been thrown aside. But in fact he followed closely in the steps of Nechayev, spoke with the Nechayev voice, and

[1] Hermann Rauschning, *The Voice of Destruction*, p. 225.

there exist long passages of his writings where the debt to Nechayev and *The Revolutionary Catechism* is made plain. "The scientific concept of dictatorship," wrote Lenin, "means neither more nor less than unrestricted power, absolutely unimpeded by laws or regulations, and resting directly upon force," a statement which Stalin quotes with approval in *Problems of Leninism*, adding, "The organs of suppression, the army and other organizations, are as necessary now, in the period of construction, as they were during the period of the Civil War." Stalin does not explain why this should be so. Nor could Lenin probably explain why it was necessary at all times to use superlatives—so many that they sometimes cancel out; but here, as elsewhere, he is only repeating the final passages of *The Revolutionary Catechism*, servilely repeating Nechayev's mindless delight in destruction for its own sake. On the eve of the October Revolution he said, "The workers, having conquered the power of government, will smash the old bureaucratic apparatus and will supplant it with a new one, and measures will immediately be taken to prevent these from degenerating into bureaucrats." But how can bureaucrats be prevented from becoming bureaucrats? The foundations of the state rest on bureaucracy, and if you do away with bureaucracy, you must do away with the state. Lenin hoped that the state would perish, by some metaphysical "revaluation of values," but in fact it did not perish, nothing was done to prevent the bureaucrats from remaining bureaucrats, they came with greater force, and they were given more far-reaching powers than they were given before. At the kernel of the whole problem of the state lies the problem of bureaucracy; Lenin had dismissed the problem with a wave of his hands. He had hoped that the army and the secret police would be abolished forever as "instruments of exploitation." Instead, they were confirmed in their powers.

THE CONTINUING TERROR

It was the inevitable consequence of Nechayev's philosophy. Unless everything, without exception, is destroyed in the revolution, the nihilist can remain in power only by the use of "unrestrictive power, absolutely unimpeded by laws or regulations and resting directly upon force." As for bureaucracy, it must become an instrument of this unrestricted force. He did not realize that we do not need to smash bureaucracy; we do need, never more desperately than in our own time, to humanize it, bring it to earth, make it viable to human needs, and only to human needs.

Lenin, placing himself at the service of nihilism, was completely careless of the suffering he caused. He possessed Nechayev's contempt for people, and said openly that he was never happier than in Siberia, where he could go shooting and be far from men. He loved men abstractly, but hated them in person. Nothing is more revealing of his iron-cold character than the story told by Gorky. Gorky had come to visit Lenin in the Kremlin. A phonograph record of Beethoven's *Appassionata* was playing. "I know nothing," Lenin said, "that is greater than the *Appassionata*. I'd like to listen to it every day. It is marvellous superhuman music. I always think with pride—perhaps it is naive of me—what marvellous things human beings can do." Then screwing up his eyes and smiling sadly, he went on, "But I can't listen to music too often. It affects your nerves, makes you want to say stupid nice things, and stroke the heads of the people who could create such beauty while living in this vile hell. And now you mustn't stroke anyone's head—you might get your hand bitten off. You have to hit them on the head without any mercy, although our ideal is not to use force against anyone. Hm, hm, our duty is infernally hard."

The Russian Revolution was, in fact, infernally hard. The *Ogpu*, under the command of Dzerzhinsky, struck out against all opposition, and even suspected opposition, with a kind of incoherent brutal rage. The theory of terror was based upon incredible simplifications. Lenin outlined the procedure, "We'll ask the man, 'Where do you stand on the question of the Revolution? Are you for it or against it?' If he is against it, we'll stand him up against the wall. If he is for it, we'll welcome him into our midst to work with us." He declared that there had never been a single revolution in history when people did not manifest salutory firmness by shooting thieves on the spot. "A dictatorship is an iron power, possessing revolutionary daring and swiftness of action, ruthless in crushing exploiters as well as hooligans." To him, all enemies had become thieves and hooligans; there was no difference between them; all must be shot.

In the first year of the revolution the death-penalty was introduced for 240 crimes, roughly the same number that were listed in the English criminal laws of the eighteenth century. People were shot for distributing pamphlets, for drunkenness, for congregating in the streets, for being out after curfew, for being an hour late in joining the revolutionary colors, for concealing food, for carrying weapons without a permit, for whispering against any facet of the regime, for actively assisting the counter-revolutionaries, and for doing nothing, or insufficient to aid the revolutionaries. Women and children were killed for being distantly related to counter-revolutionaries, or distantly related to the nobility.

Lenin's terror was a real terror, with real ends, however incoherently they were expressed. It is significant that whenever he spoke of the uses of terror, he introduced romantic phrases. He thought in terms of "revolutionary daring and swiftness of action." He would sign death-sentences without looking at the paper. He asked Dzerzhinsky once how many counter-revolutionaries there were in the prisons. Dzerzhinsky slipped a paper across the table, which read, "About fifteen hundred." Lenin marked the paper with a cross, and the next day Dzerzhinsky executed all fifteen hundred. It was as casual as that. Years before, Lenin's brother Alexander Ulianov had drawn up the program of the Petersburg Terrorists, which contained the sentence, "Convinced that terror results wholly from the absence of a minimum of freedom, we state with complete confidence that terrorist activities will cease if the Government grants this 'minimum of freedom.'"

The temper of terrorism became more virulent during the summer of 1918. Lenin wrote in his article, *Civil War in the Villages*, published in August:

> The kulak cherishes a fierce hatred for the Soviet Government and is prepared to strangle and massacre hundreds of thousands of workers. We know very well that if the kulak were to gain the upper hand they would ruthlessly slaughter hundreds of thousands of workers, would join in alliance with the landlords and capitalists, restore penal conditions for the workers, abolish the eight-hour day, and once again place the mills and factories under the yoke of the capitalists.
>
> Doubt is out of the question. The kulaks are rabid foes of the Soviet Government. Either the kulaks massacre vast numbers of workers, or the workers ruthlessly suppress the uprisings of the predatory kulak minority of the people against the government of the toilers. There can be no middle course...
>
> Ruthless war must be waged on the kulaks! Death to them! Hatred and contempt for the parties which support them—the Right Socialist Revolutionaries, the Mensheviks, and now the Left Socialist Revolutionaries! The workers must crush the kulak revolt with an iron hand, for the kulaks have formed an alliance with the foreign capitalists against the toilers of their own country.

It was all simplification, lies, a deliberate effort to incite to murder. He had become, indeed, one of those "great simplifiers," whose existence the philosopher Jacob Burckhardt had foreseen at the end of the previous century.

Terror was not, in Lenin's hands, a sharp instrument; it was a bludgeon. Once employed, it continued on its own momentum. It hit wildly, attacking whole classes, and even the proletariat, in whose defense it was instituted, recoiled under its impact. Lenin was especially pleased with its effect on the villages. "That we brought civil war to the villages," he wrote in his polemic with Karl Kautsky, "is something that we hold up as a merit."[2] Zinoviev expressed the same statement in different terms in a speech to the Red Army, "The *bourgeoisie*," he said, "will kill separate individuals, but we kill whole classes." It was left to the old revolutionary, Martov, whose name Lenin kept repeating while he lay dying, to deplore the madness of terror. "They lie," he declared, "when they say that the terror has ceased. It has only just begun. Worse still, it is part of their deliberate policy." Rosa Luxemburg said the same, but the terror went on.

Two months after the accession to power the *Ogpu* received the right to punish prisoners with "corrective labor."

It was the beginning of a new phase in the terror, one in which Trotsky played a significant part. In 1919 he wrote, "Terror must be organized," and he proposed that the whole labor force should be placed under the control of the *Ogpu*. From that moment the fate of labor was sealed. Police regimentation entered the factory. There was no possibility of protest, and it was seventeen years before a chastened Trotsky saw the error of his ways. In a new introduction to his book *The Defence of Terrorism*, published in 1935, he wrote,

[2] David Shub, *Lenin*, New York, 1948, p. 322.

THE CONTINUING TERROR

"Socialist culture implies the utmost development of the human personality: the young generations stand in need of independence, and this is wholly inconsistent with police regimentation." It was too late. The disease had spread all over Russia, and his own responsibility for the development of "corrective labor" was perhaps greater than that of any other. When Gorky protested against the use of terror, both to Lenin and Trotsky, he received from both the same answer, he was too "soft-bellied," it would be better if he returned to Capri, he knew nothing of revolutionary aims and principles. For a while Gorky fled to Berlin, regarded in Moscow as an opponent of the regime, of that mysterious dictatorship of the proletariat which was never defined and never put into practice, for the proletariat was never given power.

With supreme contempt, Trotsky stated the case against the worker, "Man is a lazy animal and he must be made to work." He meant, "Man is contemptible and must be punished." He drafted the order to militarize labor, and wrote in his book *The Defence of Terrorism*, "The key to economic organization is labor power, skilled, elementarily trained, semi-trained, unskilled or untrained. To work out methods for its accurate registration, distribution, and productive application means practically to solve the problem of economic construction." He, too, was a "great simplifier." He had ordered the peasants, under the threat of his machine-guns, to rebuild the railways in the Don area; he could do the same with the workers. "The instruments of compulsion," he remarks casually, "are already in the hands of the State." More bluntly, he declares, "The only way we can attract the labor power necessary for our economic problems is to introduce compulsory military service."[3] There were dangers ahead. He

---
[3] *The Defence of Terrorism*, p. 128.

realized only too clearly that the fiction "freedom of labor" must be declared a fiction; the laborer must have no bargaining power, and it is inconceivable that the laborer should have the right to strike. The hardest, the most disciplined people of the Soviet Union must be the laborers. But what if they refused to be militarized? He gave the answer readily. "If compulsory labor was opposed by the majority of the workers, it would be proved to be a broken reed, and so would the whole Soviet order." [4] He revelled in the idea of compulsion. "The element of socialist compulsion not only does not disappear from the historical arena, but on the contrary will still play, for a considerable period, an extremely prominent part." [5] The inventor of the perpetual revolution had invented perpetual enslavement, and when Lenin signed the document approving the militarization of labor, it was too late to call a halt. Stalin, a harder task-master than Trotsky, and with a greater understanding of the bureaucratic control of a militarized labor, has only reinforced the original edict.

Trotsky was the romantic of revolution. *The Defence of Terrorism* was written in the staff-car of his armored train, "amid," as he says, "the flames of civil war." As often happens, the romantic mind was incapable of invention. There was nothing new in the doctrine of militarized labor. Nietzsche wrote in *The Will to Power*: "Workmen should learn to regard their duties as *soldiers* do; they should receive emoluments, support, but no pay." [6] Nietzsche very carefully underlines the word "soldiers," and goes on to explain that there is no relation whatsoever between work performed and money received. The simplicity of the doctrine delighted the Bolsheviks. Similarly, Trotsky makes no efforts to defend terrorism

[4] *The Defence of Terrorism*, p. 125.
[5] *The Defence of Terrorism*, p. 118.
[6] *The Will to Power*, 763.

THE CONTINUING TERROR

in *The Defence of Terrorism:* he simply states its existence, and enlarges on this only to the extent of saying that anyone who does not see the relevance of terror is a fool:

> The State terror of a revolutionary class can be condemned morally only by a man who, as a principle, rejects (in words) every form of violence whatsoever—consequently every war and every rising. For this one has to be merely and simply a hypocritical Quaker.

This was not argument, any more than Hitler was arguing when he said, "Why babble about brutality and be indignant about tortures?" He revelled in torture and giving punishment; it was he who signed the death warrants of the Kronstadt sailors, saying in his *History of the Russian Revolution* that it was necessary to make an example. He realized too late that terror begets terror, perpetuates itself, and eternally demands to be fed, and can rarely diminish, because it is broken only by a greater terror. Marx said once, when asked for a definition of communism, "it is the pursuit of the real," but nothing was more unreal than terrorism, nothing more calculated to send the terrorist, and the one who is terrorstricken into the realm of hysteria. In the face of terror everything becomes unreal, even the state itself, and every safeguard is a trap with its mouth wide open, and every title is at the mercy of the least change in the weather of terror. Trotsky did not invent the Russian terror, but he was its prime apologist, and he seems hardly to have been conscious that the *Ogpu* was no more than the *Okhrana,* or that "militarized labor" was no more than the slavery from which the Russian peasants had been freed only sixty years before.

These, then, were the two weapons the Communists employed to maintain their power; both sprang from the free use of terror. Though the Communists delighted in dialectic, no one wrote a dialectic of the secret police, though there should have been abundant material available, for in all countries the secret police must in the nature of things follow the same course. Beginning as an instrument of oppression against the real or imagined enemies of the state, it ends by becoming the chief instrument by which a small bureaucratic ruling clique maintains its power. It uses weapons of deceit, torture and killing, not to discover the truth about the behavior and thoughts of people, but in order to instill fear, and it must instill the same fear in all the minor members of the bureaucracy, and even in the rulers, for otherwise it can never be certain of its comprehensive powers. So it happened in Germany that Himmler at the last moment, filled with a profound contempt for Hitler, decided to delegate to himself the powers of the *Führer*, and in comparable circumstances Yezhov and Yagoda, both heads of the Soviet secret police, attempted to stage *coups d'état* and assume the highest powers in the state.

Identically the same phenomenon was to be observed in the satellite countries of Soviet Russia. In October 1949, Laszlo Rajk, himself until a few months previously head of the Hungarian Ministry of the Interior, and therefore head of the secret police, was executed by orders of the Politburo. His crime was that he had set himself up against the Politburo by demanding the independence of his secret police. A secret police, like the Russian, cannot tolerate power in any other hands. So Yagoda, who had murdered and terrorized millions, was executed because "from the beginning of his vile life he had been obsessed with power." But those who had been condemned to the Siberian prison camps by him were not freed; there was no re-examination of the hundreds of thousands of people who had been tortured while he had been in command of the secret police; and the same futile, merciless terror continued as before.

THE CONTINUING TERROR

It may be—there can be no certainty in these matters—some peculiar quality in the German and Russian minds which makes them peculiarly responsive to terror. Caught in its basilisk stare, they make no effort to destroy the monster, and even make excuses for it. Nicolai Berdyaev, an opponent of the Soviet regime, an extremely intelligent theologian, a profound Christian, and a man who acknowledged the European tradition, went to great lengths to invent a theory of the "necessary expiation" which men must undergo during reigns of terror:

> A revolution always brings with it an avenger, who performs the greatest cruelties and acts of violence. The revolutionary element, i.e., the released collective subconscious, is saturated with vengeance. But those on whom the revolution wreaks its vengeance, and those whose old wrongs have caused its abuses and cruelties cannot claim to be champions of righteousness, for the revolution embodies a measure of right as compared with their wrong... Vengeance is hideous, but it is not for those whose wrongs have provoked it to denounce its hideousness. Spiritually speaking, they are the very people who ought to see a certain measure of justice in that vengeance. A revolution, like every other great and significant event in the destinies of mankind, involves me and every one of us. A revolution unites and organizes the most vindictive, envious and embittered elements of a nation. This is what gives it victory. It is the law of every revolution. Revolution is, by its very nature, devoid of grace and is the symptom of man being forsaken by God. From the moral point of view revolutions must be condemned because they create the type of man possessed by vengeance, malice and thirst for violence. They are condemned by the very expression in the eyes of the renowned leaders and by their terrible lack of spirituality. But we cannot rest content with these judgements. Moreover we cannot lightly pronounce this re-

ligious and moral condemnation. Religiously and morally we must take upon ourselves the blame for revolutions and regard them as part of our destiny.[7]

Berdyaev defends the evil in the revolution on the grounds that everyone is guilty; but everyone is not guilty. He believes, as though it was an inevitable and necessary act of faith, that the "released collective subconscious" is identical with the "revolutionary element." There is no substance for this belief. That men have the right to revolt under certain circumstances is not in doubt; what is in doubt is the justification of violence by mysticism. He never wearied of stating that one must accept the evil of revolution as an act of expiation. In his *Thoughts on the Russian Revolution*, he wrote,

> When a revolution has happened in the destiny of a nation, when it has suffered that misfortune, there is only one way out of it. One must accept the event as sent by providence, accept it like all the sufferings and misfortunes of life, as all great trials must be accepted; resist the temptations of revolution with all one's strength, remain faithful to what is sacred, go down with lamps into the catacombs, bearing the misfortunes in a religious spirit of expiation.[8]

With something of this spirit, with great holiness, the Jews sometimes accepted their fate in the concentration camps, yet it was precisely the act of expiation which the Germans desired them to perform; and in the Siberian camps there is reason to believe that the expiation of sins against the Communist State is equally encouraged. Berdyaev is prepared to be the lamb who offers himself for sacrifice. He will not fight back, for destiny rules, and he does not speak about a revolution, but the revolution which happens in the destiny of a nation.

[7] Nicolai Berdyaev, *The Destiny of Man*, pp. 265-6.
[8] Nicolai Berdyaev, *The Russian Revolution*, p. xx.

THE CONTINUING TERROR

All is destined. It is a strange philosophy, and we shall understand it better when we realize that with Berdyaev, as with so many Russian philosophers, the death-wish hovers near. "To go down with lamps into the catacombs" cannot mean anything else but to die.

The unwieldy mysticism, the schism in the Russian soul, may explain why we have never heard of a revolt of the Siberian prisoners. The devout Russian, in the utmost misery, can still dream of triumphs. Even Bielinsky, the gentlest of men, who wrote at length, and brilliantly of the coming time when there would be no more punishment, no more terror, no more slaughter and perhaps no more death, declared, "If I were a Tsar, I would be a tyrant." The disease lay deep. There are moments when one comes to believe it is inevitable that a society of sheep will beget a government of wolves. Berdyaev was not alone in finding excuses for the terror. Even foreigners came to dismiss the *Ogpu* with a wave of the hand. It was not important, and besides they did not care. The Webbs in their monumental and voluminous study called *Soviet Communism: A New Civilisation?* dismiss the secret police in a line or two. They say bluntly that the organizations guaranteeing revolutionary order and state security, the frontier guards, the constabulary forces and corrective labor camps are merged together with the secret police in "a single secret administration." [9] They never again refer to the organizations employing terror. It was characteristic of Berdyaev that he should regard *The Revolutionary Catechism* as an exercise in revolutionary asceticism, for he was determined to find religious significance in evil, and in the same way it was perhaps characteristic of the Webbs that they failed to see what they did not desire to see. But the terror remained.

[9] *Soviet Communism: A New Civilisation?* I, 161.

ZERO

With desperate fatalism the Russians accepted the terror. They did not rebel, and perhaps it was completely impossible for them to rebel. The terror was waged on so completely massive a scale that individual deaths, individual tortures and imprisonments came to mean nothing. Whole classes were uprooted and exiled, or murdered; and just as Hitler kept the attention of the Germans at fever pitch by his constant changes of direction, so Lenin and later Stalin reversed their judgments, policies and even their basic faiths in a blind, bewildering opportunism, which produced on the people the same effect—they could not guess where they were going; they knew only they were going in paths over which they had no control.

In Russia, as in Germany, the whole people were enslaved. No other civilized state possesses internal passports, but these were introduced in Russia in 1939, two years after the *Small Soviet Encyclopaedia* stated that "the custom of internal passports, instituted by the autocracy as an instrument of police oppression of the toiling masses, was suppressed by the October Revolution." Trotsky's dream of complete power over labor now came true. Workers were no longer able to travel without police permission, nor could they obtain jobs without permission from the same source. If the passport was refused, it was necessary for them within ten days to proceed to a locality 100 kilometers away, and there, too, it might not be possible for them to obtain jobs. Livelihood, at its source, was in the hands of the police. To lose one's passport was to know an ultimate degradation; without it, the laborer was completely dispossessed.

The Russian secret police permeated, and still permeates, the lives of Russian citizens in a way which is only comparable to the methods of the Gestapo. It wields the same ruthless powers; there are the same knockings on the door between the hours of eleven and two o'clock at night, there is the same bureaucratic inefficiency, and the same bureaucratic delight in simplifying all problems with a death-sentence. One summer evening, talking quietly with Kamenev and Dzerzhinsky, Stalin is supposed to have said, "To choose the victim, to prepare every detail of the blow, to gratify an implacable revenge and then to go to bed—there is nothing sweeter in this world." But the *Ogpu* was an instrument of merciless bureaucratic terror, and it is doubtful whether it knew or felt any emotion corresponding to *sweet revenge*. It obeyed orders; the orders were unbelievably irresponsible; that was all.

In Soviet Russia, bureaucratic terrorism went through many phases. The original "extraordinary commission" brought into being by the Pole, Felix Dzerzhinsky, was so wild and inaccurate an instrument of terror that it can be compared with the corresponding period during the rise of the National Socialists to power. It murdered blindly everything that lay in its path, and after the attempted assassination of Lenin in August, 1918 by Fanya Kaplan, and the assassination of the chief of the Petrograd secret police Uritsky, on the same day, it reached its peak. Within twenty days the *bourgeoisie* of Petrograd and Moscow had been decimated. Thereafter the terror followed the course of the civil war, becoming most merciless when the Red Armies gained victories. After Lenin's death there followed a period of relative quiet and readjustment. Between 1929 and 1935, the scope of terrorism immensely increased. It was the period of internal stabilization, but it was also a period which saw the gradual elimination of the Old Guard, the friends of Lenin, and original Communist Party members. This period corresponded to the defeat of the Storm Troopers in 1934. Thenceforward, Stalin was enabled to change the whole nature of the Communist experiment, and by 1935 he was restoring Russian nationalism and Pan-Slavism, and even recognizing the leadership of the Russian Orthodox Church. The Third International was dissolved; a military caste had come into being; divorce was no longer tolerated, and coeducation was forbidden; it was as though the Russian Communists were deliberately following in the path of Fascist Germany, and when Mussolini asked in an editorial in the *Popolo d'Italia* whether "in view of the catastrophe of Lenin's system, Stalin could secretly have become a fascist," he was only asking the logical question demanded by the times. From this period dates the glorification of Stalin as the *vozhd*, a Russian word which bears the exactly equivalent meaning of *Führer*, and from this date, too, there began the "terror in depth." Stalin had foreseen a war. He was not yet sure with whom the war was to be fought, but he was determined that the Russian people would obey his orders whenever the challenge came. He had uprooted whole populations, begun to colonize Siberia, and he was concerned with defections in the great cities and in the Ukraine. It was necessary that there should not be one single threat of opposition once war was engaged.

Stalin was a man who learned more from his enemies than from his friends. He learned from Hitler the whole scheme of "terror in depth." Previously, the *Ogpu* had possessed wide and arbitrary powers; now they possessed complete powers. In every city and every village, the tallest and most grandiose building belonged to the secret police. The secret police were no longer to be regarded as the watch-dogs; they were the masters. Every pretense of democracy was jettisoned. In the factories, relatively democratic during the period of American influence, the *Ogpu* now installed its managers, and the whole Far Eastern region of Siberia known as Dalstroy was given over to the secret police as their private preserve. The reign of the nihilists followed, for every factory, every village and every city possessed its nihilist chieftain responsible only to a bureaucracy which, in the nature of things, was responsible to no one, not even to Stalin.

What marks out the Soviet terror during this period was the vast strain on the national economy; the cost of a nihilist bureaucracy must always be beyond reckoning. To keep the people in a state of terrorized excitement, large-scale trials were held; all those remotely related or acquainted with the people put on trial were arrested, and usually murdered. The technique of murder was improved; the "self-sealing death" was apparently invented at this time. A prisoner ordered to walk down a concrete alleyway in a prison would be automatically shot in the back at a certain point in his progress; iron racks would thereupon descend, he would be wrapped in a tarpaulin or sheets of leaded and greased paper, and the body would be thrown mechanically into a shoot leading to the sewers. The same kind of tortures, the same desire to see the prisoners performing the rites of expiation, the same mechanical brutality was enforced in Soviet Russia as in National Socialist Germany; and there seems to have been an hysterical desire on the part of both the Russian and the German secret police to compete with each other in the art of degrading the human person. No one felt free in Russia; no one felt free in Germany. People were "liquidated" because they were thought to know too much, because they were popular, because they were unpopular, because they had once conversed with someone who had been liquidated, or was about to be liquidated, because they did not shout Stalin's name loud enough, because they were thought to be people who might not one day shout Stalin's name loud enough, or because they merely possessed an apartment which a member of the secret police desired. And just as Hitler felt least secure whenever he had destroyed opposition, so Stalin felt uneasy in the lonely eminence where he lived, all opposition ground to dust, but the fear of it increasing at every moment. It was at this time, in 1936, that the Stalin Constitution was promulgated. Under article 127: "Citizens of the USSR are guaranteed inviolability of the person: no one may be subject to arrest except by order of the court or with the sanction of the state attorney," and by article 128: "The inviolability of the homes of citizens and secrecy of correspondence are protected by law." But the nihilist loophole was contained in article 127: "The state and district attorneys' offices shall perform their functions independently of any local organs whatsoever." There were other loopholes, and perhaps the most famous of them was contained in article 12: "He who does not work shall not eat." Trotsky, the evil genius whose influence continued long after he had been officially proscribed, had stated long before, "Only one institution is empowered to say what labor is, and shall do—this institution is the State."

The *Ogpu*, "the unsheathed sword of the proletarian dictatorship," continued to possess, in spite of the Stalin Constitution, complete power over the destiny of the citizens within the state. Theoretically, since 1934 it lacked the power to sentence to death; the highest punishments it could inflict were deportation to a concentration camp, deportation to an obscure village, prison sentences, and sentences of solitary confinement. In fact, it employed the death penalty whenever it suited the purposes of the *Ogpu*, and like the Gestapo it was equally severe on all those whom it regarded as in the opposition. Masons, Jewish Zionists, anarchists, royalists, syndicalists, Leninists, Fascists, Separatists—all were gathered together under the insignia of enemies of the state, but the most potent and the most dangerous enemies were those for whom there were no names, the millions of people who still, in spite of terror, fought against it, reserving their right to praise and co-operate with all the social progress of the state.

The Soviet government, like the Nazis, made its fatal judgment on the value of men's lives. All this was inevitable from the moment when Lenin announced his casual and romantic simplifications. The law of August 7, 1933, which introduced the death penalty for the theft of *any* property belonging to the state (but everything belonged to the state), the mass deportations from the Kuban villages, the decision to let the famine take its course in the winter and spring of 1932 to 1933, all these arose from the nihilist philosophy inherent in the Nechayev doctrine. Dzerzhinsky, Menzinsky, Yagoda, Yezhov, and Beria could follow one another, die, or be executed, but the essential philosophy remained. *Because there was this philosophy, all power inevitably congregated within the secret police.*

The extraordinary similarity in method of the National Socialists and the nihilist-Communists cannot be accidental, and the same war of nerves was continually played by both on the defenseless people for the same ends. Neither searched for the "real"; both sought to heal wounds by "liquidating," "annihilating," and "making men expiate their sins." The Nazis possessed a *mystique* which, except for its extraordinary fury against the Jews, was precisely the same *mystique* as that which flowered in the Pan-Slavic dreams of the Russian nihilist-Communists, and this was inevitable, since Hitler derived his impetus from the former Russian secret police, who found the excuse for their privileged tyranny in the thought of the Third Empire ruled by Moscow, as the imperial legatee of Byzantium. So it happened inevitably that when the war came to an end, the concentration camps of the Nazis were taken over by the Russians, and the same practices and the same terrors arose from the same fertile ground. At Buchenwald in

ZERO

September 1949, there were fourteen thousand prisoners; at Sachsenhausen there were nineteen thousand; other camps were similarly filled, and the prisoners were at the mercy of the same kind of guards, and were compelled as before to wear distinctive uniforms. Nothing had changed except that there was a five-pointed red star instead of a swastika over the entrance to the camp.

Hitler had waged a war of terror by simplifying all issues to: VICTORY OR DEFEAT. The Russians did precisely the same. There could be only two possible rulers; either the dictatorship of the proletariat, i.e., the dictatorship of the Politbureau, i.e., the dictatorship of the secret police, or the dictatorship of the reviled landlords, capitalists, factory owners, German Fascists and Japanese generals, all that could be understood by the phrase "capitalist imperialism." That capitalist imperialism had died at the end of World War II, and was powerless to revive was never mentioned; the stark fear must be made starker; every radio program must announce "merciless death to the exploiters of labor," though the Soviet Government, and more particularly the Soviet secret police were the most merciless of all exploiters of labor. "What a waste of time and labor we still allow," cried Georgi Dimitrov just before his death, speaking at the National Assembly in Sofia. "We must prune our state employees. We must throw out slackers, loafers, and babblers. Death, merciless death, to all with lazy hands and lazy minds." The diseased brains of revolutionary leaders, once they come to power, see slackness everywhere; they can hardly help it, because they have worked at an inhuman fever-pitch all their lives. The phrase "merciless death" comes easy to them: it is the romantic's reward to himself—the contemplation of his own ruthless powers, the signature or the cross on the paper signifying death to the heretics, the slow burning of funereal fires. In newspaper editorials coming from eastern Europe, one might think that the phrase was simply blocked in with a rubber stamp, so casual, and insignificant, and repetitive it is. The effect is inevitable. Apathy sets in; against boundless terrors no one cares, terror becoming so commonplace that is like the hanged men dangling from the lamp-posts in the German concentration camps; when there are so many of them, they become "part of the ceremony."

The Russian terror, except in one respect, suffers from the same weakness as the German terror. It must follow the same laws, develop the same ever-increasing pitch of hysteria, become increasingly swollen with bureaucracy. The National Socialists could not harness their terror to any useful ends; the Russians could. This was the only essential difference between them, but it was an important one. The colonization of Siberia and the arctic wastes had occupied the thoughts of Peter the Great. In his will he had specifically mentioned that Russia must enlarge her boundaries eastward. In spite of the wave of colonization at the end of the last century and the systematic deportation of political prisoners to Siberia by the *Okhrana*, the process had been carried on slowly, and in general the colonization had hardly affected the land east of Verkhne-Udinsk. The discovery of gold on the Kolyma river shortly after the Communists came to power suggested that great sources of mineral wealth lay beneath the "ever-frozen earth," for in these regions the earth is perpetually frozen to a depth of ten or more meters. The secret police was given power to deport prisoners to these regions in 1930, but it was not until 1933 that the first transports of prisoners were sent to Magadan. Thereafter, the whole tendency of the secret police was to occupy more and more of eastern Siberia; and the concentration camps, which had previously spread along the line Moscow-Solovetsky now spread due east, to the very

ZERO

limits of Kamchatka and the islands facing Alaska. Most of these settlements would have remained unknown if Stalin had not been so ill-advised as to deport Polish prisoners there, for when they were released by agreement with the Polish government in 1943, they brought back with them stories of incredible hardships spent in the gold-bearing regions of the Kolyma river, where conditions were more severe than any hitherto known. By May 1930 there were roughly six hundred sixty-two thousand prisoners in Soviet concentration camps. By 1942 there were at least ten million; and the majority of these were in Siberia.

The increase over twelve years was significant of the relentless operation of the secret police machine, its necessary increase. The secret police cannot remain static. It must find larger and larger "fields of irresponsibility." Once the system of the concentration camp is introduced, it must attempt to extend its sphere of influence until the time comes when everyone who is not essentially occupied in the factories, the fields, or the bureaucracy is inevitably brought within its scope. A reservoir of surplus labor is formed, and it is this reservoir which the secret police was enabled to take *en bloc* to Siberia. The main purpose of the explorations of the Kolyma was the search for gold, and under the most heart-breaking conditions, with few implements, the prisoners were made to dig out the gold from the rock. By this time the secret police in Russia had developed to a stage corresponding to the National Socialist discovery of the incinerator; they had found the ideal punishment, which left no trace.

The barbarity of these punishments could be understood only by assuming that they had found in the arctic wastes the absolute zero of human degradation, the place where men could be completely and remorselessly dwarfed by their surroundings, and where the secret police, possessing a new and independent bureaucracy, could treat their prisoners with absolute freedom. We have seen that the value of a prisoner in the German concentration camps was one or two cigarettes. In the Kolyma area the value can be more accurately determined against gold. Between seven hundred and one thousand prisoners die for every ton of gold mined; a human life is roughly equivalent to one kilogram of gold. This was considerably higher than the German evaluation, but it was equally meaningless. Years before Lenin had said, "Gold is a capitalist trick. Ourselves, when we come to power, we shall make the urinals of gold, to show our contempt for it." There was no contempt; millions are still going to their deaths in search of the useless gold.

In Dalstroy, which means "the Far Country," the position of the secret police is unique. All the power is in their hands. Transport, government, labor, recruiting, everything that goes to form a modern state is in their hands, and Dalstroy itself is the only existing police state in the pure form. There the terror is absolute, the field of irresponsibility so great that it embraces the whole region. In our own time, Auschwitz and Dalstroy are the supreme examples of absolute terror, absolute degradation, and absolute crime. That the Soviet government is aware of the crime committed in Siberia can be shown by their repeated refusal to let independent observers enter the Kolyma area.

In the Soviet concentration camps, as in the German ones, there are complicated hierarchies, for these large camps cannot be managed without introducing a class society. Here, as in Germany, thieves and murderers receive preferential treatment; they are not marked with the signs of heresy, and therefore they are not required to expiate their crime to the same degree. The *predurki*, the camp aristocrats, form the bureaucracy; they are prisoners who are dealt with leniently.

ZERO

Below these come the *urki,* the common criminals, who are regarded as people who will help to inspire the necessary terror among the real criminals; these real criminals are divided into two classes; the *rabotyagi,* who have still sufficient strength to work and fulfill their norms, and the *dokhodyagi,* those who have lost all resemblance to human form. The name is significant, for they are final zeros of the miserable equation by which the nihilists seek to enforce their nihilist philosophy on the world. For the *dokhodyagi* there are no incinerators. It is enough that they should die.

All the efforts of the secret police, the great complex of buildings and installations, the private militia, the intelligence services, the public works systems, the secret tribunals, the highway maintenance services, the millions of informers and spies, the hierarchy of officers and their underlings, the private fleets of airplanes, ships and motorboats, the private railways, all of these could produce nothing more useful than dead men on the frozen earth and hoarded gold in the Kremlin; and the mere fact that this could happen would seem to be an unanswerable reason for abolishing gold as a medium of currency.

Meanwhile, the secret police in Russia is still developing. The frontiers of Dalstroy have been pushed back westward. There seems every reason to believe that the whole Soviet state will eventually take on the character of the administration in this Far Eastern province of Siberia. The same methods are employed in the European countries captured by the Communists. Yugoslavia broke with Russia largely because the Yugoslav dictator desired to have complete power over his own secret police rather than surrender it to the Russians. The Czechoslovak government has been more docile; it has agreed to regard its own prisoners as a slave pool, to be used by the Russians whenever they think fit. Under recent regulations all prisoners sentenced by a Soviet military court in

THE CONTINUING TERROR

eastern Germany are liable to be sent to Russia, and therefore liable to be sent to Dalstroy.

The wave of Soviet terror shows no signs of abating. It cannot abate. It must go on until it reaches barriers as absolute as itself. But just as in Germany, the terror produced apathy, so we may believe that in time the Soviet terror will produce the same apathy, and it is more likely that this will happen in countries like Poland and Czechoslovakia, where European traditions of freedom, however attenuated, still survive. In Russia, those who do not inform may be punished; everyone is encouraged to spy on everyone else, people forget to think honestly or face issues squarely, with the inevitable result that morality of all kinds subtly decays. Freedom is more than the right to speak out. It is friendship, and truth, and mental security, and knowing the difference between right and wrong. Freedom is to place the highest possible evaluation on the individual's creative ability, his usefulness to society *along his own line*. Freedom is a spiritual cleanliness impossible under police regimentation. All this is, and must be, absent in Russia, where trials are held *in camera*, confessions are obtained by drugs, and the individual's right to enjoy life and liberty is regarded as zero, for the only right belongs to the state, and the state may dispose of him as it pleases, and the state does not know that it is itself zero, because the sum of an infinite number of zeros can never be more than zero.

Nihilist-Communism remains, to torture the world for a few more years. There were good things in Communist Russia. The spread of education among the masses, the policy of absolute nondiscrimination among the races, the exaltation of labor, the promotion of health, and recreation, the special positions occupied by women and children, the effort to introduce a society where barriers between the classes became meaningless, but none of this was specifically Communist or

Marxian; the same tendencies are to be observed, more fully reinforced, in the Scandinavian countries, which are ruled by moderate Socialists. What was bad in Soviet Russia sprang from the nihilist mentality, from the outrageous and prolonged usage of the ideas which first in Russia came to birth in the mind of Nechayev.

"In a few years," said Lenin in 1917, "perhaps ten years, perhaps twenty, the state will wither away. There will be no need for these monstrously destructive engines. Men will be free to do as they please, and the state will transform itself merely into a small office dealing with the means of production." It had not happened as he foretold. The state was as far as ever away from "withering away"; it had become the embodiment of the terror. As long as the dictatorship continues, the terror must remain; for no man may hold undisputed power without terror, and the cynicism of Stalin is no less than Hitler's. It is Hitler who said, "The closer I become acquainted with physical terror, the more I asked forgiveness from the hundreds of thousands who succumb to it." [10] But it was Stalin who said, at the height of the massacres, repeating a phrase of Stavrogin's: "Do not let us be dizzy with success."

[10] *Mein Kampf*, p. 59.

IX.
The Task Before Us

IMAGINE that somewhere in the world the Nechayev monster exists. There is no need to describe him. The great Russian philosopher, Vladimir Soloviev, has already described him. The Antichrist "does not look like what he is," and therein lies the danger. He is a small man, slender and elegant, possessed of a fierce passion which no one suspects, an ascetic and a vegetarian; he wins fame by a book where he curiously mingles respect for the ancient virtues and absolute individualism, and he may have a small mustache. He goes blind for a while, and then in his thirty-third year he sets out on his mission to enslave and destroy the world. So Soloviev had described him, and every detail of Soloviev's prophecy came true in 1933.[1] It was one of the most remarkable prophecies ever made, but we need not dwell on prophecy. We can imagine the Nechayev monster of our own age as a man who completely conceals his nihilistic rage. There is no need for him to write a book, no need for him to put himself at the head of huge armies and conquer Europe and Africa first, and then lay siege to the whole world, like Soloviev's Antichrist, and there is even less need for him to hate the Jews. He can

[1] V. V. Soloviev's prophecy on the coming of Antichrist appears in his *Three Conversations*, published in Russia in 1899. A French translation by Eugène Tavernier appeared in 1916.

simply hate all men, and conceal his hatred, and determine to make an end to them. For a long while his rage may lie dormant, and then one day, suffering from a headache brought on by a bruised finger, he may say like the skeptic David Hume, "It is not contrary to reason to prefer the destruction of the whole world to the scratching of my finger." It does not take long for him to think of ways of accomplishing his purpose; we live in an age which offers the nihilist all the weapons he could desire. He reads a few books in the libraries, and decides to poison the wells. He takes *psittacosis* bacteria, or some other easily manufactured death-dealing bacteria, in a small handbag, and sets out to poison the reservoirs in all the great capitals of the world. He may even find simpler ways of destroying even more people. He works quietly and methodically; no one recognizes this harmless looking stranger who travels by air on a round ticket across the world; if there are any suspicions he can easily evade them. When the destruction is accomplished, it may please him to take over the government of the world, but it might be simpler, or more amusing, simply to watch the world becoming more chaotic. Terrified, caught up in the wave of fear, everyone distrusting everyone else, the people murder each other. The nihilist looks on. "Mass murder pleases me," he may say. "There is something very artistic in watching the experiment come to fruition: they behave exactly as I thought they would. It is astonishing how nimbly they play." He may recall Nero at the burning of Rome. A friend came up to Nero and laughed, "When I am dead, let fire devour the world." Nero answered, "No, my dear fellow, this is not the point at all—let it be while I am living." "What a fool," the nihilist says. "Nero *would* talk about it. Myself, I am quite silent." He lets the people struggle in the grip of their fears for a little while longer. "What fools they are! They never suspected me for a moment. The customs officer at Batavia should have recognized what I had in my baggage. I even told him what I had there. I said, '*Psittacosis* bacteria,' and he only laughed. We had a drink together." He remembers that executions mostly take place at dawn or dusk, because men look more inhuman in the half-light and it is easier to kill them, and he feels that it would be amusing to preserve, at this last moment of the earth's history, one of the antiquated conventions. "I will pull the switch at dusk. They don't know—poor fools—that I have ordered the whole city to be undermined with hydrogen bombs. Oh, they were slaves—just the kind of slaves I wanted. I ordered them to put the hydrogen bombs there, and they did exactly as they were told; no one even thought of removing the fuses, because they were all so afraid of me and of each other. Poor earth! It never did leave much mark on the solar system, and now it will leave less." He dreams for a while over a cigar and whiskey, remembering the more delightful things. "If I had lived, I would have created a legend," he says. "How they fought in the sewers—oh, that was the best of all." A sudden impulse to breathe clean air comes over him. He goes out in the streets of the dead city, breathes deeply and having enjoyed the sunset, he calmly returns to the room, and in the act of taking poison, he pulls the switch. "After all," he murmurs, "it would be absurd if I survived all this."

We have seen in our own age the rage of the Nechayev monster, and if he seems to us even now to be preposterous and incoherent, we forget the underlying logic beneath. We say that Hitler was mad, and in every human sense what we say is true; but no one ever suggested that the Scotch philosopher David Hume was mad. Hume described himself quite accurately when he wrote, "I am a man of mild disposition, of command of temper, of an open, social and cheerful humor, capable of attachment, but little susceptible to enmity, and of great moderation in all my passions. My company was not unacceptable to the young and careless, and I took a particular pleasure in the company of modest women. In a word, my friends never had occasion to vindicate any one circumstance of my character and conduct; not but that the zealots, we may well believe, would have been glad to invent and propagate any story to my disadvantage, but they could never find any which they thought would wear the face of probability." Yet, by insisting on the primacy of the passions, he opened the flood-gates and prepared the ground for nihilism in the modern age.

The Nechayev rage, then, may be deliberate and calm, or at least disguised by a superficial calmness. When Descartes spoke of "the disembodied will," he was inventing a new category which already possessed a long history, going back to "the will which moves itself" (*movet se ipsum*) of St. Thomas Aquinas, and to Duns Scotus; and no one could have predicted how this self-generating will would have become the basic assumption of the Romantic philosophers, and nearly everyone forgot that this self-generating will was exactly the same thing as the insolence which the Greek tragedians regarded as the cause of all errors, to be punished unmercifully by Nemesis. "You should put out insolence even more than a fire," wrote Heraclitus. Nearly two thousand years later Descartes stated his celebrated theorem, "In a certain sense the disembodied will may be regarded as infinite." Honest John Locke replied, "There is no such thing as the disembodied will; there is only the human will, and none other." But the disembodied will survived; Hitler found it in himself, and in the crowd.

When nihilism came out of the philosopher's study, it

cracked the world wide open. From that moment on, there could only be the confused war between humanity and the will, between the real and the abstract. With the industrial revolution, abstractions were beginning to win. It seems unlikely that they can be permanently defeated, though they can be held at bay. "There has been," said Coleridge, in another connection, "in some sense, a Fall." Men fell from grace when they left human values behind, and perhaps the schismatics were justified when they held to the old faiths, afraid of the new monster of change which crept over the horizon, but they fell into the same pit they imagined God was constructing for their enemies, when they called out for an inhuman revenge.

The great tragedy of our time is that mechanization cannot any longer be prevented; we become more mechanical as the machine eats into our lives. We obey the impersonal voices of the radio, we arrange our lives in accordance with a vast network of mechanical forces which no one can any longer control with perfect accuracy, and we are at the mercy of the huge abstractions which, the newspapers assure us, demand war, demand peace, declare this, that, and the other. We forget continually—such is the force of these abstractions—that there is not and cannot be any tangible thing called "Soviet Russia" or "the United States": these abstractions represent vast and unimaginable complexes of history, complex organizations of people, and industry, and soil, and love, and welfare, and hate, and death, and they are assuredly more unreal, because more incomprehensible, than the Nechayev monster. We have seen the Nechayev monsters, touched their hands, heard them speak; they at least are recognizable and familiar elements. What is strange is that we are always forgetting his perpetual presence.

There is a sense too in which the Nechayev monster repre-

ZERO

sents precisely those mechanical forces which now dominate our lives. He is the mechanical instrument who is indifferent to human lives, presiding at every car smash. He is the robot who revolts, because there is nothing left for him to do. He is the man in the leather jacket who met the Czech students as they marched up to the Hradschin Castle with waving flags, proclaiming that they wanted a state founded upon human freedom, but the vast mechanical forces represented by the man in the leather jacket were sufficient to dissuade them from marching further; they surrendered before a symbol. The Nechayev monster is the enemy of human freedom everywhere, though he declares that he destroys for the sake of freedom. The symbol of our age is not the man in the leather jacket, nor the scientist planning the destruction of remote cities, but the drunken chauffeur gazing straight in front of him, hypnotized by the horse-power at his command, unconcerned whether he is going in the right direction and hardly caring as long as he races at vertiginous speed, contemptuous of everyone else on the road, and unconvinced of the reality of the world he sees through the windshield; at a moment of boredom he presses down on the accelerator and drives into a wall. Fundamentally, the Nechayev monster is no more than personified irresponsibility, and his nihilism, like Hume's scepticism, is only irresponsibility pushed to its logical conclusion. We have spoken of the rights and duties of man; we have not yet spoken of his fields of responsibility. But it is our sense of responsibility which distinguishes us from the beasts.

Nihilism, then, is not an isolated phenomenon; it is the final expression, so far, of tendencies that have for a long time been growing stronger. These tendencies are still at work. We can oppose them in a relentlessly mechanical age only at our peril, but it is a peril that must be accepted. The doom waits. More fatal than bombs, more incorrigible than enemy weapons is the haggard man who *for no reason* is prepared to plan the destruction of the world, and it is not in the least necessary to suppose that the nihilist of the future will enjoy his nihilism any more than he has enjoyed it in the past; he will behave like this because he considers it his duty to behave in this way.

The Nechayev monster is part of our civilization. We have inherited him from the romantic past, and sometimes he may come about as the result of a flaw in the culture. He does not have to be an evil man; he may be, and often is, a man caught up in a cultural pattern where all the forces making for loyalty are condemned. He need not be insolent or unfeeling; it is simply that he has gone beyond the limits of human values, and lives in a nagging and empty world of his own. There is something eternal in him; he is always there, waiting until he can see the crack in a culture, and then he pries the crack wide-open. Baudelaire in his poem *The Seven Old Men* speaks of coming upon seven bent and evil-eyed ruffians plunging through a foul yellow fog in Paris; they had the look of men hostile to life, and Baudelaire went home to lock himself in his room, half-mad from the vision he had seen, "for they had the look of eternal beings." But it is not necessary that the men who are hostile to life should look like eternal beings; it is enough that they exist, and not all of them are in insane asylums. There is nothing in the least monstrous in the appearance of the Nechayev monster, and there is no way of detecting him.

Our hopes for survival depend upon being able to confront him on all levels, though he is invisible. We cannot spurn him. We cannot proscribe him by law, because he is indifferent to the law, or fight him with military weapons, because he has stronger weapons. He lives perhaps—for no one can precisely define his desires—for hidden power, for the sense of mastery rather than for mastery itself. He does not need to have the dictator's mania for public displays. Like Manasevich-Manuilov, like Richelieu's *éminence grise*, he prefers the shadows, and he is only happy in that shadowland where dreams, desires, and actions fuse together into nightmare. If he goes beyond the boundaries of good and evil, it is only because the landscape there is more interesting, more appetising; he has the mentality of the gangster at bay, but he is not a gangster, and commits no evil except the long-planned ultimate evil, and it may very easily happen that he will commit this evil "with the certainty of a sleep-walker," not knowing what he is doing, and therefore *unable* to care. He shadows us always; he tests the validity of our civilizations; he is entirely without fear.

In a sense we cannot oppose him even if we remembered his existence, and before the astonishing spectacle of destruction, as before the astonishing spectacle of our own inevitable deaths, we are only too apt not to remember. We pretend to ourselves that the laws will take care of him, or the powers he possesses are too small, but it is not enough to shrug our shoulders and say that he only exists in Russia, or that the police are everywhere, or that weapons of destruction are safely guarded by military guards. His name is legion. There is a Nechayev monster in everyone, not a large one, but one that might be sufficiently destructive if he ever received absolute power. We are all confused; the Nechayev monster feeds on confusion. He is inhuman, but we are often inhuman. There is in him something of the automaton, but in this mechanical age, there is something of the automaton in all of us. He does not care deeply for the lives of others, but who *does* care deeply for the lives of others? Wherever men are weakest, the Nechayev monster has the advantage of us, and at a time when the majority of men are prepared to dismiss Satan and Hell as childish heresies, Satan returns disguised as a nihilist, with power to freeze us at a glance, and Hell is only the perpetual revolution of destruction, brought about perhaps by nothing more significant than a bruised finger or a fit of spite against a Jew in Vienna; or brought about for no reason at all.

We live in an apocalyptic age. The huge figures of Satan and Hell dominate us all; we have felt Satan's breath on our necks, and already and always the flames are being lit. We cannot put out the fire. We can only guard against the flames, erect stone walls, cut down the dead wood that lets the fire spread, and beyond this we can only hope and pray. But how do we guard against Satan and Hell when they are already in ourselves?

Because Satan and Hell are so close to us, we have every reason to fear. Wherever there is nihilism there is danger of sudden death. Wherever we forget to fear, there is danger that the nihilist will enter the gates. It is almost as though wherever there is emptiness in ourselves, he is sucked in, and then the rot spreads. To say that he is unreal, that he is a phantom of our minds, is only to play into his hands. In a sense the nihilist *is* a product of our imaginations, but there are primitive tribes who fear imaginary tigers more than they fear real ones, and they have reason on their side. The Jesuit Father Dobrizhofer speaks of coming upon the tribe of the Abipones in South America. He went into their village. Someone pointed to an empty place in the center of the village, saying: "The Tiger is here." "What kind of tiger?" Father Dobrizhofer asked. "The real Tiger—the Tiger who terrifies," they answered. "How is it," the Jesuit asked, "that you should fear this imaginary Tiger when you daily hunt real tigers in the plain?" The Abipones answered: "You don't understand. We have no fear of the tigers in the plain because we kill them, because we can see them. But this imaginary tiger we do fear; we cannot see him, and we cannot kill him."

ZERO

Father Dobrizhofer went away, shaking his head. It was extraordinary; they trembled when they came to this empty place in the village. Why? But the Abipones were entitled to their fear, for the same reason that the learned Jesuit was entitled to be afraid of Satan. The empty horror in the center of the village, to be placated, to be listened to, to be understood and feared, sounds very familiar in the age of the Nechayev monsters, for the invisible horror is always more terrifying than the tangible horror, the unknown more remorseless than the known. Today, in every market-place, the unknown waits, and the knife is poised. Faced with the complexities of a mechanical civilization too intricate for any one's understanding, fascinated by the power generated in modern machines, there are already thousands of people who consciously or unconsciously are prepared to pull the switch, caring nothing at all for the consequences.

Recently a man in Canada desired to kill his wife. He sent her on a short air-journey, and arranged that his mistress should take a small package to the airplane just before it left. The package contained a time bomb, and the airplane exploded, killing everyone aboard. The man had desired to kill his wife, and he did not care in the least that twenty-two other people would also be killed, and it is conceivable that he would have cared just as little if millions of people had been killed. He did not know the names of the twenty-two people; he had never met them; had no reason to dislike them; might even have been sorry that it was necessary for them to die. In the same month, in the city of Camden, N.J., a young American-German, who brooded over religion, and collected firearms, decided that he was mortally sick of asking a Jew's permission to take a short cut across an empty lot. He decided to kill the Jew, and his whole family. He simply walked out of his house, shot the Jew and then proceeded to kill twelve other people, including a child who was staring out of the window. He withdrew to his house, surrendering quietly when the house was surrounded. Asked why he had murdered so many people in twelve minutes, the arrested man, whose name was Unruh,[2] said: "I've got a good brain." It was a characteristic answer, for murder and spiritual pride are close to one another, Nechayev's pride was intense, and in *The Possessed* Dostoyevsky has drawn the portrait of the proud murderer who thinks nothing of destroying the whole world.

These are not occasional examples. Such things are happening all the time; and in the armed forces, where men are trained to murder, the nihilists are perhaps more frequent than elsewhere. Nihilism is endemic. Acts of nihilistic fury are frequently followed by similar acts performed by those against whom the nihilist first raged. In December 1944, the Germans massacred one hundred and sixty American soldiers at Malmédy. They were lined up in a snow-covered field, eight deep and twenty abreast, and raked by machine-gun fire for three minutes. In 1946, at Dachau, seventy-three Germans were placed on trial by the American Army for their responsibility in the massacre. All were found guilty. But in order to find them guilty the Americans had employed precisely the same methods of terrorism, deceit, relentless cruelty, and fraud which the Germans had employed as their chief weapon throughout the war. According to Willis Meade Everett Jr., the prosecution teams, to extort confessions, "had kept the German defendants in dark, solitary confinement at near starvation rations up to six months; had applied various forms of torture, including the driving of burning matches under the

---

[2] The name means "unrest"; it was used in the sense of "spiritual unrest" by the Romantic novelists. Nechayev's name appears to come from the Russian: *nyet*, meaning "not," that is, he was "the one who denies."

prisoners' fingernails; had administered beatings which resulted in broken jaws and arms, and permanently injured testicles." The imitation of German methods did not end there. False confessions were obtained by mock trials, at which "the plaintiff would see before him a long table with candles burning at both ends, and a crucifix in the centre. At the other end of the table would be the prosecutor, who would read the charges, yell and scream at these eighteen- and twenty-year-old plantiffs, and attempt to force confessions from them."[3] Those who were responsible for these crimes against justice were never punished, though, as a result of Willis Meade Everett's discoveries, the death sentences on the captured Germans were commuted to imprisonment for life. The danger lies here; nihilism breeds nihilism, terror breeds terror. Once the wheel has been brought into motion, nothing is more difficult than to bring it back to a standstill—that mad, steel-glittering wheel of destruction that hovers over everyone like the threat of some primal chaos brought back to earth. This wheel is dangerous enough, but there is a point where it becomes most dangerous. This is when the wheel, running faster than anyone can control it, splits and scatters its shrapnel haphazard on all those who are within its field of destruction, and even beyond. It is at this point that words like "the Nechayev monster," "the destruction of the world," "the traffic desert," and "absolute terror" cease from being abstractions on the printed page; they become things we have to contend with every day of our lives.

How can these things be prevented?

If civilization is to survive, all that which affects our essential humanity is due for immediate, urgent re-consideration.

[3] *Time*, January 17, 1949.

THE TASK BEFORE US

We can no longer afford to experiment with our social systems without inquiring into fundamentals; and first of all it is necessary to inquire into the nature of man, what aims are proposed to him, what rights and duties are his, and what precisely is his relation to the state. At the present time no government has stated these rights and duties without equivocation, and nearly every government has accepted, or half-accepted, Hegel's dicta that "the state exists in its own right" and "the function of the true state is so to act that individuals do not exist." But it should be realized that in all these things the state, as State, is pursuing the same ends as the Nechayev monster; by treating men as numbers, cogs in a bureaucratic machine, the State inevitably comes to "destroy" men as human beings, and in the minds of their rulers men no longer possess the primacy which now belongs to the State. Hegel developed the nihilist thesis; Kant countered with the more human thesis that "the function of the true state is to impose the *minimum* restrictions and safeguard the *maximum* liberties of the people, and it must never regard the person as a thing." For Kant the State was not "a thing in itself" and possessed no other validity except that which it acquires as the representative of the popular will. For Hegel man "disappears into the state." For Kant, "the state is formed for man, and the state must obey his wishes." No two views could be more dissimilar. In general, to oppose nihilism, we must reverse all the judgments of the nihilists. The nihilist pursues *his* judgment of man to its logical conclusions—wanton violence, destructiveness, the prison camp; the anti-nihilist must pursue his judgment of man to its logical conclusions—mercifulness, creativeness, freedom. The nihilists rage against man, they are contemptuous of man, they hold that he is no more than an instrument to be shaped, something that "disappears into the state," something to be plundered or destroyed at will. His aim is the annihilation of man. Our aim should be to give each man an infinite valuation, to pay the highest honors to men, to elevate and celebrate men.

The consequences of the new doctrine inevitably follow:

1. MEN ARE INVIOLABLE, AND HUMAN LIVES ARE SACRED.

The statement must be read to mean exactly what it says. The nihilist places no value on human life; we must place the highest conceivable value. By this ruling, human life is sacrosanct, to be regarded as a trust in the sacred possession of the man himself, never to be deliberately bruised, to be cared for patiently and humbly as long as life exists. In the great Confucian phrase, "not a hair of the head may be touched."

There can be no exceptions to this, and the more exceptions we make, the more nearly we approach to the doctrine of the Nechayev monster. The life of the murderer, even the life of the Nechayev monster must be spared; for there are other ways of punishing him than by putting out his life. *Under no circumstances* may men be condemned to death, or tortured, or deliberately placed in peril. Men may place themselves in danger of their own accord; they may not be placed in danger by others. It must be recognized that the value of human life is so inconceivably great that anything which tends toward debasing this value must be destroyed, and since the nature of man is to be creative, anything that tends towards limiting his creativeness must also be destroyed. Since all men equally are inviolable, and all are sacred, and all are possessed of infinite potentialities of creativeness, no distinction may be made between the races.

This is not of course in any way a new doctrine, though it has a new application in our time, when we are no longer necessarily faced with theological Satans and theological

Hells; more immediate Satans and more immediate Hells are nearby. Satan is not now an invisible ghost; he is a very real personage, and possesses illimitable powers of destruction and the technique to destroy. Today, we are faced with the very desperate situation in which men find themselves when confronted with the Nechayev monster.

The doctrine of the sanctity and inviolability of human life was announced long ago by the mediaeval Church, and hinted at by the Greeks. "Man is the measure of all things," said Anaximander, and the great chorus of Sophocles, in the *Antigone*, only emphasizes man's prodigious place in the universe: "Most wonderful of all is man." Gregory Palamas, from his throne in Byzantium, followed the pagan tradition, though he was himself a Byzantine bishop, when he wrote, "There is nothing higher than man." According to the mediaeval theologians, men were even higher than the angels, since men could become saints, and it was impossible for an angel to accomplish miracles. The *miraculousness* of man is the theme of many mediaeval sermons; it was realized over long periods that the reverence paid to man's powers could subtract nothing from the reverence paid to God, since God included man, and Christ became man, because, says St. Aquinas, "it was fit for God to take on the dignity of man." The Benedictine Mass states specifically that Christ died that "the dignity of man may be increased." The respect for human dignity was encouraged by the Church, and Pico della Mirandola, the most humane of humanists, did not say anything contrary to the teaching of the Church or to his friendship with Savonarola when he declared that "God created man neither mortal nor immortal, neither heavenly nor earthly, only that he might be free to shape and overcome himself," and went on to suggest that "he who is a seraph, that is, a lover, is in God; and more, God is in him, and God and he are one." The renaissance princes celebrated life magnificently; they developed the codes of honor which gave increasing dignity to man, and they failed to regard human life as inviolable only because there survived, from the dark ages, a barbarous code of war. War was not necessary to them; it was a kind of terrible game played for the stakes of greater honor. "As I grow older," said Petrarch, "I see that men at war are all claws; they have not the nobility of a man at peace with himself."

The German philosophers, helpless within the stranglehold of categories, sought "the real," and found it in barren concepts: the ego, the state, necessity, will, and dream. None of these ideas contained the real, but all of them indicated their own frustrations. Meanwhile "the real" was all around them. The real is that which is most living—all that we mean by the magnificence of life.

So it is that there is only one evil—death, and it is in the landscape of this evil that the nihilist has his home. He knows death well; he knows nothing else. What is terrible is that the nihilist allies himself with death, takes on the colors of death and disease, and sees himself as the anonymous assassin, a destructive germ or a devouring flame; and against all that is creative and positive in life, he sets his mask-like face. He knows that every murder, every killing, every way in which men are wounded or hurt or spoiled is utterly senseless; and just as he allies himself with death, so he allies himself with senselessness, for they are the same thing. He deliberately neglects or rejects human power, and human glory, and he forgets or refuses to acknowledge that everything that glorifies men glorifies God as well.

It was the custom until recently to regard Gandhi as a crude agitator, and an irresponsible pacifist, whose doctrine of *ahimsa* (non-violence towards living beings) was impractical and absurd. When he debated with his disciples whether the diseased silk-worms of Nepal should be killed to protect the mulberry trees, or the mulberry trees killed to protect the silk-worms, and suggested finally that the silk-worms must be carefully collected and taken to some other place where they could live out their lives in peace; or when he suggested that a notorious murderer should be pardoned, for pardon would be more than a sufficient punishment; or when he shared his bed with his young grand-daughter, it was suggested that he was patently insane; and even now, though he is given all the honors due to a saint, he is regarded as a man who played a political game according to the purely Indian way, which can have no relevance to the West. On the contrary, everything he said has the utmost, the closest relevance to the West. He behaved at nearly all times out of a deep respect for the humanness of humanity, and his whole philosophy was based upon that respect for human beings which saw no difference between races, and which prized children more than adults, because "they possess more life." Gandhi stated his position plainly in one of his sermons. "Let me tell you why I return again and again to the *Bhagavad Gita*. You say Prince Arjuna is a soldier, and I myself practice non-violence. I do not say there should be no soldiers; I merely work for a time when murder shall not be permitted. For me Prince Arjuna is the personification of the man who strives to face the terrors of the world. He does not stand and pray only. He acts, and every action is dictated by his feeling for the goodness in men, in all men. We cannot only pray when the poor die at our doors, naked, and hungry. People are so god-like—that is why we must act for them. It is all there in the *Bhagavad Gita*." Gandhi was perhaps saying no more than the poet, Rainer Maria Rilke, who, as he lay dying of leukaemia, his blood turning to powder and his mouth black with boils, whispered, "Never forget, dear one, life is magnificent."

ZERO

Since life is magnificent, the function of men is to celebrate men, for magnificence at all times demands to be celebrated. Men must celebrate men, and the nature of man, taking an infinite pride in themselves as men, and most particularly as whole men. There is a story told by Thucydides of the Athenians who once overpowered a tribe in the Peloponnesus which had injured them greatly, and when they had the enemy army herded on the beach, naked for slaughter, they forgave them and set them free with the words, "This was not done because they were men, but because of the nature of man." Thucydides meant that it was because the nature of man is to be so god-like that they were set free. A very similar story is told in the *Talmud*, where the account of the Egyptians drowning in the Red Sea is related as it is related in the Bible, but with a very different ending. Meriam sings her song of triumph, and the song is taken up by the angels. Then God's voice is heard thundering from heaven as he orders the singing to cease, "My children are drowning," he says, "and ye would rejoice!" We must learn—it may be very difficult, but we must still learn—to rejoice in being human beings.

The Fascists and nihilist-Communists offer men the supreme excitement of playing with death; we must offer men more mature excitement, and more particularly the excitement which comes from rejoicing in themselves. We must dramatize our freedom, proclaim the new century of freedom, give proper names to the things we believe in—we should, for example, change the names of nations, and call America and all freedom-loving countries by names which are charged with meaning. Psychologically, the Soviets were right to change the name of Russia to the Union of Socialist Soviet Republics. Similarly, we should call America the Free United States of America, and so throw down the gauntlet. The Soviets were right, too, when they invented the Five-Year Plan. We should do likewise; we need to make the constructive work of the world and of individuals more exciting, and a plan at least suggests that there are deliberate aims in view, and all men are called upon to help the plan. We must dramatize freedom and the powers of the individual in a freedom-loving state, just as the Soviets dramatize tyranny. There must be far greater incentives to serve the community honestly and humbly. We need to work to destroy poverty, naming the enemy. A huge propaganda campaign should be instituted to show that poverty is as great a disease as cancer, and kills far more people; that every man deserves a good house, and sufficient remuneration if he works well; that every child should, if he makes the grade, be allowed to go to college. We have not done enough to make our commonplace freedoms exciting, though they would be exciting enough to the slaves who live behind the Iron Curtain; and we have not yet done enough to extirpate tyranny among ourselves. All the resources of propaganda, the radio, and the films should be used to give men aims worth living for. A one-year plan against poverty would have striking results in America; the whole population might be urged to destroy the evil, and they could be shown how poisonous it is; and in the next year there might be a campaign to bring about good housing; and in the third year there might be a campaign to increase the level of education. Or all these campaigns might be instituted simultaneously. What is needed is a concerted effort in which the whole nation is engaged; a war against all the evils among us, a new wave of enthusiasm inspired by the state. By such creative enthusiasms the Nechayev monsters can be held at bay indefinitely.

And all the time it is necessary to protest against corruption and injustice and the pain men inflict on men—it is even terribly dangerous not to protest. Occasionally it happened in the concentration camps that men had the strength to protest, but

ZERO

it is possible to read fifty accounts of the prison-camps without coming upon any protest, any attempt to rush the guards, any opposition: the evil of acceptance, the feeling that since nothing can be done, nothing will ever be done, lies very close to imprisoned men: fatalism takes the place of courage, and fatalism itself offers hostages to the torturers. In Odd Nansen's remarkable diary of his years in a German camp called *From Day to Day*, he describes only one protest against an execution, and it is significant that the man who protested was a Dutch Bible-searcher who shouted out with all the strength of his lungs that it was vile to hang an innocent Ukrainian boy. We must remember that it is only recently, within the lives of many now living, that the zero-judgment on human life has become a commonplace. There was a time not so long ago when people did not die like flies on the roads, when even the terrorists thought twice before killing women and children. When Kaliayev was preparing to throw a bomb at the Grand Duke Serge in 1905, he saw that the Grand-Duchess and her children were also riding in the carriage, and therefore withheld his bomb. He succeeded in killing the Grand Duke two days later, but he had shown that the absolute methods of Nechayev were entirely unnecessary even for the purpose of revolution. None of his comrades accused him of weakness. On the contrary, they accused him of possessing great strength. What is necessary is that we should never forget, never be indifferent to the human splendor; we must spare what can be spared. Looking back on his experiences in the concentration camps, Odd Nansen observed that it was the indifference of mankind which allowed these things to take place.[4] We need to view life afresh, as something positive, of infinite value, sacred and inviolable and splendid at all

---
[4] Odd Nansen, *From Day to Day*, New York, 1949, p. 485.

times; and all must be protected, and all must be assured of fellowship with their brethren. As long as this fellowship endures, we are safe from the concentration camps.

2. THE TRUE FUNCTION OF THE STATE IS TO CELEBRATE THE NATURE OF MAN.

This, too, must be read to mean exactly what it says. Kant's definition of the state as a body of elected men whose duty it is "to impose the minimum restrictions and safeguard the maximum liberties of the people, never regarding the person as a thing" is a negative definition, and places on the state no other obligation than to protect men, as though the state was essentially the policeman defending their liberties. But though this must remain one of the cardinal attributes of the state, the state itself must also be a positive and regenerative; from the state there should come the creative impulses in which all men can share.

There is nothing essentially new in this judgment of the state. There have been states in the past which were themselves the center of vast creative impulses in the arts. The Fujiwara epoch in Japan, the Gupta epoch in India, and the Tang epoch in China shared a belief in the creativeness of the people; they assisted the creativeness of the people and brought to birth great monuments, innumerable poets, and painters. The bureaucracy was secondary to the artistic achievement; the aim of the bureaucracy was not to thwart the people, or "milk" them, but to generate within them artistic passions. This was not true at all times during these periods, but at intervals, over many years, the state encouraged the arts, and saw itself as a reflection of artistic achievement. In Elizabethan England, in the Florence of Lorenzo the Magnificent, the state was an instrument for artistic creation, and in them the arts possessed a primacy which has since been lost.

ZERO

At these ages the state was a *human* thing; it had not yet become lost in a cloud of abstractions. The state celebrated the nature of man, its energies bent towards a perpetual celebration, with the result that there were continual processions, festivals and tournaments; and works of great art were accomplished on a scale which now takes our breath away.

Nearly all these states were ruled by feudal princes, who possessed together with wealth, a sense of human values, and human splendors. The state must, by its very nature, take the equivalent part of these feudal princes. Instead of becoming merely a bureaucratic machine, it must deliberately set itself towards ennobling man. It follows that the greatest rewards must be offered to those who celebrate man's humanity, and the greatest punishments must be reserved for those who commit crimes against man's humanity. Inventors, artists, poets, teachers, and social workers must be encouraged by the state and fully rewarded, while the editors of newspapers which pander to human vulgarity, the creators of vulgar films, the builders who build bad houses, the party politicians and ward-heelers who are continually debasing men by false promises, these must be punished severely; and the test of a good law must be whether it can effect an increase in human dignity.

There remains the categorical imperative, applicable to the state as to men, "Be human and be gentle." Hardly anything else can be so important. The value of theories of state vanishes in these perspectives; theories there must be, but all must be rooted in human aims, human pursuits. The heart of the matter lies here, and it is known to everyone, and no one is immune from his own humanity. What is needed is a conception of the state which takes into account the human conceptions of love, and marriage, and children, and birth, and death, and ennobles them, pays particular attention to them, gently assists them; a state where terror can have no place.

THE TASK BEFORE US

But this attitude towards the state means that the state must assume responsibility for the poor, the sick, the outcast. We are faced with the necessity of putting an end to squalor, poverty and misery, not only for the most elementary moral reasons, but because the disease which produces the Nechayev monster springs from poverty. It is in poverty and misery that the Nechayev monster begins to condemn the world which has condemned him—it is important to realize that Hitler would never have come to power if he had not possessed the rage for power which came as a result of the six years he spent starving in Vienna, and Nechayev would never have written *The Revolutionary Catechism* if he had not been born into serfdom. Men have many rights, but among them there is not included the right to starve.

It follows, also, that the fiction of the sovereign right of the state must be abandoned. The only sovereignty lies in the individual in relation to the judgment of the whole world. The individual, therefore, must be enabled to appeal against the decisions of the state. There can be no real justice if he cannot appeal beyond his own frontiers. His own basic human rights remain in danger as long as there is no Court of Rights to which he can appeal; and just as nations appeal to an international court, so ought men be allowed to appeal, and with the same sense of security. And above a certain degree of punishment, such an appeal should become mandatory.

The state must wage a bitter war against corruption of all kinds, for there lies the beginning of nihilism. The advertisers who corrupt radio audiences with gifts are neither better nor worse than the party hacks who corrupt their constituencies. The crisis of our era is essentially a moral crisis; every hint of corruption therefore makes the crisis more difficult to solve. There are also hidden forms of corruption which must be rooted out, and the bureaucracy itself, as long as it deals with men as though they are figures, is mortally corrupt. The bureaucracy, therefore, must be humanized, and the bureaucrat must continually be made to realize that he is the servant of the people, not their master. Insolent bureaucracy must not go unpunished, and absolute power must never be given to single individuals; for corruption lies in the temper of the powerful man, who gradually assumes the habit of regarding all men as his simple instruments. The edicts of statesmen must be tested for their humanness. There should be created a special department of state, called perhaps the Department of the Humanities, which will constantly watch the administration of the laws, to see that they are administered humanly. Today, not only because we choose to, but because we are in peril, we must celebrate the human aspect of the laws. This obligation is so absolute that I would have thought that some such department as the one suggested here would already have been introduced. Nor is this a new invention, for similar powers were granted to the ancient Chinese censors.

Since humanness is to be sought above all things, the state must encourage and perhaps enforce vast changes in the present administration of education. Mechanical tests for students must be abandoned; selenium cells and business machines are entirely incapable of evaluating the worth of a student, or even his knowledge. A test for maturity and capacity for growth is needed. Students should be encouraged to travel widely, and to mix widely. In the United States, for example, no student should be allowed to possess a degree until he has lived for some considerable period either in a foreign country or in a state remote from his own. A student of music should be encouraged to live among lumberjacks; a student of theology should stalk game with hunters; a science student should live for a while among a colony of painters. These are not, of course, examples to be followed to the letter. Similarly, stu-

THE TASK BEFORE US

dents must be encouraged to mix with other races, and it should be impossible for any kind of segregation to exist in universities and colleges. In all these matters the responsibility of the state and of the teachers is greater than it has ever been, for the revealed power of the Nechayev monster is in inverse proportion to the sturdy intelligence of those he desires to exploit. And in the schools, the code of humanness must be taught, and there especially it must be remembered that the great vacuum of nihilism feeds on paucity of bread, but it also feeds on paucity of spirit. Both Hitler and Stalin have resurrected the great compulsive dream-like figures of ancient military heroes; for a generation which has to fight nihilism, these heroes offer little profit, for most of them were themselves irresponsible leaders of men. The young should be reminded of those who maintained their sense of responsibility to the end. They should be taught that civilization owes most to its artists, and among artists can be found men of such widely differing talents as Mozart, Beethoven, Lincoln, Schweitzer, Kierkegaard, Whitman, and Van Gogh.

The state is faced in its colonies or mandated territories with all the dangers of becoming itself corrupt, inhuman, and bureaucratic. British rule in India was not on the whole corrupt; it was, however, inhuman, and Indian society disintegrated under British rule. Military government is rarely human, and therefore the military government of mandated territories must cease, and, except in very rare cases, the inhabitants of the mandated territories must have the power to appeal against the administration.

The state must give equal rights to women; and children must also be represented in government, for it is the grossest inhumanity that they should be deprived of a voice in the management of the state. In the last war innumerable soldiers fought although they were too young to vote. Women and children are the natural enemies of the Nechayev monster, for they possess a sense of humanness which men lose only too easily. Though there are occasional exceptions to the rule, women commit far fewer crimes than men, are far less vindictive, and are more concerned with the survival of their children than men. It is significant that as early as 1922 the National Socialist party issued an order that on no account would women ever be admitted into the higher offices of the party. All the arguments that can be brought against women in government fail when confronted with the extraordinary fact that aggressiveness and bureaucratic efficiency are largely male qualities; and in the current sense an "efficient" bureaucracy is not what is needed. What is needed is simply a bureaucracy that can speak in human terms. Women have so far failed to assume their responsibilities in government, and for this reason they are guilty of not exercising the authority and responsibility that is rightly theirs.

Above all, the state must abjure the methods of terror; it dare not tolerate third-degree punishment, or any kind of physical punishment whatsoever. Our hopes for survival depend upon being capable of confronting terror at all levels; and we cannot use these mechanical weapons for fear that they will overpower us. We must be able to discern in our civilization all those elements which make for terror. We can resist terror only when we can recognize it for what it is—a despicable trick, a game of mirrors, continually attempting to distort the humanity of people. The main weapon of terror is dehumanization; it feeds on secrecy, ridicule, threats and rumors; it dare never show itself in the daylight, for then it would be seen to be so contemptible and so offensive to human dignity that it would be abolished by the awakened fury of healthy individuals. And even in the war against nihilism, we dare not use nihilist weapons.

THE TASK BEFORE US

Meanwhile, we have to face the possibility that there will be another war, and that in this war there will be the same senseless massacres, the same pathetic belief in the powers of the nihilists to create a new world, the same torture chambers, the same use of incinerators, and the same mass graves. To avoid this war every conceivable kind of psychological and social preparation is necessary, and the attack must be taken into the enemy camp:

3. THERE MUST BE WAR TO THE DEATH AGAINST NIHILISM, AGAINST ALL THE OFFICIAL AND UNOFFICIAL POWERS WHICH DEGRADE MEN.

This does not in the least mean that we must immediately launch an attack on Russia, or even that we should fight with physical weapons. It does mean that we must make a sharp differentiation between those parts of the communist experiment which represent social progress, and those parts which represent *The Revolutionary Catechism*. The use by the Soviet Government of a vast and powerful secret police, its inhuman punishments, and its relentless system of organizing men's lives must be answered by the offer of increasing liberty within the democracies. Just as terror assures its own survival only by increasing its field of irresponsibility, so liberty ensures its survival only by increasing its field of responsibility, by allowing greater and greater freedoms within the law. But the attack against nihilism must be carried on by something infinitely more relentless than our own example. Every psychological weapon—radio, films, scholarships, the newspapers —must be placed at the service of those who are fighting the nihilist conspiracy; and these weapons must be sharpened. Armies of free men must be sent abroad to represent the democracies in their fight against nihilism. The present strength of the Catholic Church in Europe lies in the fact that it is prepared to use the weapons of its opponents, because these weapons are precisely those which it has employed for nearly two thousand years—it has formed cells in Communist districts, and it forms still closer and more powerful cells in the countries where it is officially repressed. We must learn to do the same. We cannot fight the Communists without employing these cellular organizations. We must learn, too, to call things by their right names. It is useless to hold the Communists in detestation: present day Communism results from the tragic marriage of two contrary doctrines—the doctrine of socialist progress and the doctrine of Nechayev. In as far as they work for the social welfare of men, they deserve our praise; in as far as they enslave men, they deserve themselves to be enslaved. "Civilization," said Mr. Justice Jackson at the Nuremberg Trial, "would not survive if these crimes were committed again." But they *are* being committed in all the lands occupied by the Russians, and civilization is therefore in perpetual danger. There can be no compromise. Against the Nechayev monsters the war is eternal. And the great tragedy of our time is that while the rest of the world moves towards the formation of states where men are encouraged to have a greater responsibility for their fellows, the schizophrenic Politiburo is split hopelessly between the extremes of humanness and cruelty.

The dangers are all around us, and must be faced. We cannot escape from the Nechayev monsters even if we desired to. The consequences in inhumanity if we fail are more terrible than any conceivable acts of war. There were incinerators and mass graves a little while ago, there were places where the surface of the earth moved like a wave above the buried innocents who were still alive; and soon enough, unless we fight the corruption of nihilism with every conceivable mental weapon, we shall find ourselves in the position of the young Russian who unwittingly found himself beside the black vacuum of a ditch filled with the dead and dying:

> When we had been brought up to the anti-tank ditch and were lined up alongside this fearful grave, we still believed we had been fetched in order to fill in the ditch with earth or to dig new ones. We did not think we had been brought there to be shot, but when we heard the first shots from the automatic guns trained on us, I realized we were about to be murdered. I immediately hurled myself into the ditch and hid between two corpses. Thus, unharmed and half-fainting, I lay until nearly evening. While lying in the ditch, I heard several of the wounded call to the gendarmes shooting them, "Finish me off, blackguard!"—"You missed me, scoundrel! Shoot again!"
>
> Then, when the Germans went off for dinner, an inhabitant from my village called from the ditch, "Get up, those of you who are still alive." I got up, and two of us began to drag out the living from underneath the corpses. I was covered with blood. A light mist hung over the ditch—steam arising from the rapidly congealing mass of dead bodies, from the pools of blood and from the last breaths of the dying.[5]

Among those of us who have survived there is only one answer: "Be human, celebrate your humanity and tenderness towards each other, for the darkness is all around you. By every act of corruption, however small, by every effort to degrade human beings, by every physical punishment you inflict, you bring the terror nearer. Take warning. There is not much time."

Then, if we succeed in banishing the monster, it may be that in the end he will have served his purpose. "That which in the beginning was as poison," says the *Bhagavad Gita*, "is in

[5] *Nuremberg Trials*, VII, 63.

the end as the waters of life." By opposing, and by being compelled to oppose the Nechayev monster with all our might, we may arrive sooner than anyone expected at the stage when every man will attempt to increase the human dignity of his fellows, and it is even possible that some such realization as this is the next step in the processes of *human* evolution.

Index

Abetz, Otto, 77, 78
Abipones, 241, 242
Acron, 90
Aeneas, 95
Aeneid, 93
Agrippa, 110
Ainu, 105
Alexander the Great, 196
Alexander II, 35, 36, 38, 63, 66
Alexandria, 92, 110
Alexis, 33
Andreev, Leonid, 55
Anglo-Saxons, 103
Angst, 123
Antichrist, 82, 233
Antigone, 247
Appassionata, 209
Appian, 93
Athenaeus, 92
Augustus, 92, 95
Aurelian, 92
Auschwitz, 146
Austen, Jane, 175
Austria, 157
Avvakum, Archpriest, 79, 81, 100

Babeuf, François, 2
Bacchae, 91

Baghdad, fall of, 58
Bakhmetiev Fund, 19, 26, 30
Bakhunin, Mikhail, 5, 6, 14, 25, 26-30, 31, 33, 40, 50, 83
Barrabas, 110
Baudelaire, Charles, 7, 128, 239
Beethoven, 257
Benedictine Mass, 247
Berchtesgaden, 179
Berdyaev, Nicolai, 217-219
Beria, Lavrenti, 225
Berlin, 154
Bhagavad Gita, 249, 261
Biarritz, 65
Bielinsky, 219
Blackstone, Sir William, 131
Blanc, Louis, 2, 15
Blanqui, Louis, 2, 15
Blick ins Chaos, 104
Boergermoor, 154
Bogorodetsky, 32, 38
Brand-marks, 163
Brandt, Dr., 162
Braun, Eva, 185
Breslau, 154
Brigandage, 20
Brotherhood of Fire, 83
Brothers Karamazov, The, 52

Buchenwald, 225
Buddhism, 56
Burckhardt, Jacob, 212
Byzantium, 225

Camden, N. J., 242
Camillus, Marcus Furius, 91
Carabas, 110
Carthage, 93-95, 104, 106
Castrated, The Society of the, 82
Catherine the Great, 20
Catholic church, 260
Cato the Younger, 93, 94
Chamberlain, Houston Stewart, 122
Chang Hsien-chung, 58, 96, 99
Chernichevsky, Nikolai, 33, 39
China, 96, 105
Ch'ing Dynasty, 109
Chunagtse, 99
Citizen, The, 68
Civil War in the Villages, 211
Coleridge, Samuel Taylor, 237
Concerning the Ultimate Things, 128
Confucius, 246
Committee of Public Safety, 31
Commune, The, 30
Communist Manifesto, 205
Count of Monte Christo, The, 57
Crime and Punishment, 17, 18, 137
Crimean Tartars, 87
Cyclone B, 164, 171
Czechoslovakia, 157

Dachau, 146, 153, 154, 243
Dadaists, 54
Dalstroy, 222, 229, 230

Dandy, 7, 45
Dark Night, The, 109
Defence of Terrorism, The, 212-215
Demon, The, 45
Descartes, 236
Destiny of Man, The, 218
Deutsch, Otto, 38
Dialogue aux enfers, 64, 66
Diary of a Writer, The, 45, 53, 206
Dido, 93
Dimitrov, Georgi, 226
Dionysus, 91
Dobrizhofer, Father, 241, 242
Dokhodyagi, 230
Dolgorusky, Makar, 180
Dostoyevsky, Fedor, 17, 30, 33, 45, 46, 47, 49, 50, 52, 68, 99, 102, 137, 177, 180, 206, 243
Drenteln, General, 37
Dubno, 140
Duerrgoy, 154
Dukhobors, 82
Duns Scotus, 236
Dzerzhinsky, Felix, 209, 210, 221, 225

Ego and His Own, The, 198
Egypt, 91
Eichmann, Adolf, 173, 187
Eliot, T. S., 104
Ennius, 93
Etruria, 91
Euripides, 91
European Revolutionary Alliance, 5
Everett, Willis Meade, 243, 244
Existence, 207

INDEX

Fathers and Sons, 16
Fegelein, 185
Fichte, J. G., 45
Figner, Vera, 35
Flaubert, Gustave, 15
Frank, Hans, 187, 188
Frankfurter Zeitung, 72
Frazer, Sir James, 110
Freemasons, 120, 130
French Revolution, 14
From Day to Day, 250
Fujiwara epoch, 253

Gandhi, 248-49
Gapon, Father, 69
Gestapo, 124, 126, 161, 172, 173, 220
Giaour, 45
Gisevius, Hans Bernd, 121
Gluke, General, 136
Gödsche, Hermann, 65, 67
Goebbels, Joseph, 58, 171, 172
Goering, Hermann, 125
Goethe, Johann Wolfgang von, 16
Golden Bull, 131
Golem, 190
Golovinsky, 66
Götterdämmerung, 183
Gorky, Maxim, 209, 213
Grazhdanin, 68
Great Schism, 62, 82, 105
Grynszpan, Herschel, 156
Gupta epoch, 253

Han Dynasty, 96
Heidegger, Martin, 189
Hegel, G. W. F., 45, 101, 204-207, 245

Helmno, 158
Heraclitus, 236
Herod, 110
Herzen, Alexander, 26
Herzl, Theodor, 67
Hess, Rudolf, 72
Hesse, Hermann, 100, 104
Heydrich, Reinhard, 162
Himmler, Heinrich, 132, 164, 172, 183, 191, 216
Hippocrates, 165
Hiroshima, 106
History of the Russian Revolution, 72, 215
Hitler, Adolf, 7, 30, 43, 58, *passim*.
Hobbes, Thomas, 53
Hölderlin, Friedrich, 44, 205
Hollywood, 106
Holy Synod, 36
Hradchin Castle, 238
Hulagu, 58
Human worth, under Nazis, 136, 137; under Soviet, 229
Hume, David, 175, 234, 235
Hutler, Johann, 72

Illyrian Wars, The, 93
Infantile Sickness of Leftism in Communism, 58
Inquisitor, 160, 161, 165
Issayev, Grigory, 35
Ivan the Terrible, 63, 72, 84, 85-87, 94, 105, 180, 182
Ivanov, Ivan, 22, 23, 24, 46, 53
Ivano-Voznessensk, 2

Jackson, Justice, 260

Jack the Ripper, 118
Japan, 105
Jehovah's Witnesses, 120, 130, 139
Jesuits, 29
Jesus, 81, 110
Jewish Nationalist Movement, 67
Jews, 66, 110, 120, 130, 139, 152, 153, 189, 225
Joly, Maurice, 64, 66, 67, 71, 72
Josephus, 88
Jung, C. G., 115

Kafka, Franz, 92, 196
Kaliayev, 252
Kaltenbrunner, 187
Kamchatka, 228
Kamenev, Lev, 221
Kant, Immanuel, 101, 204, 245
Kapital, Das, 25
Kaplan, Fanya, 221
Karamazov, Dmitri, 104
Karmazinov, 50
Karski, Jan, 132
Katkov, Mikhail, 53
Kautsky, Karl, 212
Keitel, Wilhelm, 133-136
Kern, Erwin, 177
Kierkegaard, S. A., 257
Kirillov, 30, 46, 47, 48, 49, 58
Kishinev, 70
Kolyma, 227, 228, 229
Komisarev, General, 68, 70
Kropotkin, Pëtr, 33
Kuomintang, 108, 110
Kurbsky, Andrei, 85

Lebensraum, 114

Lenin, Nikolai, 7, 30, 41, 43, 58, 79, 202, 204, 211, 220, 221, 229
Leningrad, 179
Les Soirées de St. Pétersbourg, 126
Levachov, Count, 32, 34
Liao Dynasty, 99
Lictors, 92
Lidice, 134
Life of a Great Sinner, The, 46
Lincoln, Abraham, 255
Lin Tung-chi, 97, 98
Li Po, 96
Livy, 91
Locke, John, 236
Lorenzo the Magnificent, 13
Lovell, William, 44
Lucretius, 95
Lu Hsun, 109
Luther, Martin, 100
Luxemburg, Rosa, 212

Machiavelli, Nicolo, 29, 65, 143, 144, 197
Machtergreifung, 153
Magadan, 227
Magic Mountain, The, 53, 54
Maistre, Joseph de, 127, 128, 224
Malmédy, 243
Manasevich-Manuilov, Ivan, 66, 68, 69, 240
Manifeste Dada, 55
Mann, Thomas, 53, 54, 101
Mao Tse-tung, 99
Marmelodov, 137
Martians, 106
Marx, Karl, 25, 26, 40, 41, 206, 207
Maya, 105, 170

INDEX

Meaningless sacrifice, 88
Mein Kampf, 72, 111, 112, 113, 120, 139, 145, 178, 192
Melos, destruction of, 104
Melville, Herman, 195
Menzinsky, 225
Merezhkowski, Dmitri, 82
Meshchersky, Prince, 68, 69
Metullus, Caecilius, 93
Mezentsev, 22
Michelet, Jules, 14
Miliukov, Paul, 81
Mirsky, Leon, 37, 38
Mitwerda, 169
Montesquieu, 65
Moscow, burning of, 87, 104
Mozart, Wolfgang Amadeus, 255
Mussolini, Benito, 222
Muspilli, 178, 188, 191, 194
Mysteries of Udolpho, The, 65

Nacht und Nebel Decree, 142, 143
Nansen, Odd, 252
Narodnaya Rasprava, 25
Narodnaya Volya, 35, 36, 37, 63, 69
Naphta, 53, 54
Napoleon I, 57, 58
Napoleon III, 64
National Socialism, 58, 62, 72, *passim*
Nechayev, S. G., *passim*
Nemesis, 236
Nero, 234
Newman, Ernest, 84
New York, 106
Nibelungenlied, 142
Nietzsche, Friedrich, 197

Nihilist, *passim*
Nikhon, Archbishop, 17, 79, 81
Nilus, Sergei, 67, 68, 70, 71
Nuremburg Laws, 154
Nuremburg Trials, 133, 134, 141, 158, 166, 180, 198, 261

October Revolution, 208, 220
Ogarev, Nikolai, 19, 21, 25, 26, 27, 31, 50
Ogpu, 209, 212, 215, 219, 221, 224
Okhrana, 63, 66, 67, 69, 70, 227
Old Guard, 221
Opritchina, 72, 84, 85, 87
Oradour-sur-Glane, 134
Oranienburg, 154
Oryevsky, General, 66
Other China, The, 98
Ouspensky, 22, 24
Outlaws, The, 177

Pajou de Moncy, 24
Palamas, Gregory, 247
Pan-Slavism, 69, 70, 225
Pauline Epistles, 83
Perovskaya, Sophie, 63
Peter and Paul, 82
Peter the Great, 32, 33, 227
Petersburg, 1, 3, 24
Petrarch, 248
Petrovsk Park, 23
Pico della Mirandola, 247
Pliny, 110
Plutarch, 90
Pogroms, 66
Polyakov, 25, 26
Polybius, 94
Popolo d'Italia, 222

267

Possessed, The, 45, 46, 47, 48, 50, 52, 53, 177, 243
Predurki, 229
Principles of Revolution, The, 24, 58
Protocols of the Wise Men of Zion, 67, 70, 71, 72
Proudhon, Pierre J., 15
Ptolemy Philadelphus, 92
Pugachev, Emelyan, 20, 21, 204
Punic Wars, 91

Rabotyagi, 230
Radcliffe, Mrs. Anne, 65
Rajk, Laszlo, 216
Raskolnikov, 17, 105
Raskolniki, 17, 105
Rasputin, Grigori, 70
Ratchkovsky, General, 66, 68, 69
Rath, Ernst vom, 156
Rathenau, Emil, 177
Rauschning, Hermann, 58, 61, 76, 138, 180, 183, 185, 189, 190, 203, 207
Ravelin, Alexis, 32, 33, 38
Raw Youth, A, 180
Razin, Stenka, 20, 21, 80
Red Cross, 133
Remusat, Mme. de, 57
Retcliffe, Sir John, 65
Revolutionary Catechism, The, passim
Richter, Jean-Paul, 44
Rimbaud, Arthur, 15
Robbers, The, 57
Rohm, Ernst, 176
Romulus, 90
Rosenberg, Alfred, 72
Rostov-on-the-Don, 161

Rothschilds, 67
Rousset, David, 129, 130, 131
Rudenko, General, 134, 135
Russian Revolution, 70, 79, 218

Sabine women, 90
Sachsenhausen, 226
Sade, Marquis de, 72
Salomon, Ernst von, 177
Samurai, 96, 104
Sartre, Jean-Paul, 128, 129
Scheman, Ludwig, 142
Schiller, Johann von, 57
Selene Cleopatra, 92
Serge, Grand Duke, 252
Seyss-Inquart, Artur, 198, 199
Shadows, 55, 56
Shatov, 45, 180
Shigalov, 46, 48, 52, 102
Shiraev, 34, 35
Shore-dwellers, 83
Shub, David, 42, 322
Sicily, 94
Sigfiolli, 194
Sigmund, 194
Sirin, 202
Siva, 91
Small Signs Prophesy Great Events, 67
Small Soviet Encyclopaedia, 220
Solovetsky Monastery, 80
Soloviev, V. V., 233
Sophocles, 247
Sorel, Georges, 15
Soviet Communism: A New Civilisation?, 219
Spain, 157
Speer, Albert, 78, 171, 172, 199, 200, 201

INDEX

Spirit of Christianity and Its Destiny, 205
Stalin, 220, 232
Stalin Constitution, 224, 232
Stavrogin, 46, 48, 52, 102
Stirner, Max, 198
Storm Troopers, 117, 152, 153, 154, 156, 221
Story of a Traitor, The, 176
Streicher, Julius, 150
Strempkowski, Adolf, 31
Stürmer, Der, 150, 174
Syracuse, 104
Szechuan, 58, 96

Tabun, 202
Tacitus, 95, 125
Talandier, 27, 29
Talmud, 250
Tamerlane, 58
Tang Dynasty, 96, 253
Taoism, 96-100
Tarnkappe, 142
Tartar Horde, 87
Tattooing, 163
Tazzling Mill, The, 14
Tcherkassov, Prince, 24
Ten Commandments for the Conduct of a German Soldier, 133
Third Division, 3, 22, 34, 38, 63
Third International, 222
Thirty Years War, 105
Thomas Aquinas, 236, 247
Tieck, Ludwig, 44
Tkachev, Peter, 3, 24
Tohuwabohu, 178, 185
Tolstoy, Leo, 99, 189
To the Bitter End, 121

To the Finland Station, 57
"Traffic desert," 136, 244
Treatise on Human Nature, 175
Treblinka, 159
Trepov, General, 22
Trevor-Roper, H. R., 58, 200
Triumph, the Roman, 88, 89, 90, 91, 92, 93, 103, 149
Trotsky, Leon, 72, 111, 212-215, 220
Troy, 95
Tsara, Tristan, 55
Turgeniev, Ivan, 16
Twilight of the Gods, The, 30

Ukraine, 140, 222
Univers Concentrationnaire, L', 129-131
Unruh, 243
Uritsky, 221

Vaillant-Couterier, Mme. Claude, 168
Van Gogh, Vincent, 255
V-bombs, 200
Verkhne-Udinsk, 227
Verkhovensky, Pyotr, 46, 47, 48, 49, 50
Via Sacra, 90
Vienna, 114
Virgil, 93
Vistula, 181
Voluspa, 188
Vozhd, 222

Wagner, Richard, 15, 83, 84
Wagner, Walter, 195
Wanderers, 82

ZERO

Warring Dynasties, 99
"Way of Heaven," 97
Webb, Sidney, 219
Weininger, Otto, 104, 128, 184
Welles, Orson, 106
Werewolves, 58, 194
What should be done?, 39
White Sea, 82
Whitman, Walt, 255
Will to Power, The, 197, 214
Wilson, Edmund, 57
Winter Palace, 69
Wirth, Chancellor, 176
Witte, Count Sergei, 70
Wolkenbrand, 188

World Revolutionary Alliance, 6, 21, 22, 25, 27

Yagoda, 216, 225
Yanov, 161
Yezhov, 216, 225
Yuman Pass, 96

Zasulich, Vera, 4
Zemski Sobor, 32
Zen Buddhism, 96
Zenobia, 92
Zhelyabov, Andrei, 34, 35, 63
Zinoviev, Grigori, 212
Zossima, Father, 52

www.ingramcontent.com/pod-product-compliance
Lightning Source LLC
Chambersburg PA
CBHW070726160426
43192CB00009B/1329